The Architectural Uncanny

The Architectural Uncanny

Essays in the Modern Unhomely

Anthony Vidler

The MIT Press
Cambridge, Massachusetts
London, England

This book was set in Baskerville by DEKR Corporation and was printed and bound in the United States of America.

Library of Congress Cataloging-in-Publication Data

Vidler, Anthony.
    The architectural uncanny : essays in the modern unhomely /
Anthony Vidler.
        p.   cm.
    Includes bibliographical references and index.
    ISBN 0-262-22044-X (hb); 0-262-72018-3 (pb)
    1. Architecture and literature.   2. Architecture in literature.   3. Architecture, Modern—20th century—Psychological aspects.   4. Literature, Modern—19th century—History and criticism.   5. Critical theory.   I. Title.
PN56.A73V53   1992
720'.1'04—dc20   91-38900
                                                                          CIP

10 9 8 7

In memory of
Alvin Boyarsky

Contents

Preface ix

Introduction 3

I Houses

Unhomely Houses 17
Buried Alive 45
Homesickness 57
Nostalgia 63

II Bodies

Architecture Dismembered 69
Losing Face 85
Trick/Track 101
Shifting Ground 117
Homes for Cyborgs 147

III Spaces

Dark Space 167
Posturbanism 177
Psychometropolis 189
Oneirism 199
Vagabond Architecture 207
Transparency 217

Notes 227

Acknowledgments 249

Index 251

Preface

Intrigued by the unsettling qualities of much contemporary architecture—its fragmented neoconstructivist forms mimetic of dismembered bodies, its public representation buried in earthworks or lost in mirror reflection, its "seeing walls" reciprocating the passive gaze of domestic cyborgs, its spaces surveyed by moving eyes and simulating "transparency," its historical monuments indistinguishable from glossy reproductions—I have been drawn to explore aspects of the spatial and architectural uncanny, as it has been characterized in literature, philosophy, psychology, and architecture from the beginning of the nineteenth century to the present. Marked by its origins in romantic thought, the theme of the uncanny serves to join architectural speculation on the peculiarly unstable nature of "house and home" to more general reflection on the questions of social and individual estrangement, alienation, exile, and homelessness.

Architecture has been intimately linked to the notion of the uncanny since the end of the eighteenth century. At one level, the house has provided a site for endless representations of haunting, doubling, dismembering, and other terrors in literature and art. At another level, the labyrinthine spaces of the modern city have been construed as the sources of modern anxiety, from revolution and epidemic to phobia and alienation; the genre of the detective novel owes its existence to such fears—"the unsolved murder is uncanny," wrote the psychoanalyst Theodor Reik.

But beyond this largely theatrical role, architecture reveals the deep structure of the uncanny in a more than analogical way, demonstrating a disquieting slippage between what seems homely and what is definitively unhomely. As articulated theoretically by Freud, the uncanny or *unheimlich* is rooted by etymology and usage in the environment of the domestic, or the *heimlich*, thereby opening up problems of identity around the self, the other, the body and its absence: thence its force in interpreting the relations between the psyche and the dwelling, the body and the house, the individual and the metropolis. Linked by Freud to the death drive, to fear of castration, to the impossible desire to return to the womb, the uncanny has been interpreted as a dominant constituent of modern nostalgia, with a corresponding spatiality that touches all aspects of social life.

Perhaps this explains why, following the lead of literary and psychoanalytic criticism after Lacan and Derrida, a number of contemporary architects have seized on this domain for their own study of domesticity and its discontents in projects that attempt deliberately to provoke disquiet and unease, to reveal the hidden terrors of the house. Such projects assume a critical role once reserved for literature and social thought in their emulation of the conditions of estrangement through architectural and urban form. Although powerless in the face of actual homelessness, their different versions of a spatial uncanny nevertheless articulate ways in which architecture works with respect to the dedomesticated subject. As analytical diagrams of the embodied gaze constructed by a prosthetic architecture, they press the notion of theoretical discourse in architecture to its limits, at the same time forcing political discourse to reformulate its paradigms of spatial analysis.

In the following book, I have not attempted an exhaustive historical or theoretical treatment of the subject; nor have I constructed or applied any comprehensive theory of the uncanny based on phenomenology, negative dialectics, or psychoanalysis. Rather I have chosen approaches that seem relevant to the interpretation of contemporary buildings and projects provoked by the resurgent interest in the uncanny as a metaphor for a fundamentally unlivable modern condition. In this sense the book is at once historical, serving to situate contemporary discourse in its own intellectual tradition, and theoretical, investigating the difficult relationships between politics, social thought, and architectural design in an era when the realities of urban existence and the ideals of the neo-avant-garde have never seemed so far apart.

Part I is concerned with the uncanny as a literary, aesthetic, philosophical, and psychoanalytical concept from Schelling to Freud.
Freud's 1919 essay on the uncanny provides a theoretical starting
point for a discussion of the genre of the uncanny tale among nine-
teenth- and twentieth-century authors, including Freud's own favorite example, E. T. A. Hoffmann. I trace the history of the spatial
uncanny as it develops out of the aesthetic of the sublime to its full
exploitation in the numerous "haunted houses" of the romantic period imagined by Victor Hugo, Thomas De Quincey, Charles Nodier,
and Herman Melville. Melville's reflection on the secret recesses of
domesticity leads to a discussion of the role of the uncanny in the
fantasies of burial and return that were inseparable from the historical and archaeological self-consciousness of the nineteenth century.
The uncanniness of archaeology in its excavation of sites from Pompeii to Troy, supplied a guiding metaphor for Freud in his development of psychoanalysis, and provided the incentive for his
disquisition on the fear of being buried alive, a test case in his psychoanalytical study of the uncanny as a peculiar kind of fear, posi-
tioned between real terror and faint anxiety. Tinged with late
nineteenth-century nostalgia, as evoked by the melancholic reveries
of Walter Pater, the uncanny became an equally powerful trope for
imaging the "lost" birthplace, against the deracinated home of postindustrial society, in the writings of critics of modernity from Gaston
Bachelard to Martin Heidegger.

These themes offer a conceptual starting point for the examination
of a number of contemporary architectural and urban projects that
implicitly or explicitly pose the question of the unhomely in modern
culture. In part II I examine the complex and shifting relations
between buildings and bodies, structures and sites, that have characterized the attempt to destabilize the conventions of traditional
architecture in recent years, with reference to the critical theories of
estrangement, linguistic indeterminacy, and representation that have
served as vehicles for avant-garde architectural experiment. Here the
question of the unhomely becomes particularized, embodied in architectural forms that seek to express the precarious relationship
between psychological and physical home; Freud's analysis of the
uncanny effects of dismembered bodies is especially redolent for the
interpretation of an architectural fragmentation that rejects the traditional embodiment of anthropomorphic projection in built form.

Thus the work of Coop Himmelblau in Vienna, founded by Wolf D. Prix and H. Swiczinsky in the late sixties, has programmatically questioned the traditional verities of architecture through neoconstructivist forms expressly designed to challenge the notion of the bourgeois *Heimlichkeit* by means of the demotion of the classical body from its privileged place in architectural theory and practice. Conceived through a design process that resembles a kind of automatic writing, Coop Himmelblau's projects attempt to recuperate an immediate connection between body language and space, the unconscious and its habitat. Signs of this dismembering of the corporeal figure in building are equally, if less dramatically, present in the effacement of monumental representation in James Stirling's Staatsgalerie in Stuttgart, a building that, despite its appeal to classical archetypes, refuses to put up a traditional facade. Bernard Tschumi's project for the new park of La Villette in the northeast of Paris exploits references to modernism's own critique of classical anthropomorphism in photography and film. Tschumi's *folies,* late twentieth-century versions of eighteenth-century park pavilions, join film theory and the genre of the *bande dessinée* or illustrated comic book to create an aesthetic of calculated disequilibrium.

Equally committed to an architecture that, in his words, "decomposes" classical humanist forms, the New York architect Peter Eisenman has been influenced by the radical criticism of philosophical language developed by Jacques Derrida. Resisting the superficial resonances of the word "deconstruction," Eisenman derives the forms of his half-buried structures from geomorphic traces that respond, perhaps unwittingly, to the problem of architecture's death as theorized by Hegel.

Concluding this section on the mutations of the bodily analogy in recent architecture, I identify the characteristics of what might be called a bio- and a techno-uncanny as represented in the work of the New York architects Elizabeth Diller and Ricardo Scofidio. Based on a close analysis of dadaist and surrealist investigations of the mechanical body, their projects treat of architecture and its attendant objects as prosthetic devices with a sinister life of their own, engendering peculiar contaminations of the biological and the technological. Their research is thrown into focus by the recent theorization of cybernetic culture by feminists such as Donna Haraway, who introduces the concept of the cyborg, a being that knows none of the nostalgia associated with birth but which presents all the spectral effects of the double, as a heuristic device through which to rethink the political relations of gender.

In part III, I turn to the implications of the uncanny for urbanism, and especially for the interpretation of its spatial conditions. Following Freud's tantalizing accounts of the uncanny effects of getting lost in a city, and conscious of the modernist fascination with the isolated *flâneur* from Breton to Benjamin, I look at the ways in which psychology and psychoanalysis have found in cities a topos for the exploration of anxiety and paranoia. I describe what might be called a posturbanist sensibility that, from surrealism to situationism, has stood against the tendency of modern urbanism to create so many *tabulae rasae* for the building of cities without memory. Preoccupied with traces and residues—the material of the dreamwork—rather than with the new, writers and architects have increasingly found ways to chart the underground reverberations of the city. In their ascriptions, territoriality becomes unfixed, camouflaged and dug-in, in so many ironic emulations of military and geopolitical strategy; subjectivity is rendered heterogeneous, nomadic, and self-critical in vagabond environments that refuse the commonplaces of hearth and home in favor of the uncertainties of no-man's-land.

The Office of Metropolitan Architecture (OMA)—beginning in 1972 with Elia Zenghelis, Rem Koolhaas, and the artists Madelon Vriesendorp and Zoe Zenghelis and practicing in London, Holland, and Greece—has consistently exploited the psychological associations of urban architecture by postsurrealist juxtapositions and ironically reformulated modernist visions. Koolhaas's book *Delirious New York*, published in 1978, applied a version of Salvador Dalí's "paranoid critical method" to urban architecture and laid the groundwork for his later, independent work in Europe, as well as charting an intellectual path that has been followed and transformed by younger Dutch architects, such as Wiel Arets and Wim van den Bergh. As founding editors of the Dutch journal *Wiederhalle*, Arets and van den Berg have based their work on a continuing investigation of the role of memory and desire in the city. More closely allied to surrealist roots in his reading of André Breton and Raymond Roussel, John Hejduk has developed a form of modernism that has always resisted the positivities of functionalism in favor of provocation. Hejduk's mobile constructions, emblematically housing a Kafkaesque gamut of

modern occupations, are designed to stage guerrilla assaults on privileged urban sites from Vladivostock to Berlin. Each of these architects has a common interest in the intangible but palpable realm of
the unconscious as a domain to be exploited by architecture and the
city. The notions of the found object and the readymade are here
seen to be applied to the building as a whole that, in its relations to
the mind and to other buildings, triggers associations and operates,
so to speak, as a vehicle for the kind of uncanny mechanisms already
explored in Breton's *Nadja* or Aragon's *Paysan de Paris*.

I conclude by assessing the place of the modern subject in architecture as it has been reformulated through contemporary psychoanalytic theory. The modernist ideal of the universal subject,
represented through transparency and criticized by a more opaque
postmodernism, has recently resurfaced in the aesthetic programs of
many public competitions, notably those for the Parisian *grands projets*.
The participation of such an aesthetic, which inevitably involves reflection and mirroring, in a society of spectacle committed to the
suppression of all phenomenological depth, would indicate that the
long tradition of anthropomorphic embodiment in architecture has
been finally broken, with spatially uncanny consequences.

This book was written over the last five years supported in part by
grants from the John Simon Guggenheim Foundation, the National
Endowment for the Humanities, and two sabbatical leaves of absence
from Princeton University. Certain chapters were originally pub-
lished in response to requests from a number of individuals: Suzanne
Stephens (*Skyline*), Hubert Damisch and Jean-Louis Cohen (*Critique*),
Michael Hays (*Assemblage*), Alessandra Ponte and Marco De Michelis
(*Ottagono*), Georges Teyssot and Pier Luigi Nicolin (*Lotus Interna-
tional*), Ignazio Solà Morales (*Quaderns*), Toshio Nakamura (*A+U*),
Mary Wall (*AA Files*), and France Morin (The New Museum for
Contemporary Art, New York). Peter Brooks, Michael Fried, Raphael
Moneo, Mark Taylor, Bernard Tschumi, and Susan Suleiman were
kind enough to provide interdisciplinary forums for discussion. Mark
Cousins offered important comments and Hal Foster encouraged me
to explore the uncanny in its contemporary contexts. My colleagues
and friends at Princeton, including Beatriz Colomina, Alan
Colquhoun, Elizabeth Diller, Ralph Lerner, Robert Maxwell, and
Mark Wigley, have contributed significantly to the development of
my ideas. Participants in my graduate seminars in criticism and theory

at Princeton have forced me to refine my arguments. The Doctoral Program in Architecture at the Georgia Institute of Technology invited me to present the work in its incomplete state, and the responses of faculty and students were important for its revision. Peter Eisenman has been a consistently provocative critic and his questions have helped to frame many of the central chapters of the book. At the MIT Press, Roger Conover has been supportive of the project throughout; I am especially grateful for Matthew Abbate's editorial precision. Without the intellectual example of Emily Apter, whose observations and perceptive advice have informed its writing since the beginning, the book could not have been written.

I dedicate the book to the memory of a friend and interlocutor, Alvin Boyarsky, who as Director of the Architectural Association School of Architecture in London created a unique place for architectural debate. It was at his insistence that a first draft of this book was brought together as a series of lectures and seminars given at the AA in 1989, and the present work owes much to his affectionate criticism.

Paris, Summer 1991

The Architectural Uncanny

Introduction

Something is uncanny—that is how it begins. But at the same time one must search for that remoter "something," which is already close at hand.

Ernst Bloch, "A Philosophical View of the Detective Novel"

The contemporary sensibility that sees the uncanny erupt in empty parking lots around abandoned or run-down shopping malls, in the screened trompe l'oeil of simulated space, in, that is, the wasted margins and surface appearances of postindustrial culture, this sensibility has its roots and draws its commonplaces from a long but essentially modern tradition. Its apparently benign and utterly ordinary loci, its domestic and slightly tawdry settings, its ready exploitation as the *frisson* of an already jaded public, all mark it out clearly as the heir to a feeling of unease first identified in the late eighteenth century.

Aesthetically an outgrowth of the Burkean sublime, a domesticated version of absolute terror, to be experienced in the comfort of the home and relegated to the minor genre of the *Märchen* or fairy tale, the uncanny found its first home in the short stories of E. T. A. Hoffmann and Edgar Allan Poe. Its favorite motif was precisely the contrast between a secure and homely interior and the fearful invasion of an alien presence; on a psychological level, its play was one of doubling, where the other is, strangely enough, experienced as a replica of the self, all the more fearsome because apparently the same.

At the heart of the anxiety provoked by such alien presences was a fundamental insecurity: that of a newly established class, not quite at home in its own home. The uncanny, in this sense, might be characterized as the quintessential bourgeois kind of fear: one carefully bounded by the limits of real material security and the pleasure principle afforded by a terror that was, artistically at least, kept well under control. The uncanny was, in this first incarnation, a sensation best experienced in the privacy of the interior. Ernst Bloch was not the first to remark that "the setting in which detective stories are enjoyed the most is just too cozy. In a comfortable chair, under the nocturnal floor lamp with tea, rum, and tobacco, personally secure and peacefully immersed in dangerous things, which are shallow."[1] The vicarious taste for the uncanny has been a constant in modern culture, only intensified by shifts in media.

But the uncanny, as Walter Benjamin noted, was also born out of the rise of the great cities, their disturbingly heterogeneous crowds and newly scaled spaces demanding a point of reference that, while not refuting a certain instability, nevertheless served to dominate it aesthetically. Here the privileged point of view—of Hoffmann's observer keeping his careful distance from the marketplace, looking through "The Cousin's Corner Window" with opera glasses; of Poe and of Dickens watching the crowd; of Baudelaire losing himself in the swarming boulevards—attempted to preserve a sense of individual security that was only precariously sustained by the endless quest of the detective tracking his clues through the apparent chaos of modern urban life.[2]

In the context of the nineteenth-century city, the alienation of the individual expressed by writers from Rousseau to Baudelaire was gradually reinforced by the real economic and social estrangement experienced by the majority of its inhabitants. For Benjamin Constant, writing in the aftermath of the French Revolution and Napoleonic Empire, urban estrangement was a consequence of the centralization of the state and the concentration of political and cultural power, where all "local customs" and community bonds were brutally severed: "Individuals, lost in an isolation from nature, strangers to the place of their birth, without contact with the past, living only in a rapid present, and thrown down like atoms on an immense and leveled plain, are detached from a fatherland that they see nowhere."[3] For Marx, writing some thirty years later, individual estrangement had become class alienation. As he noted in the *Economic and Philosophical Notebooks* of 1844, the development of the rent system had rendered "home" a temporary illusion at best.

> We have said . . . that man is regressing to the *cave dwelling*, etc.,—but he is regressing to it in an estranged, malignant form. The savage in his cave—a natural element which freely offers itself for his use and protection—feels himself no more than a stranger, or rather feels as much at home as a *fish* in water. But the cellar-dwelling of the poor man is a hostile element, "a dwelling which remains an alien power and only gives itself up to him insofar as he gives up to it his own blood and sweat"—a dwelling which he cannot regard as his own hearth—where he might at last exclaim: "Here I am at home"—but where instead he finds himself in *someone else's* house, in the house of a *stranger* who always watches him and throws him out if he does not pay his rent.[4]

Here the question of "the stranger," which was to be a central notion in the sociology of Georg Simmel and his followers after the turn of the century, was joined with political urgency to what Hegel had called *Entfremdung* and Marx named *Entäusserung*.

This sense of estrangement was intellectually reinforced by the disturbingly transient qualities of the twin foundations of certainty for the nineteenth century—history and nature. The uncanny habit of history to repeat itself, to return at unexpected and unwanted moments; the stubborn resistance of nature to the assimilation of human attributes and its tragic propensity to inorganic isolation, seemed, for many, to confirm the impossibility of "living comfortably" in the world. Estrangement, in these terms, seemed a natural consequence of a conception of history, of the implacable impulsion of time that, while sweeping away the past in favor of the future, was necessarily uncertain only about the present. The remedies to such uncertainty, which ranged from revolution to restoration, from reform to utopia, were equally caught in the dilemmas of temporality, tied to the inhospitable context of the here-and-now at the same time as imagining a there-and-then. This anxiety of time, as expressed in the intellectual attempts to imagine impossible futures or return to equally impossible pasts, was accompanied by a fascination with the consequences of time's errors—the dystopian effects of unwonted interference with the natural development of things, on the one hand, and the psychological effects of past and future shock on the other.

Gradually generalized as a condition of modern anxiety, an alienation linked to its individual and poetic origins in romanticism, the uncanny finally became public in metropolis. As a sensation it was no longer easily confined to the bourgeois interior or relegated to the imaginary haunts of the mysterious and dangerous classes; it was seemingly as disrespectful of class boundaries as epidemics and plagues. Perhaps this is why, from the 1870s on, the metropolitan uncanny was increasingly conflated with metropolitan illness, a pathological condition that potentially afflicted the inhabitants of all great cities; a condition that had, through force of environment, escaped the overprotected domain of the short story. The uncanny here became identified with all the phobias associated with spatial fear, including "la peur des espaces" or agoraphobia, soon to be coupled with its obverse, claustrophobia.

Thus psychologized, the uncanny emerged in the late nineteenth century as a special case of the many modern diseases, from phobias to neuroses, variously described by psychoanalysts, psychologists, and philosophers as a distancing from reality forced by reality. Its space was still an interior, but now the interior of the mind, one that knew no bounds in projection or introversion. Its symptoms included spatial fear, leading to paralysis of movement, and temporal fear, leading to historical amnesia. In each case, the uncanny arose, as Freud demonstrated, from the transformation of something that once seemed homely into something decidedly not so, from the *heimlich,* that is, into the *unheimlich.*

In his essay on the uncanny, published in 1919, Freud took as his own starting point for an enquiry into personal and aesthetic estrangement the complex significations of the German word for "uncanny," *das Unheimliche,* literally the "unhomely."[5] On one level, Freud's "Das Unheimliche" was ostensibly a study of a literary genre and an aesthetic sensation, and Freud's close reading of E. T. A. Hoffmann's short story "The Sandman" has become celebrated and much commented upon in literary criticism. As a contribution to the psychoanalytic study of literature, "The Uncanny" takes its place with such works as Otto Rank's *The Double* and Marie Bonaparte's study of Poe.[6] But behind Freud's wartime interest in this theme, and underlying the complex argument of the essay itself, there seems to have been a larger, socio-psychoanalytical interest.

[For Freud, "unhomeliness" was more than a simple sense of not belonging; it was the fundamental propensity of the familiar to turn on its owners, suddenly to become defamiliarized, derealized, as if in a dream] On the surface an innocuous inquiry into the psychological dimensions of the literary uncanny, his essay in fact precipitated the uncanny into the more disturbing territory of the death drive. Written in the aftermath of Freud's attempts to grapple with the traumas of war, starting with "Thoughts for the Times on War and Death" and "On Transience" of 1915–1916, continuing with "Mourning and Melancholia," and concluding with his preface to a collective study on war neuroses, "The Uncanny" seems to incorporate, albeit in an unstated form, many observations on the nature of anxiety and shock that he was unable to include in the more clinical studies of shell shock. Equally, it seems to anticipate in many respects the extension of psychoanalysis to social concerns, beginning with *Beyond the Pleasure Principle* of 1920. Themes of anxiety and dread, provoked by a real or imagined sense of "unhomeliness," seemed particularly appropriate to a moment when, as Freud noted in 1915, the entire "homeland" of Europe, cradle and apparently secure house of western civilization, was in the process of barbaric regression; when the territorial security that had fostered the notion of a unified culture was broken, bringing a powerful disillusionment with the universal "museum" of the European "fatherland."[7] The site of the uncanny was now no longer confined to the house or the city, but more properly extended to the no man's land between the trenches, or the fields of ruins left after bombardment.

In a moment when history seemed to have been brutally arrested, the uncanny reinforced its traditional links with nostalgia, joining what for many writers after the war seemed to be the "transcendental homelessness" that Georg Lukács saw as the modern condition.[8] "Homesickness," nostalgia for the true, natal home, thus emerges in the face of the massive uprooting of war and ensuing Depression as the mental and psychological corollary to homelessness. It was in this context that philosophers from Martin Heidegger to Gaston Bachelard wistfully meditated on the (lost) nature of "dwelling," through nostalgic readings of the poets of the first, romantic uncanny. For Heidegger, the *unheimlich*, or what Hubert Dreyfus prefers to translate as "unsettledness," was, at least in his formulation of 1927, a question of the fundamental condition of anxiety in the world—the way in which the world was experienced as "not a home." In Dreyfus's terms,

Not only is human being interpretation all the way down, so that our practices can never be grounded in human nature, God's will, or the structure of rationality, but this condition is one of such radical rootlessness that everyone feels fundamentally unsettled (*unheimlich*), that is, senses that human beings can *never* be at home in the world. This, according to Heidegger, is why we plunge into trying to make ourselves at home and secure.[9]

It was, of course, for this security that, following the Second World War, Heidegger himself searched; attempting to trace the roots of preanxious dwelling and exhibiting a profound nostalgia for the premodern, his later writings have formed the basis of a veritable discourse on dwelling that has been taken up by latter-day phenomenologists and postmodernists alike.[10]

This coincidence of the sensibility of exile, intellectual and existential, with the forced nomadism and lived homelessness of the Depression only reinforced the growing feeling that modern man was, essentially and fundamentally, rootless: "Homelessness is coming to be the destiny of the world," wrote Heidegger in his celebrated "Letter of Humanism" in 1947.

At the same time, for the modernist avant-gardes, the uncanny readily offered itself as an instrument of "defamiliarization" or *ostranenie;* as if a world estranged and distanced from its own nature could only be recalled to itself by shock, by the effects of things deliberately "made strange." Expressionist artists and writers from Kubin to Kafka explored the less nostalgic conditions of the modern uncanny, pressing the themes of the double, the automat, and derealization into service as symptoms of posthistorical existence. Symbolists, futurists, dadaists, and of course surrealists and metaphysical artists found in the uncanny a state between dream and awakening particularly susceptible to exploitation. In this way, the uncanny was renewed as an aesthetic category, but now reconceived as the very sign of modernism's propensity for shock and disturbance.

"Estrangement from the world," noted Adorno, citing Freud's essay on the uncanny, "is a moment of art." For Adorno, indeed, the secret movement of the uncanny was the only way to explain why "the most extreme shocks and gestures of estrangement emanating from modern art—seismograms of a general, inescapable mode of response—are closer to us than past art which merely seems close because of its historical reification."[11] The artistic techniques of estrangement, he argued, rendered art less alienated than the condition they seek to address:

There is no denying that the antagonistic condition Marx called alienation was a powerful leaven for modern art. However modern art was not simply a replica or reproduction of that condition but has denounced it in no uncertain terms, transposing it into an *imago*. In so doing modern art became the opposite other of an alienated condition. The former was as free as the latter was unfree.[12]

Adorno supports his observations by citing Freud's dictum "that the uncanny is uncanny only because it is secretly all too familiar, which is why it is repressed."[13] The familiarity of estrangement in modern art, Adorno concluded, as opposed to the distance of the apparently familiar "classic" artwork, was a result of the very "repression" of modern art's effects; its dismissal by contemporary critics was in fact a sign of its secret comprehensibility.

Thus historicized, the uncanny might be understood as a significant psychoanalytical and aesthetic response to the real shock of the modern, a trauma that, compounded by its unthinkable repetition on an even more terrible scale during World War II, has not been exorcised from the contemporary imaginary. Estrangement and unhomeliness have emerged as the intellectual watchwords of our century, given periodic material and political force by the resurgence of homelessness itself, a homelessness generated sometimes by war, sometimes by the unequal distribution of wealth.

If, in this way, the uncanny has found its place as a way to think the two "postwars" after 1919 and 1945, its reemergence as an aesthetic sensibility since the mid-sixties seems at once a continuation of its privileged position in the "negative dialectics" of the modernist avant-garde—a role given double force by the self-conscious ironization of modernism by postmodernism—and a product of the new technological conditions of cultural representation. A postmodern uncanny has been construed, the product of the rereading of Freud by Lacan and Derrida but also of the application of critical theory to the analysis of popular culture.[14] For Lacan, the uncanny formed the starting point for his examination of anxiety, the very "image of lack";[15] for Derrida, the uncanny lurks behind the unstable links between signifier and signified, the author and the text;[16] for Baud-rillard, its propensity for the double, for the elision between reality and fiction, its insistent trompe l'oeil, gives it a central role in the explication of the simulacrum.[17]

The interpretative force of the uncanny has, in turn, been renewed in literature and painting but above all in film, where the traces of its intellectual history have been summoned in the service of an entirely contemporary sensibility. The domestic and suburban un-canny of David Lynch's *Blue Velvet*, and, more recently, of his televi-sion series "Twin Peaks," draws its effect from the ironization of all the commonplaces of a half-century of uncanny movies; while the metropolitan uncanny of Wim Wenders's *Wings of Desire* plays on a post–World War II reenvisioning of Benjamin's historical uncanny. The emergence of a genre of science fiction exploring the ramified dimensions of cyberspace and its inhabitants, cyborgs, epitomized by William Gibson's now classic *Neuromancer*, has voiced a peculiarly contemporary sense of haunting: that provoked by the loss of tradi-tional bodily and locational references, by the pervasive substitution of the simulated for the "real," in the computer's virtual reality. Contemporary feminist critics, from Sarah Kofman to Kaja Silver-man, finally, have reread Freud with skepticism, noting the obvious difficulties of a theory that privileges a male response to the "uncanny trauma" of woman's lack.[18]

More directly in the tradition of Marx and Simmel, and writing in the context of the reemergence of racism and the increase in real homelessness, Julia Kristeva has remarked on the coincidence of "strangeness" and "depersonalization," already present in Freudian theory, as she traces the long history of strangers, those phantom beings closer to ourselves than we would want to realize, and with needs, as demonstrated by Michael Ignatieff and Tzvetan Todorov, that are not at all dissimilar to our own.[19] In a perceptive reading of the postcolonial "nation" in space and time, Homi Bhabha has simi-larly reappropriated the uncanny to speak of the return of "the migrants, the minorities, the diasporic" to the city, "the space in which emergent identifications and new social movements of the people are played out." What he calls "the perplexity of the living" might be, in these terms, interpreted through a theory of the uncanny that de-stabilizes traditional notions of center and periphery—the spatial forms of the national—to comprehend how "that boundary that secures the cohesive limits of the western nation may imperceptibly turn into a contentious *internal* liminality that provides a place from which to speak both of, and as, the minority, the exilic, the marginal and emergent."[20]

As a concept, then, the uncanny has, not unnaturally, found its metaphorical home in architecture: first in the house, haunted or not, that pretends to afford the utmost security while opening itself to the secret intrusion of terror, and then in the city, where what was once walled and intimate, the confirmation of community—one thinks of Rousseau's Geneva—has been rendered strange by the spatial incursions of modernity. In both cases, of course, the "uncanny" is not a property of the space itself nor can it be provoked by any particular spatial conformation; it is, in its aesthetic dimension, a representation of a mental state of projection that precisely elides the boundaries of the real and the unreal in order to provoke a disturbing ambiguity, a slippage between waking and dreaming.

In this sense, it is perhaps difficult to speak of an "architectural" uncanny, in the same terms as a literary or psychological uncanny; certainly no one building, no special effects of design can be guaranteed to provoke an uncanny feeling. But in each moment of the history of the representation of the uncanny, and at certain moments in its psychological analysis, the buildings and spaces that have acted as the sites for uncanny experiences have been invested with recognizable characteristics. These almost typical and eventually commonplace qualities—the attributes of haunted houses in Gothic romances are the most well known—while evidently not essentially uncanny in themselves, nevertheless have been seen as *emblematic* of the uncanny, as the cultural signs of estrangement for particular periods. An early stage of psychology was as a result even prepared to identify space as a *cause* of the fear or estrangement hitherto a privilege of fiction; for an early generation of sociologists, "spatial estrangement" was more than a figment of the imagination, but represented precisely that mingling of mental projection and spatial characteristics associated with the uncanny.

From this point of view the architectural uncanny invoked in this book is necessarily ambiguous, combining aspects of its fictional history, its psychological analysis, and its cultural manifestations. If actual buildings or spaces are interpreted through this lens, it is not because they themselves possess uncanny properties, but rather because they act, historically or culturally, as representations of estrangement. If there is a single premise to be derived from the study of the uncanny in modern culture, it is that there is no such thing as an uncanny architecture, but simply architecture that, from time to time and for different purposes, is invested with uncanny qualities.

Yet the contemporary sense of the uncanny, as I shall attempt to demonstrate, is not simply a survival of a romantic commonplace, or a feeling confined to the artistic genres of horror and ghost stories. Its theoretical exposition by Freud, and later by Heidegger, places it centrally among the categories that might be adduced to interpret modernity and especially its conditions of spatiality, architectural and urban. As a frame of reference that confronts the desire for a home and the struggle for domestic security with its apparent opposite, intellectual and actual homelessness, at the same time as revealing the fundamental complicity between the two, *das Unheimliche* captures the difficult conditions of the theoretical practice of architecture in modern times. As a concept that itself has recurred with differing effects in the last two centuries, it serves as an interpretative model that cuts through the periodizations of historians according to categories such as romanticism, modernism, and postmodernism, as a way of understanding an aspect of modernity that has given a new meaning to the traditional Homeric notion of "homesickness."

Equally, consideration of the theory of the uncanny allows for a rewriting of traditional and modernist aesthetic theory as it has applied to categories such as imitation (the double), repetition, the symbolic, the sublime. Questions of gender and subject might be linked to the continuing discourse of estrangement and the Other, in the social and political context of racial, ethnic, and minority exclusion. The resurgent problem of homelessness, as the last traces of welfare capitalism are systematically demolished, lends, finally, a special urgency to any reflection on the modern unhomely.

But it is in this very confrontation with social and political practice that the aesthetic theory of estrangement finds an apparently intractable and unyielding test. The formal and critical *expression* of alienation, as the first avant-gardes found to their chagrin, does not always neatly correspond to the work of transforming or even ameliorating such conditions in practice. Formal explorations of defamiliarization based on carnivalesque reversals of aesthetic norms, substitutions of

Read again /

the grotesque for the sublime, the uncanny for the domestic, can all too easily be construed as decoration or caricature. Faced with the intolerable state of real homelessness, any reflection on the "transcendental" or psychological unhomely risks trivializing or, worse, patronizing political or social action.

This said, I would still want to suggest the possibility that the theme of the uncanny, considered both historically and in its post-Freudian dimensions, opens questions that are larger than their simple illustration in architectural projects, questions that have stubbornly refused solution in politics as in design and that seem still pertinent to our late twentieth-century condition. In this sense, I want to use the different connotations of the theme both suggestively and critically, understanding its various textual and architectural manifestations as problematic contributions to a yet unfinished history that pits the homely, the domestic, the nostalgic, against their ever-threatening, always invading, and often subversive "opposites."

For if the theoretical elaboration of the uncanny helps us to interpret the conditions of modern estrangement, the special characteristics of architecture and urbanism as arts of spatial definition allow us to advance the argument into the domain of the tangible. Here it is that the "void" described by *posthistoire* philosophy is almost uncannily repeated in the world, that the question of the "unhomely home" finds its most poignant expressions and equally troubling solutions. This occurs on a number of interrelated levels, both literal and phenomenal. On the literal plane, the "empty spaces" appropriated or created by urbanism—the clearing of vacant or occupied territory—are paralleled on the phenomenal plane by the tabula rasa imagined by modernist utopias, to the point where both levels intersect in the commonplaces of modern urban development. The task of filling these voids—what Ernst Bloch has termed the "hollow spaces of capitalism"—is given over to architecture, which is forced, in the absence of a lived past, to search for posthistorical grounds on which to base an "authentic" home for society.[21] Thus, on an even more literal level, architecture finds itself "repeating" history, whether in traditional or avant-garde guise, in a way that itself gives rise to an uncanny sense of déjà vu that parallels Freud's own description of the uncanny as linked to the "compulsion to repeat." The apparently irreconcilable demands for the absolute negation of the past and full "restoration" of the past here meet in their inevitable reliance on a language of architectural forms that seem, on the surface at least, to echo already used-up motifs *en abîme*.

Deployed in this way, the uncanny might regain a political connotation as the very condition of contemporary haunting; what in the sixties was so overtly a presence in theory and practice, a presence that largely denied the formal in architecture in favor of social practice, utopian or material, is now, in the nineties, apparently suppressed by an ostensibly nihilistic and self-gratifying formalism. But the political, I would argue, cannot be so easily eliminated from cultural practice, and it is precisely the point at which it reerupts within the very formal techniques of its repression that it takes on the characteristics of the uncanny. It was Jeffrey Mehlman who first pointed to the inherent nature of revolutions to provoke, through repetition in practice and in text, a kind of *unheimlich* effect.[22] In the present work I would simply note that, in contemporary architecture, the incessant reference to avant-garde techniques devoid of their originating ideological impulse, the appearance of a fulfilled aesthetic revolution stripped of its promise of social redemption, at least approximates the conditions that, in Freud's estimation, are ripe for uncanny sensations. If I feel a personal uncanny in the face of such a repression of the political, it is perhaps for this reason: that, within many of the projects that pretend to a radical disruption of cultural modes of expression, there still lurks the ghost of avant-garde politics, one that is proving difficult to exorcise entirely. "This uncanny," wrote Freud, "is in reality nothing new or alien, but something which is familiar and old-established in the mind and which has become alienated from it only through the process of repression. . . . The uncanny [is] something which ought to have remained hidden but has come to light" (U 64).

I
Houses

Unhomely Houses

Some languages in use today can only render the German expression "an *unheimlich* house" by "a *haunted* house."
Sigmund Freud, "The Uncanny"

By far the most popular topos of the nineteenth-century uncanny was the haunted house. A pervasive leitmotiv of literary fantasy and architectural revival alike, its depiction in fairy tales, horror stories, and Gothic novels gave rise to a unique genre of writing that, by the end of the century, stood for romanticism itself. The house provided an especially favored site for uncanny disturbances: its apparent domesticity, its residue of family history and nostalgia, its role as the last and most intimate shelter of private comfort sharpened by contrast the terror of invasion by alien spirits. Edgar Allan Poe's "The Fall of the House of Usher" was paradigmatic: "With the first glimpse of the building, a sense of insufferable gloom pervaded my spirit. . . . The feeling was unrelieved by any of that half-pleasurable, because poetic, sentiment with which the mind usually receives even the sternest natural images of the desolate or terrible."[1]

And yet the House of Usher, in Poe's description, while evoking premonitions of "shadowy fancies," exhibited nothing untoward in its outer appearance. Its "bleak walls" and "vacant eye-like windows" were stark, but any sentiments of doom were more easily attributed to the fantasies of the narrator than to any striking detail in the house itself. Indeed, when looked at objectively, its ancient stones, carvings, tapestries, and trophies were all familiar enough. The "atmosphere" that surrounded the house, its smell of the grave that "had reeked

"Something in between the dream and awakening."

familiar/ unfamiliar

up from the decayed trees, and the grey wall and the silent tarn," was difficult to account for: "vague sentiments," seemingly the products of a *dream*. The slow realization that these were properties of the house, embedded in the very stones that possessed a fatality in themselves, that the house was itself an uncanny power, came unwillingly, against all reason, the more disquieting for the absolute normality of the setting, its veritable *absence* of overt terror. The effect was one of the disturbing unfamiliarity of the evidently familiar: "While the objects around me . . . were but matters to which, or to such as which, I had been accustomed from my infancy—while I hesitated not to acknowledge how familiar was all this—I still wondered to find how unfamiliar were the fancies which ordinary images were stirring up."[2]

But in Poe's paradigmatic haunted house, all the tell-tale signs of haunting were present, systematically culled from his romantic predecessors. The site was desolate; the walls were blank and almost literally "faceless," its windows "eye-like" but without life—"vacant." It was, besides, a repository of centuries of memory and tradition, embodied in its walls and objects; the walls were marked by the "discoloration of ages" and crumbling stones; the furnishings were dark, the rooms vaulted and gloomy; it was, in fact, already a museum, a collection such as that assembled by Alexandre du Sommerard in the Hôtel de Cluny, here preserved in memory of a family. Finally, the family itself was almost extinct, doomed by a history that lent the air of the tomb, the family vault, to this once-living abode; its fabric was reminiscent of "old wood-work which has rotted for some years in some neglected vault, with no disturbance from the breath of the external air."[3]

The house was then a crypt, predestined to be buried in its turn, an event prefigured in the "barely perceptible fissure" that ran vertically from roof to foundations. Inside, painted by Usher himself, was what seemed to be the image of its own tomb, a scene that in its character seemed to his narrator the most uncanny of all in its "abstraction":

One of the phantasmagoric conceptions of my friend, partaking not so rigidly of the spirit of abstraction, may be shadowed forth, although feebly, in words. A small picture presented the interior of an immensely long and rectangular vault or tunnel, with low walls, smooth white, and without interruption or device. Certain accessory points of the design served well to convey the idea that this excavation lay at an exceeding depth below the surface of the earth. No outlet was observed in any portion of its vast extent, and no torch or other artificial source of light was discernible; yet a flood of intense rays rolled throughout, and bathed the whole in a ghastly and inappropriate splendor.[4]

Abandoned houses, real or imaginary, had a similar effect on the viewer. Those described by Victor Hugo on the islands of Jersey and Guernsey, veritable figures of his own unhomely exile, shared characteristics with the House of Usher, with the difference that they were "haunted" not by some imaginary family spirit but by virtue of the superstitions of the islanders.

It sometimes happens, in Jersey or Guernsey, that in the countryside, or even in the town, when passing through some deserted spot or a street filled with people, you will see a house with a barricaded entrance; holly obstructs the door; one knows not what hideous layers of nailed planks fill the windows of the ground floor; the windows of the upper floors are at once closed and open, all the casements are barred but all the window-panes are broken.

Such a house, killed by its very emptiness and the superstitions that have built up in the region, "is a haunted house [*une maison visionée*]. The devil comes there in the night."[5]

Among these "dead houses" one in particular fascinated Hugo, an empty house in the Guernsey village of Pleinmont. He returned three times in seven years to sketch it from various angles and used it as a central motif in *Les Travailleurs de la mer*. Drawn in brown ink and wash, this small, two-story stone cottage seemed to have little out of the ordinary about it. With its four windows, walled up on the ground floor, its single door, pitched roof, and chimney, it seems no more than the archetypical "child's house," a commonplace compilation of the fundamental elements of dwelling. As Hugo himself noted, "the site is fine, the house is good. This house, built in granite and two stories high, is surrounded by grass. It is in no way ruined. It is perfectly habitable. The walls are thick and the roof solid. Not a stone is lacking in the walls, not a tile from the roof." Nevertheless, it had the reputation of being haunted, and despite its simplicity, "its aspect was strange." Firstly, the deserted site, almost entirely surrounded by the sea, was perhaps too beautiful: "The site is magnificent, and consequently sinister." Then the contrast between the walled-up windows on the ground floor and the open, empty windows on the upper floor, "opening onto the shadows of the interior," gave a quasi-an-thropomorphic air to the structure: "One would say that the empty holes were two gouged-out eyes." An enigmatic inscription over the closed-up door added to the mystery and told of a building and abandonment before the Revolution: "ELM-PBILG 1780." Finally, the silence and emptiness contributed the aura of a tomb; "one thought one saw a sepulcher with windows allowing the specters to look out." It is by such mysteries, adding to local lore, that Hugo explains the haunting. Who were the original inhabitants? Why the abandonment? Why no present owner? Why no one to cultivate the field? These questions, all inexplicable without some unknown and metaphysical cause, added to the atmosphere: "This house is uncanny at midday; what is it at midnight? Looking at it one looks at a secret. . . . Enigmas. Sacred horror is in these stones. This shadow inhabiting these walled-up rooms is more than a shadow; it is the unknown."[6] Thus guarded by terror, the house, as Hugo develops the narrative, becomes paradoxically secure for those unaffected by the haunting; it is the home of smugglers and renegades, exiles and fugitives. Only those on the margin would feel at home in so disquieting an abode. The legend of a crime committed in the house, an indelible act from which it has never recovered, thus rejoined the present it sheltered, and the circle of a home killed by memories was completed in this image of a tomb inhabited by its robbers: "The house, like man, can become a skeleton. A superstition is enough to kill it. Then it is terrible."[7]

Such "terror," however, was not exactly equivalent to that pre-scribed by Edmund Burke; in the hierarchy of romantic genres, the uncanny was intimately bound up with, but strangely different from, the grander and more serious "sublime," the master category of aspiration, nostalgia, and the unattainable. Thus Poe, attempting to define the peculiar feeling evoked by the House of Usher, had dis-tinguished it sharply from the more terrifying sensations normally attendant on the sublime: "There was an iciness, a sinking, a sickening of the heart—an unredeemed dreariness of thought which no goad-ing of the imagination could torture into aught of the sublime."[8]

Traditionally, of course, all the subgenres of the sublime—the gro-tesque, the caricature, the fairy story, the melodrama, the ghostly romance, and the horror story—were considered to be subversive of its overarching premises and its transcendent ambitions. While Burke had traced the sublime to its fundamental source in terror, he readily admitted that not everything that induced terror was sublime.[9] By the same token, Kant's description of a sublimity residing entirely in the mind, as it was drawn to "think the unattainability of nature," did not apply to all ideas of things unattainable. Lurking behind all attempts to achieve sublime expression were a host of pitfalls that ranged from the bathetic to the nonsensical; rhetoricians from Longinus to Jean Paul Richter had understood this tendency of the sublime to fall into the ridiculous, an opposite, moreover, that shared many characteristics with its more serious antecedent. "Ugliness," stated Burke, "I imagine to be consistent enough with an idea of the sublime. But I would by no means insinuate that ugliness of itself is a sublime idea unless united with such qualities that excite a strong terror."[10]

The uncanny, however, was perhaps the most subversive of all, not only because it was easily trivialized but also because it seemed at times indistinguishable from the sublime. Burke himself had included this ill-defined but increasingly popular sensation among those associated with the obscurity that provoked terror, along with the night and absolute darkness: "How greatly the night adds to our dread in all cases of danger," he observed, "and how much the notions of ghosts and goblins, of which none can form clear ideas, affect minds."[11] Such was the threat of the uncanny throughout the romantic period that Hegel, in his vain effort to preserve the memory of an authentic sublime in the Hebrew texts, tried to close the door on this province of "magic, magnetism, demons, the superior apparitions of clairvoyance, the disease of somnambulism," banishing these dark powers from the clear and transparent realm of art. But he was nevertheless forced to admit the general preoccupation of his contemporaries with those "unknown forces" wherein "there is supposed to lie an indecipherable truth of dreadfullness which cannot be grasped or understood."[12]

More than eighty years later, Freud recognized that the uncanny was, at least in its received connotations, an aesthetic category that lay directly within the boundaries of "all that is terrible," that is, within the traditional sublime (U 339). But he set himself the task of identifying "what this particular quality is which allows us to distinguish as 'uncanny' certain things within the boundary of what is 'fearful.'" It was almost with delight that he undertook to explore, against those "elaborate treatises on aesthetics which . . . prefer to concern themselves with what is beautiful, attractive and sublime," feelings of an apparently opposite kind, those of unpleasantness and repulsion (U 339–340). To explore, that is, the margins of the sublime against its acknowledged center. For Freud, the uncanny evidently presented itself as an especially useful instrument with which to deflate an empty aesthetics on behalf of psychoanalytical knowledge, a skirmish that mirrored his more general attack on metaphysical psychology:

> The subject of the uncanny . . . is undoubtedly related to what is frightening—to what arouses dread and horror; equally certainly, too, the word is not always used in a clearly definable sense, so that it tends to coincide with what excites fear in general. Yet we may expect that a special core of feeling is present which justifies the use of a special conceptual term. One is curious to know what this common core is which allows us to distinguish as "uncanny" certain things which lie within the field of what is frightening. (U 339)

The sensation of "uncanniness" was, then, an especially difficult feeling to define precisely. Neither absolute terror nor mild anxiety, the uncanny seemed easier to describe in terms of what it was not than in any essential sense of its own. Thus it might readily be distinguished from horror and all strong feelings of fear; it was not uniquely identified with the parapsychological—the magical, the hallucinatory, the mystical, and the supernatural did not necessarily imply "uncanniness"; nor was it present in everything that appeared strange, weird, grotesque, or fantastic; it was the direct opposite, finally, of the caricatural and the distorted, which, by their exaggeration, refused to provoke fear. Sharing qualities with all these allied genres of fear, the uncanny reveled in its nonspecificity, one reinforced by the multiplicity of untranslatable words that served to indicate its presence in different languages.

Indeed, Freud's initial attempt at comparative lingustic definition foundered immediately in the face of *unheimlich, inquiétant, sinistre, lugubre, étrange, mal à son aise, sospechoso, de mal aguëro, siniestro,* and of course "uncanny," itself untranslatable. Greek offered simply ξένος (strange, foreign), and Latin only *locus suspectus,* or "uncanny place" (U 341–342). And yet, despite Freud's irritation, the total effect of this assemblage of words certainly delimits, if not the word, at least a field of connotation, a set of attributes. Thus the uncanny would be sinister, disturbing, suspect, strange; it would be character-ized better as "dread" than terror, deriving its force from its very inexplicability, its sense of lurking unease, rather than from any clearly defined source of fear—an uncomfortable sense of haunting rather than a present apparition. Here the English word is perhaps more helpful than Freud was willing to admit: literally "beyond ken"—beyond knowledge—from "canny," meaning possessing knowl-edge or skill.[13]

The psychologist Ernst Jentsch, in an essay of 1906 that Freud used as a starting point for his own investigation, had already pointed to the intimate relations between psychology and language: "Our German language seems to have created a fairly happy construction with the word *unheimlich*. Without doubt it seems to express that somebody who has an uncanny experience is not quite *zu Hause* [at home] in the matter, that he is not *heimisch* [homely], that the affair is foreign to him."[14] Jentsch attributed the feeling of uncanniness to a fundamental insecurity brought about by a "lack of orientation," a sense of something new, foreign, and hostile invading an old, familiar, customary world. As summarized by Freud, he

ascribes the central factor in the production of the feeling of uncanniness to intellectual uncertainty; so that the uncanny would always, as it were, be something one does not know one's way about in. The better oriented in his environment a person is, the less readily will he get the impression of some-thing uncanny in regard to the objects and events in it. (U 341)

Despite Freud's reluctance to accept the limits of this explanation—Jentsch's definition was, he concluded, "incomplete"—it nonetheless underlined a first relation of the uncanny to the spatial and environ-mental, that of "orientation," of "knowing one's way about."

For Freud's purposes, the multiple significations and affiliations of the German word *unheimlich* were more promising. They served at once to clarify the operations of the uncanny as a systematic principle as well as to situate its domain firmly in the domestic and the homely, thence to permit its decipherment in individual experience as the unconscious product of a family romance. To this end, Freud delib-erately approached the definition of *unheimlich* by way of that of its apparent opposite, *heimlich*, thereby exposing the disturbing affilia-tions between the two and constituting the one as a direct outgrowth of the other.

Drawing on two nineteenth-century dictionaries with lengthy citations, Freud allowed his argument, so to speak, to unfold by itself (U
342–347).[15] Thus in Daniel Sanders's *Wörterbuch* of 1860, *heimlich* is
first defined as "belonging to the house or family," as "not strange,
familiar." It is associated with the intimate, the "friendlily comfortable," "the enjoyment of quiet content, etc., arousing a sense of
agreeable restfulness and security as in one within the four walls of
his house." Sanders evokes a host of examples: "'To destroy the
Heimlichkeit of the home.' 'I could not readily find another spot so
intimate and *heimlich* as this.' 'We pictured it so comfortable, so nice,
so cozy and *heimlich*.' 'In quiet *Heimlichkeit*, surrounded by close
walls.'" Swabian and Swiss authors seemed especially susceptible to
such notions, as Sanders localized the term in its regional and picturesque spelling: "'How *heimelich* it seemed to Ivo again of an evening, when he was at home.' 'It was so *heimelig* in the house.' 'The
warm room and the *heimelig* afternoon.' . . . 'The cottage where he
had once sat so often among his own people, so *heimelig*, so happy.'"
The word *heimlich* is thereby linked to domesticity (*Häuslichkeit*), to
being at home (*heimatlich*) or being neighborly (*freundnachbarlich*).[16]
    And yet, lurking behind such images of happiness and erupting
through Sanders's own examples, there is the burden of what is
definitely not *heimlich*: "The man who till recently had been so strange
to him"; "the Protestant landowners [who] do not feel . . . *heimlich*
among their Catholic inferiors"; "that which comes from afar [which]
assuredly does not live quite *heimelig* among the people." Already
conscious of the intrusion of the stranger, Sanders himself seems
worried that, as he warns, the original "form of the word deserves
to become general in order to protect this perfectly good sense of
the word from becoming obsolete"; he fears that *heimlich* will turn on
itself and take on the sole meaning of its second major acceptation,
that of "concealed, kept from sight, so that others do not get to know
of or about it," as in "To do something *heimlich*, i.e., behind someone's
back . . . *heimlich* places (which good manners oblige us to conceal)."
From home, to private, to privy ("the *heimlich* chamber"), to secret
and thereby magic ("the *heimlich* art"), was an all-too-easy slippage.
Thence, Sanders noted, it was a small step to *unheimlich*: "Note especially the negative 'un': eerie, weird, arousing gruesome fear:
'Seeming quite *unheimlich* and ghostly. . . . 'Feels like an *unheimlich*

horror.' '*Unheimlich* and motionless like a stone image.' 'The *unheimlich* mist called hill-fog,'"[17]

Similarly, the brothers Grimm, indefatigable collectors of folklore and myth, defining the word *heimlich* in their own *Deutsches Wörterbuch* (1877), traced the idea of the homely, that which belongs to house and home, a sentiment of security and freedom from fear, as it gradually took on the ominous dimensions of its apparent opposite, the unhomely:

4. *From the idea of "homelike," belonging to the house, the further idea is developed of something withdrawn from the eyes of strangers, something concealed, secret.* . . . "Heimlich" is used in conjunction with a verb expressing the act of concealing. . . .

Officials who give important advice which has to be kept secret in matters of state are called *heimlich* councilors; the adjective, according to modern usage, has been replaced by *geheim* [secret]. . . .

Heimlich, as used of knowledge—mystic, allegorical: a *heimlich* meaning, *mysticus, divinus, occultus, figuratus. Heimlich* in a different sense, as withdrawn from knowledge, unconscious. . . . *Heimlich* also has the meaning of that which is obscure, inaccessible to knowledge.

The notion of something hidden and dangerous . . . is still further developed, so that "heimlich" comes to have the meaning usually ascribed to "unheimlich." Thus: "At times I feel like a man who walks in the night and believes in ghosts; every corner is *heimlich* and full of terrors for him."[18]

Freud was taken with this slow unfolding of the homely into the unhomely, pleased to discover that "*heimlich* is a word the meaning of which develops in the direction of ambivalence, until it finally coincides with its opposite, *unheimlich*" (U 347). Sanders had even produced a citation that demonstrated "that among its different shades of meaning the word *heimlich* exhibits one which is identical with its opposite, *unheimlich*." This excerpt, from the dramatist Karl Ferdinand Gutzkow, included the phrase "We call it *unheimlich;* you call it *heimlich*." But Freud the psychoanalyst was even more intrigued by the first part of the passage:

"The Zecks are all *heimlich*." . . . "*Heimlich*? . . . What do you understand by *heimlich*?" "Well . . . , they are like a buried spring or a dried-up pond. One cannot walk over it without always having the feeling that the water might come up there again." "Oh, we call it *unheimlich;* you call it *heimlich*."[19]

This sense of a once-buried spring bursting forth unexpectedly, of the *unheimlich* compared to a disquieting return, was confirmed by other examples in Sanders that joined the notion of *heimlich* as "concealed" to the sense of something "buried." Thus if sleep was in some way "*heim'lig,*" so cemeteries were "quiet, lovely, and *heimlich,* no place more fitted for their rest," and burial was no more than "To throw into pits or *Heimlichkeiten.*" "I have roots that are most *heimlich,*" cried an author cited by Sanders, "I am grown in the deep earth."[20] In this sense, the *unheimlich* seemed to emerge beneath the *heimlich,* so to speak, to rise up again when seemingly put to rest, to escape from the bounds of home.

Such an ascription was confirmed for Freud by an aphorism again quoted in Sanders and taken from the philosopher Schelling: "*Unheimlich* is the name for everything that ought to have remained . . . secret and hidden but has come to light."[21] It was this phrase that Freud seized upon as the vital clue to his investigation; recurring as a leitmotiv throughout the essay, it offered a veritable "principle" that, intimating a prepsychoanalytic version of "the return of the repressed," permitted him to go beyond the simple "intellectual uncertainty" posited by Jentsch. Indeed the entire argument of "The Uncanny" was to devolve around this apparently simple statement, finally only understandable, according to Freud, by the concept of repression.

Schelling's felicitous "definition" of the uncanny had in fact been extracted by Sanders from the *Philosophie der Mythologie* of 1835, Schelling's late attempt to synthesize the history of religion with the anthropology of cults. Here Schelling had proposed an origin for the uncanny that was itself joined to the origins of religion, philosophy, and poetry. His formulation, anticipating Nietzsche, asserted the necessary existence of the uncanny as a force to be overcome, a first step toward the birth of poetry. Speaking of the Homeric songs, for him among the purest examples of the sublime, Schelling proposed that they were precisely the result of an initial suppression, the civilized subjugation of mystery, myth, and the occult. Like the birth of the Apollonian out of the Dionysian, and with similar effects, the Homeric sublime was founded on the repression of the uncanny:

Greece had a Homer precisely because it had mysteries, that is because it succeeded in completely subduing that principle of the past, which was still dominant and outwardly manifest in the Oriental systems, and in pushing it back into the interior, that is, into secrecy, into the Mystery (out of which it had, after all, originally emerged). That clear sky which hovers above the

Homeric poems, that ether which arches over Homer's world, could spread itself over Greece until the dark and obscure power of that uncanny principle which dominated earlier religions had been reduced to the Mysteries (all things are called uncanny which should have remained secret, hidden, latent, but which have come to light); the Homeric age could not contemplate fashioning its purely poetic mythology until the genuine religious principle had been secured in the interior, thereby granting the mind complete outward freedom.[22]

This account of the "uncanny principle," besides providing a convenient starting point for Freud—as based on a primal repression, a slaying of the father ("Homer," stated Schelling, "is not the father of mythology, mythology is the father of Homer")[23]—summarized the idea of *unheimlich* as evoked by the romantics. At once a psychological and an aesthetic phenomenon, it both established and destabilized at the same time. Its effects were guaranteed by an original authenticity, a first burial, and made all the more potent by virtue of a return that, in civilization, was in a real sense out of place. Something was not, then, merely haunted, but rather revisited by a power that was thought long dead. To such a force the romantic psyche and the romantic aesthetic sensibility were profoundly open; at any moment what seemed on the surface homely and comforting, secure and clear of superstition, might be reappropriated by something that should have remained secret but that nevertheless, through some chink in the shutters of progress, had returned.[24]

Among the foremost practitioners of the uncanny—what Hegel called that genre of "visionary notions," where "nothing is expressed except a sickness of the spirit," where "poetry runs over into nebulousness, insubstantiality, and emptiness"—Hegel cited the writer E. T. A. Hoffmann, who had for all intents and purposes made the uncanny a genre of his own. It was precisely this aura of indecipherability that attracted Freud to Hoffmann. Hoffmann's stories, further, seemed to present themselves as completely worked examples of Schelling's "theory of the uncanny" in all its possible permutations.

It was in no way accidental that Hoffmann's almost systematic exploration of the relations between the homely and the unhomely, the familiar and the strange, extended to an equally subtle examination of the role of architecture in staging the sensation and in acting as an instrument for its narrative and spatial manifestations. Hoffmann was himself an amateur architect, stageset designer, and "collector" of strange houses; as a writer and musician the architect he most admired was Karl Friedrich Schinkel, whom he commissioned to design the sets for his opera *Undine*.[25] But the place of architecture in Hoffmann's idea of the uncanny was secured by more than simple allegiance to a talented designer. For romantics of Hoffmann's generation, architecture was central to the task of representing nature, a veritable microcosm of the social and natural world. Kant, after all, had turned it into a metaphor for his entire philosophy, explaining by means of the architectonic the structural relations of thought; for the Young Germans, after Goethe, architecture was, in its Gothic or classical incarnations, a vision of aesthetic perfection—classical as a norm, Gothic as witness to the birth of the nation. Schiller, Schelling, the brothers Schlegel, and later Hegel made architecture a central concern of their aesthetics. Hölderlin, Novalis, and Clemens Brentano found material for their Orphic visions in the temples and fora of an antique Golden Age. Caspar David Friedrich depicted the ruins and traces of a symbolic perfection destroyed by time and the elements. Hoffmann, despite his accentuated irony, found in architecture the tangible sign of a musical harmony unattainable in sound. He also "designed" with meticulous care the settings of his stories, delineating spaces that, sympathetically as it were, resonated to the psychological dimensions of his characters, not simply the illustrations of primitive Gothic terror but the constructed equivalents of the psychological uncanny in architecture.

There are numerous haunted houses in the tales of Hoffmann. The house of the archivist Lindhorst in "The Golden Pot" ("Der Goldne Topf"), for example, is to all intents and purposes a house like any other on its street. Only its door knocker displays signs of the uncanny within. But inside, what might seem to be the familiar spaces of libraries, greenhouses, and studies might turn at any moment into fantastic, semiorganic environments: rooms formed of palms, their gilded leaves covering the ceiling, their bronze trunks standing like organic columns; tropical gardens lit by no outside source of light. Less fantastic but more uncanny, the uninhabited dwelling described in "The Deserted House" ("Das öde Haus") presents itself to the street, like Hugo's ruin, with its openings blocked; its dilapidation strange in comparison with its magnificent boulevard setting, the house was like "a square block of stone pierced by four windows, forming two stories only, a ground floor and a first floor;

. . . cracked and decayed. . . . The four windows were fast shut. Those belonging to the ground floor had been walled up."[26] Finally, Rossitten Castle in "The Deed of Entail" ("Das Majorat") seems only romantic from the outside, a gloomy ruin cursed by the fate of its owners; inside, the rapid transitions from comfortable and secure to uncomfortable and insecure produce a semi–dream effect similar to that of the familiar turned strange.

None of these houses exhibits the structure of the uncanny as well as that described in the tale of "Councillor Krespel" ("Rat Krespel"), however. First published in 1818, then included in the first volume of the *Serapion Brethren (Die Serapions Brüder)* the following year, this story sets out the relationship between the uncanny and architecture without relying on the apparatus of dream, of haunting, or of mystery.[27]

The story opens with an apparently incidental description of the building of a house; on the surface, indeed, as the narrator notes, this is no more than an illustration of one of "the craziest schemes" of this Councillor, himself "one of the most eccentric men" (K 80). The house, described as having been the gift of a local lord in payment for legal services, was built at the bottom of the Councillor's garden according to his own somewhat peculiar specifications. Having bought and assembled all the building materials, stacked and cut the stones, mixed the lime, and sifted the sand, the Councillor had proceeded to amaze the neighbors by refusing all architectural help, directly employing a master mason, journeymen, and apprentices on the work. What was more extraordinary, he had neither commissioned nor drawn up a plan for the house, but had simply excavated a perfectly square foundation for the four walls. These, following his instructions, were built up by the masons, without windows or doors, just as high as the Councillor indicated. Despite the evident madness of this procedure, the builders seemed happy enough, plentifully supplied with food and drink. One day Krespel shouted "Stop!" and the walls were complete (K 80–81).

Then the Councillor began a most strange activity, pacing up and down the garden, moving toward the house in every direction, until, by means of this complex triangulation, he "found" the right place for the door and ordered it cut in the stone; similarly, walking into the house, he performed the same method to determine each window and partition, deciding, seemingly spontaneously, their position and

size. The house was then finished. To celebrate his new home, Krespel invited the builders and their families, but no friends, to a feast
at which he played the violin. The result of his maneuvers was a
home "presenting a most unusual appearance from the outside—no
two windows being alike and so on—but whose interior arrangements
aroused a very special feeling of ease" (K 82).

This short, anecdotal introduction serves in Hoffmann's story to
present the peculiar character of the musician, lawyer, and violin-
maker Krespel, whose beautiful but ill-fated daughter Antonia, blest
with an uncannily harmonious singing voice, is trapped within the
house, unable to sing lest she die of the effort. In the light of the
tale that follows, which recounts the story of Antonia's seduction and
final death song, the description of Krespel's crazy house might seem
to be one more nonsensical trait of its owner, or at best a literary
conceit. The crazy house would then be merely a picturesque fragment, a lively introduction to the tale.

On another level, however, the very eccentricity of Krespel in
refusing an architect, the disastrous effects of whose professional
drive had been demonstrated in Goethe's own "architectural" novel
Elective Affinities, might lead us to read Hoffmann's preface as in itself
carrying a moral. Perhaps, in the antics of the Councillor, Hoffmann
is gently satirizing the myth of the "natural architect," a myth common to the Enlightenment and romantic period alike. In this fable,
the architect would be depicted as a Rousseauesque figure, who, left
alone in the primeval woods, knew immediately how to build, establishing indeed the very laws of architecture in the raising of the first
columns and the framing of the first beams. Krespel as the "antina-
tural" designer, then, would only make a mess out of his primitive
and clumsy gestures, demonstrating, as Hoffmann loved to demonstrate, the negative values of sentimental myths. Following this line
of reading, we might also suppose that by refusing the help of an
architect (a modern professional) and by employing masons (traditional builders and geometers), Krespel would be a paradigm of the
romantic patron, returning to the "roots" of a truly German building
by restoring the wisdom of the craft guilds.

Or perhaps Krespel's house should be taken as a kind of paradigm
of the beautiful in architecture. Its foundation was erected, after all,
on a perfect square; remembering that Krespel was a musician, we
might think of the relations, endlessly drawn in classical theory, be-

tween architecture and music, whereby architecture is said in its geometrical harmonies to echo those of music. This too was a favorite romantic analogy: Schelling had announced that "architecture is in general frozen [congealed] music," and had cited the myth of Amphion, who had with his lyre caused the stones to join together to form the walls of Thebes.[28] This idea of architecture as concrete music was widely commented on. In his *Maxims and Reflections* Goethe turned the phrase into "petrified music," and, recalling the myth of Orpheus, qualified his understanding of architecture by finding it a sort of "expired harmony": "the sounds fade away but the harmony lives on."[29] In this sense, Krespel's house might be seen as a large music box, singing on behalf of its occupant, Antonia, who is held mute, save for the first time she was heard to sing, when, finally, the house shone with reflected radiance: "the windows lighted up more brightly than usual." There is little in the crazy exterior of the house to recall the petrified harmonies of Orpheus, those "rhythmic walls" evoked by Goethe, but then Krespel was an extremely unorthodox musician.[30]

Here, along the lines of this synaesthetic analogy, the house might be interpreted as a direct replication in stone of the musical personality of Krespel, replicating not just his outer eccentricity but also his inner soul. We are told that his outer behavior, indeed, is a direct reflection of his inner emotions:

There are men from whom nature or some peculiar destiny has removed the cover beneath which we hide our own madness. They are like thin-skinned insects whose visible play of muscles seems to make them deformed, though, in fact, everything soon returns to its normal shape again. Everything which remains within us becomes action in Krespel. (K 92)

Thus the apparently "mad" gestures and "irrational" leaps of the Councillor are no more than the external expressions of his spirit, which remains healthy, despite, or maybe because of, the madness on the surface. The chaos of the outer facades of his house, compared to the sense of order within, would be an analogue to this condition of reversed repression. Such a pattern of reversals runs through the whole story, which on every level throws into opposition the terms of apparent madness or evil and revealed sanity or good. The *mise-en-abîme* of upside down and inside out finds its crystallization and prefiguration in the house.

This characterization leads us to a final observation that condemns us no longer to circulate, so to speak, around the house as a metaphor, but permits us to cross over the threshold of an edifice whose structure coincides with the mood of the story and proposes thereby a method for its interpretation. The house, we remember, was described as a house "unusual" from the outside, and homely inside,

presenting a most unusual [*tollsten,* "mad" or "crazy"] appearance from the outside—no two windows being alike, and so on—but whose interior arrangements aroused a very special feeling of ease [*Wohlbehaglichkeit,* "coziness," "well-being"]. Everyone who went there bore testimony to this. (K 82)

That is, in the terms we have been using, the house was homely inside but most unhomely outside, illustrating Freud's intuition that from the homely house to the haunted house there is a single passage, where what is contained and safe is therefore secret, obscure, and inaccessible, dangerous and full of terrors; that "*heimlich* is a word, the meaning of which develops toward an ambivalence until it finally coincides with its opposite, *unheimlich*."

But Krespel's house, viewed in these terms, is a structure that in fact reverses the general drift of the uncanny movement from homely to unhomely, a movement in most ghost stories where an apparently homely house turns gradually into a site of horror. Krespel's house makes no attempt to hide its uncanniness on the exterior. In this context, it should be remembered that in fabricating the house Krespel's activities were themselves decidedly *unheimlich*:

"Make way!" cried Krespel, who then ran to one end of the garden and paced slowly toward his square building. When he came close to the wall, he shook his head in dissatisfaction, ran to the other end of the garden and again paced toward the wall with the same result. He repeated this tactic several times, until finally, *running his hard nose against the wall,* he cried, "Come here, come here men. Make me a door right here." (K 82, my emphasis)

Like a blind man with only his cane and his nose to guide him, Krespel did not, like normal men, see something and then point to it, but rather ran toward something and then touched it. If he saw at all it was with a very "close up," almost haptic, vision. This impression is confirmed in the story when he is described the next day as moving like a drunken or blind man: "He looked as if he would bump into or damage something at any moment," but by some uncanny sense he avoided breaking the cups on the table and was able to maneuver around a full-length mirror that he initially thought was a void.

Only a partially blind man would be tricked by such a mirror into thinking it was a void. Again, after dinner, fabricating miniature bone objects out of the remains of the rabbit, he is described as operating like a nearsighted jeweler whose eyes enlarge small things, but to whom large things are out of focus. And yet, in literal terms, Krespel can obviously see; it is rather as if he consciously represses the full faculties of sight in order to exercise others, deeper and more potent. This repression of the eye will find its explanation in other uncanny stories by Hoffmann, notably that selected by Freud as the locus of the uncanny itself, "The Sandman" ("Der Sandmann"), a story where the "lust of the eye," as Walter Pater would call it, is played out in every conceivable combination.[31]

In "Der Sandmann," Hoffmann, as Freud observed, privileges the power of the eye; indeed a quantitative reader would estimate more than sixty pairs of eyes described, not to mention the sack of eyes carried by the legendary Sandman, or the "myriad" eyes figured by the flashing eyeglasses of the barometer dealer Coppola, or the incessant repetition of veiled references to eyes in gazes, glances, and visions. The roles of all these oculi might be seen as dividing into two. On the one hand there are the eyes that see everything clearly as it is in the world, like the eyes of Klara, "bright" and "childlike," which see "only the bright surface of the world" (S 287). These are eyes that stop in front of appearance. On the other, there are the more powerful eyes, those of the Sandman, and perhaps of Nathanael, however clouded with sand, eyes that see beyond appearances. The former, clear-sighted eyes are described as mirrors: they reflect the outside world, even as Klara's eyes are "like a lake by Ruïsdael, in which the pure azure of a cloudless sky, the woodlands and flower bedecked fields, and the whole bright and varied life of a lush landscape are reflected" (S 290). The latter, dark-sighted eyes are described as flashing with inner light, with fire; they project rather than reflect, thrusting inner forces onto the outside world, working on it to change and distort it. To the possessors of such potentially lethal intruments, simple mirrors seem lifeless: "'Look at me,' says Klara to Nathanael, 'I have still got my own eyes'; Nathanael looked into Klara's eyes; but it was death that, with Klara's eyes, looked on him kindly" (S 293). Those who possess only mirrors, those of the homely eyes, however, are not afraid of losing them: the Sandman will not, Klara affirmed, "harm my eyes" (S 287).

But those with inner, uncanny eyes are always fearful of losing their powers of sight; disconnected from the physical eye, the mental eye can all too easily be extinguished, or even vanquished by stronger eyes. Thus Freud will interpret the fear of losing sight as a substitute for the dread of castration, citing "the substitutive relation between the eye and the male organ which is seen to exist in dreams and myths and fantasies" (U 352). In this way, after the father's death, the Sandman appears as destroyer, divider, castrator, impelling Nathanael toward a destructive anxiety of (visual) influence.

There is in *Der Sandmann*, however, a third category of eyes, those mechanical copies that, fabricated either to imitate real eyes, as in the doll Olympia, or to extend the powers of real eyes, as glasses or telescopes, all seem to take on uncanny roles. The spyglass sold by Coppola to Nathanael thus possesses the ability to bring Olympia's artificial eyes to life: "As he continued to look more and more intently through the glass it seemed . . . as if the power of vision were only now starting to be kindled; her glances were inflamed with ever-increasing life" (S 297). The spyglass has the further power to reduce real eyes to dead ones, as when, casually taking out the glass from his pocket to focus on a strange bush pointed out by Klara, Nathanael looks through it accidentally into Klara's own eyes and is immediately transported to his final vision of the dismembered Olympia, the wooden doll. These mechanical eyes, then, are doubles, the products of art embellishing nature. They add to the already formidable powers of the natural eye, and more often than not they trick it. They are the veritable instruments of trompe l'oeil.

Art as the double of nature, doubling the frightening double existence of man himself, an existence divided between the ego and the ego that observes itself, was a familiar theme in Hoffmann and in romantic literature as a whole. Hoffmann's story entitled "The Doubles" ("Die Doppelltgänger") plays between a painter and his own double, and the double life that is in his art. In another tale, *The Devil's Elixirs (Die Elixiere des Teufels)*, art's doubling of nature is referred to the story of Pygmalion who, through desire, brought his statue of Galatea to life. In this case, Hoffmann rewrites this Ovidian story, turning the statue into a painting that uncannily comes to life for its painter Francesko. In both instances the doubling of art, which succeeds in tricking the eye, is viewed as inherently dangerous. Thus at the end of "The Doubles," Haberland the painter renounces the real Nathalie in favor of a pure ideal that remains in his mind, while in *The Devil's Elixirs*, Francesko's living Venus is a force of the Devil. Art, first invented to ward off the threat of extinction, as in the tracing of a lover's shadow on the wall, is transformed into the demonic sign of death; in this way, as Freud demonstrated, art itself takes on the aspect of the uncanny.

Art is then uncanny because it veils reality, and also because it tricks. But it does not trick because of what is in itself; rather it possesses the power to deceive because of the projected desire of the observer. As Jacques Lacan has noted, the fable of Zeuxis painting grapes that were mistaken by the birds for real fruit implies not that the painter had painted perfect grapes but simply that the eyes of the birds were deceived: "a triumph of the gaze over the eye." Conversely, when the painter Parrhasios triumphed over Zeuxis by depicting a veil on the wall, so lifelike that Zeuxis observed, "well, now show us what you have painted behind it," what was at stake was the *relation* between the gaze of the observer, full of desire to possess, and the trick of the painting.[32] Hence the sinister relation between the double, which is both mask and presentation, and the evil, voracious eye, which demands to be deceived by itself.

No wonder then that Councillor Krespel repressed the power of his eye, deliberately forcing himself to be shortsighted. Krespel was no doublt privileging touch and hearing, the primary senses of the musician; he was also, in the context of a romantic mythology that endowed sight with the sinister properties of destruction—the evil eye—and dissimulation—masking—achieving a kind of willed innocence, through a childlike perception of the world of objects. Only by so doing could he fabricate a house that was not an evil "double," a willed projection of his worst passions, but that was, rather, a house that contained his inner self, whole and untroubled within. And this would be why the outside of the house seemed *unheimlich* and the inside *heimlich;* as a blind transcription, an automatic writing of his undivided soul, it operated as a return route, a passage back from the uncanny to the homely. Even as the Councillor's strange behavior is read by the Professor as an indication that "tomorrow he'll be jogging along at his donkey-trot as usual," so the unfamiliar outside of the house is a sure indication of familiarity within. "What comes from the earth," the Professor observes, "Krespel returns to the earth, but he knows how to preserve the Divine" (K 92). His crazy house, before the age of analysis, was a mechanism of self-preservation.

In this respect, the house was a therapeutic instrument: Krespel found in this mask of madness a way to rebuff the world and achieve inner composure. This was, after all, a canny way to follow what Hoffmann called his "Serapions Prinzip," which brought together the secular brotherhood in his series of tales of the same name. In this ideal, the outer world was used as a lever to set the inner world of the artist in motion by means of a clear sense of the boundaries between poetry and life. For this the artist had to cultivate a special kind of composure, a *Besonnenheit* or mental state that controlled the release of images and translated stimuli from the outer world into the spiritual domain. As Maria Tatar has concluded, "without this gift, the painter's canvas remains empty, the writer's manuscript consists of blank pages, the composer's score contains not a single note and the artist in general is branded a madman by society."[33] Krespel, before the age of analysis, had preserved his poetic self by means of an artificial boundary, a house that was, in a special sense, a mirror of his soul.

Krespel's house, in its peculiar relationships between exterior and interior, takes its place among many uncanny houses throughout the nineteenth century. Through them, inside and outside, like *heimlich* and *unheimlich,* became the privileged topoi of the uncanny. Thus the typical context for the telling of ghost stories, the apparently homely interior that gradually turns into a vehicle of horror, was described in numerous versions: a cheerful household, generally following dinner, the men smoking pipes before the blazing fire, the women sewing, the children allowed to stay up late. This was the nostalgic evocation of the *veillée,* a "cottage" vision of house and home especially relished in the age of rural displacement and urban emigration. In such a secure setting, stories of terror might be tasted with delight; many writers insisted on the need for a storm outside, to reinforce by contrast the snugness within. Thus the setting of Hoffmann's "Uncanny Guest" ("Der unheimliche Gast"), where "the four ingredients, autumn, a stormy wind, a good fire, and a jorum of punch" engendered a strange sense of the awesome, provoked a fear of the

supernatural, that was then deliciously prolonged by stories that reminded the listeners of the spirit world surrounding them.[34]

Similarly, Thomas De Quincey, an adept in the art of evoking
dreams of terror, sometimes with the artificial help of opium, was
equally convinced of the need for a secure vantage point from which
to start the interior journey. The site of his reveries, stimulated by
laudanum, was a simple white cottage, formerly owned by Wordsworth, in the valley of Grasmere. "Embowered by flowering shrubs,"
this was a homely house, in a sheltered valley, with its simple rooms
lined with books and warmed by cheerful hearths.[35] De Quincey, too,
insisted on the need for winter and a storm outside for his adventures
of the mind, as, almost innocently, he sipped from the ordinary
decanter containing the deceptive liquid, an instrument of those
fantasies of the architectural sublime that he remembers being described by Coleridge, himself inspired by faulty recollection of Piranesi's *Carceri* etchings.[36]

Building on an already rich tradition of Piranesi "misreading" from
Horace Walpole through Loutherbourg to William Beckford, De
Quincey adumbrated the first romantic meditation on what might be
called the spatial uncanny, one no longer entirely dependent on the
temporal dislocations of suppression and return, or the invisible slippages between a sense of the homely and the unhomely, but displayed
in the abyssal repetitions of the imaginary void.[37] The vertical labyrinth traced by De Quincey images the artist, Piranesi, caught in a
vertigo *en abîme* of his own making, forever climbing the unfinished
stairs in the labyrinth of carceral spaces. The passage is celebrated:

> Creeping along the sides of the walls, you perceived a staircase; and upon
> it, groping his way upwards, was Piranesi himself: follow the stairs a little
> further, and you perceive it come to a sudden abrupt termination, without
> any balustrade, and allowing no step onwards to him who had reached the
> extremity, except into the depths below. Whatever is to become of poor
> Piranesi, you suppose, at least, that his labors must in some way terminate
> here. But raise your eyes, and behold a second flight of stairs still higher:
> on which again Piranesi is perceived, by this time standing on the very brink
> of the abyss. Again elevate your eye, and a still more aerial flight of stairs is
> beheld; and again is poor Piranesi busy on his aspiring labors: and so on,
> until the unfinished stairs and Piranesi both are lost in the upper gloom of
> the hall.[38]

De Quincey goes beyond a simple Burkean delight in the indeterminacy of ruins, in the sublime, to intimate a fully developed spatial

uncanny. Arden Reed has noted the relations to the Freudian uncanny both in the "omnipotence of thought" displayed by De Quincey's hypnagogic visions and in the space of endless repetition constructed by a reading that conflates all the *Carceri* into a single chain of mental-spatial associations.[39] Such repetition, as Derrida has observed in connection to Freud's own repetition of Neitzsche's affirmation of the "eternal return of the same," has a devilish quality to it; thus, speaking of Freud's own text *Beyond the Pleasure Principle,* Derrida notes: "The entire text has a diabolical movement, it mimes walking, it walks without ceasing, but does not advance; it regularly traces out one more step but does not allow the gain of an inch of ground."[40] This endless drive to repeat is then uncanny, both for its association with the death drive and by virtue of the "doubling" inherent in the incessant movement without movement.

Piranesi's drawings, indeed, served many romantics as (always misread) tropes of spatial instability signifying an abyssal drive toward nothingness. De Quincey's report of his conversation with Coleridge gave rise to a long tradition of Piranesi (mis-)interpretation, in which the prison etchings, variously described as dreams, drug-induced deliria, and prisons of the mind, take on the aspect of labyrinths through which the artist wanders, metaphors of the romantic mind.

In this way, Charles Nodier, without acknowledgment but evidently creatively rereading De Quincey, develops the theme with relish in a short story he entitles, significantly enough, "Piranèse," published in 1836, a fable of proto-Borgesian dimensions that evokes the space of interior reflection as a symbol of the endless growth of libraries, the repetition of Babel, the doubling without original of the world in the book.[41] Characterizing a kind of illness that he calls "monomania of reflection" (*monomanie réflective*), Nodier finds its spatial analogue in the vagaries of what he calls Piranesi's "castles in Spain." Here the romantic bibliophile drew a striking distinction between the conventions of the sublime as exhibited in the paintings of John Martin and the strange interior "nightmares" of Piranesi:

The ruins of Piranesi are about to collapse. They groan, they cry. . . . The effect of his great buildings is no less extraordinary. They produce vertigo, as if one were measuring them from on high, and when you search for the cause of the emotion that inspires you, you are surprised to tremble in fear on one of their cornices, or to see all the objects turn beneath your eyes from the capital of one of their columns.

But *Piranesi's nightmare did not consist in this. I am sure that Martyn [sic] had the nightmare of space and multitude. Piranesi certainly had the nightmare of solitude and constraint, of the prison and the coffin, of he who lacks air to breathe, voice to cry out and place to struggle.*[42]

In this way Nodier distinguishes the general space of the sublime—that of height, depth, and extension, as characterized by Burke—from that of the uncanny—that of silence, solitude, of internal confinement and suffocation, that mental space where temporality and spatiality collapse. The vertigo of the sublime is placed side by side with the claustrophobia of the uncanny. Thus, imagining a palace built by Piranesi, perhaps the "Ampio magnifico collegio," Nodier contrasts the "imposing grandeur" and "overwhelming magnificence" of the exterior with the interior, still encumbered by the wood and masonry of construction. Nothing is finished, nothing is complete or clear:

The great stair that twists and turns, and the deep vestibule, and the long gallery that leads far off to an even narrower stair, are so obstructed with temporary constructions that it is almost impossible to conceive that the workers can make their way out, and in the imagination one thinks to hear them lament, cry, shout with exhaustion, famine, and despair.

Within this construction, Nodier, like De Quincey, places Piranesi himself, with one foot on the first step, his gaze fixed on the interior whence "an invincible destiny" forces him to climb to the topmost level. This "strange obsession," brought to his spirit by sleep, is both dream and an emblem of the more general fate of the romantic genius: "He must climb, amidst obstacles and dangers, either triumphing or dying." The abyssal space of this ascent is similar to that described by De Quincey, but highly elaborated as a scene of repetitive stages toward infinity.

Oh, how will he make his way, the poor Piranesi, between these close-pressing beams and fragile scaffolds that bend and creak? How will he advance across these unstable posts that are joined to each other by narrow and shaky joists? . . . across this mass of ill-laid stones that overhang and beneath these low and perilous vaults . . . ? One would follow with unease the subtle path of the lightest lizard!
    Piranesi climbs nevertheless, and, even though the mind can hardly imagine it, Piranesi arrives.—He arrives, alas, at the foot of a building similar to the first, access to which presents the same difficulties, menacing him with the same perils, demanding the same effort, in yet greater proportion, mag-

nified by his tiredness, exhaustion, and also his old age. . . . Nevertheless, Piranesi climbs again; he must climb and climb and arrive.—And he arrives.

He arrives, overburdened, decrepit, broken, feeble as a shadow; he has arrived at the bottom level of a building similar to the first buildings. . . .

In this way, Piranesi climbs on forever through a space that, still pictorially controlled by the laws of perspective, diminishes while repeating, "until the moment when [the buildings] are lost at a distance hardly measurable by the imagination." At this point, even Piranesi himself, "Piranesi who regards each new building with terror, who climbs, who walks, who arrives, near to ceding to the inexpressible sadness of never arriving the end of his suffering," becomes "imperceptible . . . like a black point on a fading level almost lost in the depth of the skies." Beyond this, Nodier asserts with some relief, "there is nothing but space."[43]

This long and deliberately exhausting *promenade architecturale* has, for Nodier, the function of delineating the space of "morbid sleep," of the "intolerable torture" involved in the monomania of internal reflection, where "all impressions are prolonged without end, where every minute becomes a century." It serves as the prelude to an equally uncanny exploration of the mental space of Count G., a rich bachelor, who, having determined to retire from the world, planned the restoration of the interior of his chateau according to the "fantastic plan of a Piranesian palace." The literal construction of such a space, a "labyrinth of stones," hides the solitary retreat of the proprietor, who, like some character from De Sade's *120 Jours,* defends himself from the world by an almost impassable network of broken connections: "galleries which were only to be circumnavigated with patience and courage; narrow stairs, alternatively mounting and descending, cut by dark and confusing corridors which led nowhere. . . ." Only the narrowest passerelle, to be crossed with terror, led to the Count's apartment, an almost impenetrable asylum, where for three years the proprietor lived in solitary meditation "like the stylite on his column." Found peacefully in death on his bed, at the heart of this interiorization of Babel, he had succeeded in attaining a degree of "alienation" that was not, Nodier stresses, the madness described by the doctors. Like that distantiation (also described by Nodier) achieved by a scholar who, desiring solitude, retreated from the world in an apartment strung with cables on which he balanced further and further from the door, this was a "strange alienation that leaves free all the other faculties of high intelligence . . . the fanaticism of perfectibility.[44] Such interiority was, in Nodier's terms, the true site of the uncanny, the final place of resistance against "the progress of progress."[45]

The passage from homely to unhomely, now operating wholly in the mind, reinforced the ambiguty between real world and dream, real world and spirit world, so as to undermine even the sense of security demanded by professional dreamers. Following Kant's prescription for the achievement of delight through terror through certain knowledge of safety—"provided our own position is secure, [the aspect of terrifying natural phenomena] is all the more attractive for its fearfulness"—the aesthete of terror succeeded in barricading the walls against nature in order to indulge a taste for fear. But with the locus of the uncanny now shifted to the mind, such barriers were difficult to maintain, dissolving readily into the fabric of the dream, haunting the site of its own dread.

Thus the *veillée*, or "stay-up-late evening" as Michael Riffaterre translates the title of Rimbaud's poem,[46] becomes itself uncanny, its security belied and clouded by its anticipated end, from the nights when, as in Hoffmann's story, Nathanael's father awaits the arrival of the Sandman, sitting silently in his armchair "blowing out billows of smoke till we all seemed to be swimming in clouds" (S 278), to that evening described by Rimbaud when mantle shelf and wallpaper merge with the dream of a voyage, only to return as the sign of normalcy and thereby of death.

The light returns to the roof post. From the two sides of the room, commonplace scenes, harmonious elevations merge. The wall facing the watch-man is a psychological succession of fragments of friezes, atmospheric bands, geological faults.—Intense and rapid dream of sentimental groups with beings of all characters among all appearances.[47]

It is out of the meeting of such a *veillée* and the modern city that Rimbaud would develop his own vision of the Piranesian abyss—the "Villes" of *Illuminations*.

From Hoffmann to Rimbaud, in short stories and in many *veillées*, smoke is thus an agent of dissolution by which the fabric of the house is turned into the depth of the dream; in the same way, as an instrument of the sublime, smoke has always made obscure what otherwise would have seemed too clear.

Nothing seemed to be more settled, more at home, than the life of the narrator of Melville's short story "I and My Chimney" as he sat contentedly puffing his pipe beside an equally puffing chimney stack.[48] Resisting modernization and determined to maintain an amicable pact between himself and his old, silent friend, the chimney, this narrator has indeed captured the imagination of those who have seen something pragmatic and sturdily "American" in finding the center of the home in the fire: a tradition of settler origins, rooted in the anthropology of Semper and finding its architectural expression in the Prairie homesteading of Frank Lloyd Wright.[49]

Certainly the narrator loved his chimney; it provided warmth and stability for the entire house, as structure and function; it did not, like his wife, "talk back," and it represented, symbolically enough, a last bastion of the good past against the intrusions of a bad present. And yet the chimney, as he readily admitted, was something of a tyrant. Twelve feet square at the base, four feet wide at the top, it completely usurped the center of the house, permitting no passage from one side to another, forcing the inhabitants into continual peripheral movement. So strong was its presence, indeed, that the narrator had become its slave. The chimney was master of the house; its "owner" stood behind it, deferring to it on every count, finally protecting it from destruction by withdrawing from the outer world and mounting a continuous vigil lest it be demolished while his back was turned. Fear pervades this story: fear of being deprived of a "backbone" with the removal of the chimney; fear of losing the "one permanence" of the dwelling; fear of confrontation with the wife; fear, given the chimney's shape and vertical power, of loss of manhood.

The chimney provided another kind of support also. It was the central object of the narrator's fantasy life; at once a reminder of the distant pyramids of Egypt and the dark Druidical ritual standing stones, it stood for the entire romantic history of origins, an ur-monument, both life-giving and life-taking, harbinger of the eternal fire and tomb of kings. It was further an instrument of knowledge, an observatory pointed toward the heavens. In its bulk almost incommensurable, irreducible to the mathematical calculations of the architect (contemptuously called "Scribe"), it could not be cut down to size. Its inner recesses hiding unknown mysteries and its external walls impermeable and silent, it was, as Hegel would have characterized it, the perfect type of *symbolic* architecture, an object not yet separated from the magical world of demons or the projected fantasies of men. Around this pyramid-tomb the house deployed itself, depending on the chimney for sustenance and support; because of its position, it was a kind of labyrinth protecting the inner center from profane intrusion. The resulting confusion of rooms, each forced to act as a passage to the next, one with as many as nine doors, generated a complex network of relations: "almost every room like a philosophical system, was in itself an entry, or passageway to other rooms and systems of rooms, a whole suite of entries in fact." Like the daydreamer whose mental map these rooms seemed to emulate, "going through the house you seem to be forever going somewhere and getting nowhere." Indeed, one might entirely lose one's way: "it is like losing oneself in the woods; round and round the chimney you go, and if you arrive at all it is just where you started and so you begin again and get nowhere."[50]

We are reminded of the similar pattern of uncanny repetition in Freud's description of his strange experience of a particular quarter in a provincial town, "the character of which could not long remain in doubt," as painted women filled the windows of the small houses.

I hastened to leave the narrow street at the next turning. But after having wandered about for a time without inquiring my way, I suddenly found myself back in the same street, where my presence was now beginning to excite attention. I hurried away once more, only to arrive by another *detour* at the same place yet a third time. Now however a feeling overcame me which I can only describe as uncanny. (U 359)

Freud compared this "involuntary repetition" that transformed a peaceful Italian town (Genoa) into a site of Piranesian claustrophobia to being lost in the mist in a mountain forest, where "every attempt to find the marked or familiar path may bring one back again and again to one and the same spot," or to the experience of being lost in "a dark, strange room," "looking for the door or the electric switch," colliding time after time with the same piece of furniture (U 359). Melville's narrator had a similar sense of helplessness before the uncanny might of his chimney, and he seemed equally unwilling to track down the unconscious motivations of his "involuntary" acts.

This need to veil the source of dependency was mirrored in the narrator's resistance to deciphering or interpreting his hermetic chimney. It was as if his own body were threatened with extinction. He preferred the pyramid to remain a primal force, before writing, resisting all explanation, like the hieroglyphs before Champollion. Even when, as a last resort to persuade the owner to demolish the chimney, the architect invented the fiction of a "reserved space hermetically closed . . . a secret chamber . . . hid in darkness," the narrator refused to search. Not because he did not believe in its existence, but rather the opposite: he believed too much in mysteries. What the chimney concealed, its and his nether world, should remain concealed. "Infinite and sad mischief," he held, "has resulted from the profane bursting open of secret recesses," thus precisely repeating Schelling's principle. By this means, a kind of tacit treaty was reached between the subversive and comforting powers of the house, allowing it, during the life of its owner at least, to remain a home.

Buried Alive

What had formerly been the city of Pompeii assumed an entirely changed appearance, but not a living one; it now appeared rather to become completely petrified in dead immobility. Yet out of it stirred a feeling that death was beginning to talk.

Wilhelm Jensen, Gradiva[1]

Bound to sit by his chimney until he died, Melville's narrator was, in a very real sense, buried alive—a condition intensified by the similarity of the chimney itself to an Egyptian pyramid. Here Melville was rehearsing another familiar trope of the uncanny, one that nicely intersected with the archaeological interests of the nineteenth century, and whose literary exploration followed, almost chronologically, the successive "rediscoveries" and excavations of antique sites— Egypt, Pompeii, Troy. As Freud was later to note, the uncovering of what had been long buried not only offered a ready analogy to the procedures of psychoanalysis but exactly paralleled the movements of the uncanny itself: "To some people the idea of being buried alive by mistake is the most uncanny thing of all" (U 366).

Of all sites, that of Pompeii seemed to many writers to exhibit the conditions of unhomeliness to the most extreme degree. This was a result of its literal "burial alive" and almost complete state of preservation, but also of its peculiarly distinct character as a "domestic" city of houses and shops. The circumstances of its burial had allowed the traces of everyday life to survive with startling immediacy. The pleasures of Pompeii, in comparison to those of Rome, were, all visitors agreed, dependent on its homely nature. Its streets, shops, and houses seemed to the traveler from the north at once intimate and private. Chateaubriand, who passed through in 1802, was struck by the contrast between "the public monuments, built at great cost in granite and marble," typical of Rome, and the "domestic dwellings," built with "the resources of simple individuals," of Pompeii: "Rome is only a vast museum; *Pompeii is living antiquity*."[2] He even dreamed of a new form of nonmonumental museum, which would leave in place the tools, furniture, statues, and manuscripts found among the ruins (and normally displaced to the museum at Portici), with the roofs and walls of the houses rebuilt as a mise-en-scène of everyday life in ancient Rome. "One would learn more about the domestic history of the Roman people, the state of Roman civilization in a few restored promenades of Pompeii, than by the reading of all the works of antiquity," he observed, proposing in this way an anticipation of the folk museums of the twentieth century: "It would only need a little brick, tile, plaster, stone, wood, carpentry, and joinery . . . a talented architect would follow the local style for the restorations, models for which he would find in the landscapes painted on the very walls of the houses of Pompeii." Thus, at little cost, "the most marvelous museum in the world" might be created, "a Roman town conserved in its entirety, as if its inhabitants had just left a quarter of an hour before."[3]

Other writers, from Winckelmann to Le Corbusier, have attested to this humble, workaday quality of the ruins: the so-called Villa of Diomedes, the House of the Faun, the House of Championnet, the House of the Baker were only a few of those dwellings painstakingly described and "restored" by generations of architectural students. The sense of having intruded on a domestic scene not long abandoned was increased by the plethora of household goods uncovered by the excavations, some of which were carefully left in place for the benefit of visitors, but also by the intimate glimpses into the customs, mores, and even sexual life afforded by the wall paintings. What had been shrouded for reasons of prudery in museums was displayed as part of a complete panorama, a veritable ethnographic study, on the walls. Pierre-Adrien Pâris carefully copied the priapic bas-relief on the wall of a small shop, while the young Flaubert found it the only memorable ornament of the town.[4]

And yet, despite the evident domesticity of the ruins, they were not by any account homely. For behind the quotidian semblance there lurked a horror, equally present to view: skeletons abounded. In the soldiers' quarter, as Creuzé de Lesser noted, "the judges perished with the accused," and the remains of the prisoners were still chained to the walls. As opposed to the death of Herculaneum, which according to popular mythology was slow—"the lava filled up Herculaneum, as the molten lead fills up the cavities of a mold," wrote Chateaubriand—that of Pompeii was sudden. Gérard de Nerval recreated the terrifying vision of the fiery rain of ashes, suffocating and burning those in flight; hidden until the mid-eighteenth century, this hideous destruction was revealed side by side with its less disturbing and apparently more normal context. The archaeological gaze was pitiless: "in the middle of the last century the scholars began to excavate this enormous ruin. Oh! incredible surprise; they found a city in the volcano, houses under the ash, skeletons in the houses, furniture and pictures next to the skeletons."[5] The town was evidently no common archaeological site, its ruins bleached by the sun and exorcised of social memories: history here seem to be suspended in the gruesome juxtaposition of these grisly remains and their apparently homely surroundings. Chateaubriand's folksy museum was, in fact, still inhabited.

This dramatic confrontation of the homely and the unhomely made Pompeii a locus of the literary and artistic uncanny for much of the nineteenth century, whether in the mystical formulations of Nerval, the popular melodramas of Bulwer Lytton, the full-blown romanticism of Théophile Gautier, or the dream narratives of Wilhelm Jensen. *L'étrange, l'inquiétant, das Unheimliche,* all found their natural place in stories that centered on the idea of history suspended, the dream come to life, the past restored in the present. Pompeii, in contrast to the conventional settings of haunting and horror, possessed a level of archaeological verisimilitude matched by historical drama that made of it the perfect vehicle, in a century obsessed by the fugitive relations between past and future, for what Gautier variously called "l'idéal rétrospectif," "la chimère rétrospectif," "le désir rétrospectif," or, in relation to Pompeii, "l'amour rétrospectif."[6] The special characteristic of this retrospective vision was its unsettling merging of past and present, its insistence on the rights of the unburied dead, its pervasive force over the fates of its subjects. In Pompeii, it seemed, history, that solid realm of explanation and material fact, was taking a kind of revenge on its inventors.

In these terms, Pompeii evidently qualified as a textbook example of the uncanny on every level, from the implicit horror of the domestic to the revelations of mysteries, religious and otherwise, that, in Schelling's view, might better have remained unrevealed. Gautier's tale "Arria Marcella" insistently contrasted the banal and the extraordinary, the trivial and the momentous, the sublime and the grotesque aspects of the town: the brilliance of the light and the transparency of the air were opposed to the somber tint of the black volcanic sand, the clouds of black dust underfoot, and the omnipresent ashes. Vesuvius itself was depicted as benign as Montmartre, an old fellow like Melville's chimney owner, quietly "smoking his pipe" in defiance of his terrifying reputation. The juxtaposition of the modern railway station and antique city; the happiness of the tourists in the street of tombs; the "banal phrases" of the guide as he recited the terrible deaths of the citizens in front of their remains: all testified to the power of the place to reproduce, quite systematically, the structures of the uncanny.[7]

On a purely aesthetic level, too, Pompeii seemed to reflect precisely the struggle identified by Schelling between the dark mysteries of the first religions and the sublime transparency of the Homeric hymns, but in reverse, as if reenacting the battle in order to retrieve the uncanny. For what the first excavations of Pompeii had revealed was a version of antiquity entirely at odds with the sublime vision of Winckelmann and his followers. The paintings, sculptures, and religious artifacts in this city of Greek foundation were far from the Neoplatonic forms of neoclassical imagination. Fauns, cupids, satyrs, priapi, centaurs, and prostitutes of every sex replaced the Apollonian grace and Laocoönian strength of Winckelmann's aesthetics. The mysteries of Isis and a host of Egyptian cults took the place of high philosophy and acropolitan rituals. Archaeology, by revealing what should have remained invisible, had irredeemably confirmed the existence of a "dark side" of classicism, thus betraying not only the high sublime but a slowly and carefully constructed world of modern mythology. Schelling, with Goethe and Schiller a true believer in the "congealed music" of classical architecture, had already noted this undermining archaeology in his ambiguous assessment of the temple sculptures of Aegina, "perfected" as much as possible by Thorvaldsen but betraying all the distortions characteristic of a presublime art. Their masklike features, he proposed, embodied a "certain character of the uncanny," the product of an older mysterious religion showing through.[8]

Perhaps the least forgivable aspect of this archaeological treason was its blatant display of classical eroticism, a world hitherto circumlocuted and circumscribed but now open to the view of tourists and the interpretation of historians. Not only did such a scandalous unmasking support a literature of dubious quality, from d'Hancarville to de Sade, but it also, as the next generation of romantics demonstrated, dangerously unsettled the apparatus of classical aesthetics. For of all the disturbing fragments found in the city, it was the erotic traces that most exercised the imaginations of those who, from Chateaubriand to Gautier, were themselves concerned to undermine the high sublime.

One of the more fascinating remains of Pompeii, described in detail by many early visitors, and with relish by every guide, was a fragment of scorched earth found beneath a portico of the House of Diomedes and kept in the museum at Portici. Chateaubriand noted:

The portico that surrounds the garden of this house is made up of square pillars, grouped in threes. Under this first portico, there is a second: there it was that the young woman whose breast is impressed in the piece of earth I saw at Portici was suffocated.[9]

This simple but lugubrious "impression" became the focus of a series of meditations, each a reflection on its predecessor, the burden of which was the strange way in which nature in its own death throes had, so to speak, become its own artist: "Death, like a sculptor, has molded his victim" (Chateaubriand). The coincidence with the story of Pygmalion and Galatea was too close to avoid, and it was somehow satisfying, if depressing, to find the classical theory of imitation thus trumped by fate. The sculptor whose creation was so lifelike that she seemed to blush at his embrace, who fell in love with and "married" his ivory statuette, was now replaced by nature, or even better, history, which had molded its own work of art from the life, turning, in a reversal that caught the romantic imagination, living beauty into dead trace. And, following the hardly subdued erotic subtext of the buried city, this trace was not simply a mummified body or skeleton but the ghost of a breast, a fragment that, in an age preoccupied with the restoration and completion of broken statues, demanded to be reconstituted, in imagination at least.

As a fragment, this negative petrified sign of *nature morte* easily took its place among other similar fragments in literature and art that at once signaled an irretrievable past and evoked an unbearable desire for future plenitude: the Belvedere Torso, the Elgin Marbles, the Venus de Milo. But unlike these, the Pompeiian *terre cuite* in its isolated anatomical specificity represented a far more brutal cutting of the body, and thus imposed a greater interpretative effort. Its status was more that of the lost arm of the Venus de Milo than of the statue itself. Its archaeological equivalent would perhaps be the posthole of a hut or the pattern of woven cloth retained in dried mud.

The cutting of the body into significant parts, each representative of the perfect beauty of the whole, was of course a commonplace of classical aesthetics. Zeuxis after all had assembled the type of beauty by the selection and combination of the best parts of his models. It was precisely against this kind of mechanical imitation that Winckelmann and his students had fought, proposing in its stead a kind of preromantic Neoplatonism, an enthusiastic idealism. But the romantics themselves, while agreeing with Winckelmann's dislike of the copy, nevertheless invested the fragment with more than fragmentary significance. Forced to reconcile the material existence of fragments—the increasing quantity of bits and pieces from the past piled up in the basements of the new museums—with their organicist metaphysics, they preferred to take the fragment as it was and cultivate it as an object of meditation.

In Schlegel's celebrated formulation, the fragment, "like a small work of art, should be totally detached from the surrounding world and closed in on itself like a hedgehog." This closure, turning the fragment in on itself like an aphorism, on one level monumentalized it and allowed it to be framed and stabilized in the context of its historical origins. On another level, however, it released a kind of metahistorical potentiality by virtue of its incompletion, forming part of an imaginary dialogue, "a chain or a crown of fragments." In this way the fragment might become a "project," the "subjective germ of an object in becoming," a "fragment of the future." As Schlegel concluded, "numerous works of the Ancients have become fragments. Numerous works by Moderns are fragments from their birth."[10]

If the status of Chateaubriand's "piece of earth" was enhanced in these terms, it was even more so by its role as an object of impossible love, a theme given full play in Gautier's "Arria Marcella." In this story of the buried city as uncanny habitat, the "hero," Octavien, loses himself in a "profound contemplation":

> What he looked at with so much attention was a piece of coagulated black ash bearing a hollowed imprint: one might have said that it was a fragment of a mold for a statue, broken in the casting; the trained eye of the artist had easily recognized the curve of a beautiful breast and a thigh as pure in style as that of a Greek statue. It was well known, and the least of guidebooks pointed it out, that this lava, cooled around the body of a woman, had retained its charming contour.[11]

Out of such contemplation was engendered the uncanny dream of Arria Marcella's feast, where Octavien, long an admirer of statues, who had been known to cry out to the Venus de Milo, soliciting an embrace from "her marble breast," was finally brought face to face with the original of the molded copy. She, true to his desires, "surrounded his body with her beautiful statuelike arms, cold, hard, and rigid as marble." The reversal is clear and pointed directly by Gautier: the living body, impressed in its mold of earth, when revived took on the attributes of the artistic imitation. Classical aesthetics was thereby rendered dead, in favor of the life of "natural" fragments, themselves destined to be completed only by the powerless form of dreamed desire.

According to this analogy, we might also interpret the dreamlike "restoration" of the fragmented buildings of Pompeii that, in Gautier's tale, preceded Octavien's meeting with his Galatea. In this already strange night, a "nocturnal day" where the bright moonlight seemed to disguise the fragmentation of the buildings, repairing "the fossil city for some representation of a fantasy life," Octavien noted a "strange restoration" that must have been undertaken since the afternoon at great speed by an unknown architect:

> This strange restoration, made between the afternoon and the evening by an unknown architect, was very troubling to Octavien, certain of having seen the house on the same day in a sorry state of ruin. The mysterious reconstructor had worked quickly enough, because the neighboring dwellings had the same recent and new aspect.[12]

Such a dream of the past restored, like some exact copy of an architectural student's *restitution* for the Ecole des Beaux-Arts, acted, like the vision of Arria Marcella, to return history not to life but to death: "All the historians had been tricked; the eruption had not taken place." Archaeology with its precise materialism had overcome temporality at least for a moment. It would be tempting to read into Gautier's narrative an implicit attack on restorers, Beaux-Arts and medievalist alike, as they searched desperately to make contemporary historical monuments out of the remains of the past.

But where, in the too-complete visions of a literal architect, whether restorer or conservator, the aesthetic effect verged on a touristic sublime, all too often a response to something that through endless rerepresentation and reproduction had become a copy of itself— Carcassonne, the Acropolis, and of course Pompeii itself would be examples—the effect of the uncanny in Gautier's treatment was less predictable. The sublime, as defined by Kant, stemmed primarily from a feeling of inadequacy in the face of superior powers; the mental state of the uncanny, tied to the death or frustration of desire, remained both sublime and a threat to its banalization. In the version described by Gautier it was a harbinger of a living death in the face of which the historical fate of Pompeii's inhabitants seemed almost preferable. Thus Octavien, returning to the site of his dream, finding the remains of Arria, "resting obstinately in the dust," despaired and was suspended in the same state of coldness, distance, banality as the statue he desired. In the same manner, d'Aspremont, in another tale by Gautier, "Jettatura," having courted death in a duel only to slay his opponent in the ruins of Pompeii, leaves the city like "a walking statue," finally to die by his own hand, his body never to be found.[13] Those who courted the remains of the buried alive evidently risked sharing the same fate.

In an apparently strange reversal, however, the tombs in Pompeii, city of the dead, were, unlike the catacombs of Naples and Rome, rarely the subjects of necropolitan meditations. To Octavien's companions, indeed, they were positively pleasant: "This road lined with sepulchers which, according to our modern feelings, would be a lugubrious avenue in a town . . . inspired none of that cold repulsion, none of those fantastic terrors that our own lugubrious tombs make us feel." Rather the visitors experienced "a light curiosity and a joyous fullness in existence" in this pagan cemetery. Like shepherds in Arcadia, they frolicked, conscious of the fact that in these tombs "in place of a horrible cadaver" were only ashes, "the abstract idea of death" and not the object itself.[14]

Such pleasure in the face of a ritualized death contrasted with the terror felt at the untimely death of the inhabitants under the eruption; it seemed to exorcise, in some way, the uncanny effect of the guide's recital of the death of Arria Marcella: "'It was here,' said the Cicerone in his nonchalant voice, the tone of which hardly matched the sense of his words 'that they found, among seventeen skeletons, that of the woman whose imprint can be seen in the Museum at Naples.'"[15] The fear stimulated by *l'amour rétrospectif* was countered by the security, almost *heimlich*, to be found in tombs "embellished by art," as Goethe had it. Ritually placed ashes were part of a human plan; naturally created, they were a terrifying catastrophe.

Freud commented on this fear of being buried alive, which he linked to other uncanny tropes common in nineteenth-century literature such as the forces of animism, witchcraft, magic, the evil eye, and especially the "*Gettatore,* that uncanny figure of Roman superstition," that had, fifty years before, also inspired Gautier (U 365–366). His long analysis of Hoffmann's tale "The Sandman" persuaded him that on one level Schelling had been correct in ascribing the feeling of the uncanny to the return of "a hidden familiar thing that has undergone repression and emerged from it." In this way, the fragment—"dismembered limbs, a severed head, a hand cut off at the wrist" (U 366)—might be related to the castration complex, and superstition itself might be traced to the return of a primitive fear, long buried but always ready to be awakened in the psyche. In this sense, Freud reinterpreted Schelling's definition in terms of a recurrence of the repressed, the uncanny as a class of morbid anxiety that comes from something "repressed which *recurs*." Thus the phenomenon of haunting:

Many people experience the feeling [of the uncanny] in the highest degree in relation to death and dead bodies, to the return of the dead, and to spirits and ghosts. . . . There is scarcely any other matter . . . upon which our thoughts and feelings have changed so little since the very earliest times, and in which discarded forms have been so completely preserved under a thin disguise, as of our relation to death. (U 364)

Freud, himself an amateur archaeologist, was well aware of the uncanny effects of Pompeii: he had devoted a long essay to the analysis of Wilhelm Jensen's fantasy *Gradiva,* in which a young archaeologist found the original of his model—a bas-relief of a young girl "splendid in walking"—amidst the ruins of the city.[16] Jensen's Pompeiian fantasy was indeed a reworking of Gautier, with the addition of the archaeologist's dream content. But Freud, in this analysis, strangely refused any direct reference to the uncanny, or even to the buried discoveries of archaeology, preferring to enunciate the principles of the interpretation of dreams as represented in fiction. Perhaps this in turn was his own repression, for in *The Interpretation of Dreams* itself he had fully explored the question of the *unheimlich* with reference to one of his own dreams, one that incorporated both the fear of being buried alive and the desire for a fully restorative archaeology. It was also, as he noted, "strangely enough," an account of a dream that "related to a dissection of the lower part of his own body," a kind of self-fragmentation.[17]

In this dream, which he attributed to the reading of a popular melodramatic novel by Rider Haggard, *She,* Freud found himself, following the self-dissection scene, driving in a cab through the entrance of his own apartment house, thence to make his way over an Alpine landscape, and finally to arrive at a primitive "wooden house" within which were men lying on benches along the walls. His interpretation, refusing the more obvious reference to *She* as a dramatization of the return of the repressed, a figure of woman triumphant over history on the model of Arria Marcella, turned instead to his archaeological fantasies:

The wooden house was also, no doubt, a coffin, that is to say, the grave. . . . I had already been in a grave once but it was an excavated Etruscan grave near Orvieto, a narrow chamber with two stone benches along its walls, on which the skeletons of two grown men were lying. . . . The dream seems to be saying: "If you must rest in a grave let it be an Etruscan one." And, by making this replacement, it transformed the gloomiest of expectations into one that was highly desirable.[18]

Much later, in *The Future of an Illusion,* Freud was more explicit on this desire for archaeological fulfillment:

The sleeper may be seized with a presentiment of death which threatens to place him in the grave. But the dream-work knows how to select a condition that will turn even that dreaded event into a wish-fulfillment: the dreamer sees himself in an ancient Etruscan grave which he has climbed down into, happy to find his archeological interests satisfied.[19]

If the uncanny stems, as Freud argues, from the recurrence of a previously repressed emotional affect, transformed by repression into anxiety, then fear of live burial would constitute a primary example of "this class of frightening things."

> To some people the idea of being buried alive by mistake is the most uncanny thing of all, and yet psychoanalysis has taught us that this terrifying fantasy is only a transformation of another fantasy which had originally nothing terrifying about it at all, but was qualified by a certain lasciviousness—the fantasy, I mean, of intra-uterine existence. (U 367)

Here the desire to return to the womb, displaced into the fear of being buried alive, would exemplify Freud's uncanny, as "in reality nothing new or alien, but something which is familiar and old established in the mind and which has become alienated from it only through the process of repression." In turn, the impossible desire to return to the womb, the ultimate goal represented by nostalgia, would constitute a true "homesickness":

> It often happens that neurotic men declare that they feel that there is something uncanny about the female genital organs. This *unheimlich* place, however, is the entrance to the former *Heim* [home] of all human beings, to the place where each one of us lived once upon a time and in the beginning. . . . In this case too, then, the *unheimlich* is what was once *heimisch*, familiar; the prefix *un* is the token of repression. (U 368)

Perhaps it was out of homage to the power of an archaeology that refused to hide what it had laid bare that Freud hung on the walls of his consulting room, just above the famous couch, a large photograph of the rock temple of Ramses II at Abu Simbel, and this beside a bas-relief in plaster copied from the Museo Chiaramonti in the Vatican portraying one of the Horae, goddesses of vegetation, otherwise known as the "Gradiva" relief that inspired Jensen.

Homesickness

The perpetual exchange between the homely and the unhomely, the imperceptible sliding of coziness into dread, was, in Hoffmann and De Quincey, a carefully arranged affair, where architecture operated as a machine for defining boundaries that in the end were to be overcome. In Melville, the divisions, while still essentially embodied in physical spaces and objects, are less clear: between literal conceal-ment and projected fantasy, settled comfort and lurking dread, the smoke raised an ill-defined wall. We are even left in some doubt whether the house and its chimney are not in fact some elaborate symbol for the mind of the narrator, at home in its unhomely thoughts. In Walter Pater's fragment "The Child in the House," however, there is no longer any question: memory of the house and the house itself have become subsumed in the dream.[1]

At first the dream of Florian seems homely enough; it parades as the very essence of remembered homeliness—for, as we are told, "in Florian the sense of home was singularly intense," as "the special character of his home was so essentially homelike," a repetition that, like that of the term "behind" by the narrator in Melville's story, tends to undermine itself by positive assertiveness. The remembered attributes of Florian's childhood house, however, confirm this picture: its trees, garden, walls, doors, hearths, windows, furnishings, even its scent contributing to make it the very type of home, a typicality reinforced by its position in the English Home Counties and their homely landscapes. So secure was this house to the child Florian that even the fog and smoke that occasionally drifted in from the nearby town held no ominous air. It was in every way a "place 'inclosed' and 'sealed.'"

But of course this house was only a remembered house, and this itself recalled in a dream. Its aspect was clear, but "as sometimes happens in dreams, raised a little above itself," heightened, half-spiritual, and merged with the knowledge, later acquired, of its essential impermanence. In retrospect, watching the growth of his soul in the house from a distance, Florian would give significance to things that held only a vague portent for him as a child. The dream rapidly became a history of the growth of fear, a tracing of the sources of what, to the child, were uncanny sensations, and remained, with the adult, the permanent springs of unease. Windows were, so to speak, left half-open inadvertently; a "cry in the stair, sounding bitterly through the house," heralded the news of Florian's father's death; a visit to the churchyard provoked questions as to the nature of a final resting place.

Finally, Florian's house became haunted: a "certain sort of figure that he hoped not to see," a shadow of the father, remained each night by his bed and did not entirely leave in the morning. The move from this childhood home simply confirmed this foreknowledge of death, the death of the child of course, but also of security and of homeliness. Returning for an instant to the already abandoned rooms, "lying so pale, denuded and meek," the "aspect of the place touched him like the face of one dead." Henceforth the soul would have no rest but in nostalgia, in that malady provoked by all apparently secure enclosures, homesickness. The childhood home was transformed into no more than a locus for dreams, for what Pater called "that clinging back towards it" that lasts for a long time and eventually spoils all anticipated pleasure.

In Pater's palely sublime dream, the return of a sense of primary narcissism gave an uncanny aura to the memory of the house, a repetition of something half suppressed in the mind, of the once-intimate relationship between ideas and things. It was at least significant for literary history and the establishment of the Proustian mode that Florian's dream was stimulated not by actually revisiting the site of childhood, nor by hearing a description of it that awakened memories, but by the simple conjuring of the "name of the place." Henceforth the uncanny will manifest itself no longer in the prolonged and artistically delivered ghost story but in the fragmentary, chance occurrence of a word, a phrase that, suspended as it were in ordinary discourse, demands as one of a series of such linguistic fragments of a once-whole past, to be interpreted.[2]

The domestic nostalgia of memory was, for Pater, only the private locus of a deeply felt nostalgia at the passing of history itself. In the last essay of his collection *The Renaissance*, Pater evokes the haunting figure of Winckelmann in the nineteenth century, a figure whose discourse of antiquity formed the classical imaginary for Goethe and Hegel as for Pater himself, who had followed the pale traces of Winckelmann's dreams in his own *Marius the Epicurean* some eighteen years later. Pater characterizes Winckelmann through a late historicist lens as "of an abstract type of culture, consummate, tranquil, withdrawn already into the region of ideals," a Winckelmann already neoclassicized by Goethe and canonized by Hegel. The author of the *History of Ancient Art* and the champion of high Greek culture is lauded for capturing "the charm of the Hellenic spirit," a melancholic dreamer alien to his own country and to that he adopted. Pater lends all of the faintness and remoteness that the classical has come to have in the last quarter of the nineteenth century to the interpretation of this first Hellenist; he draws a picture of a wandering and unfortunate spirit, born out of his rightful place and time, dedicated to the resuscitation of a distant culture. Winckelmann's own nature, indeed, seemed to Pater "itself like a relic of classical antiquity, laid open by accident to our alien, modern atmosphere." Against the "color" of modernity, and the "heat and profundity" of the Middle Ages, Winckelmann followed the "preeminent light" of the Hellenic, its transparency, rationality, and desire for beauty, bathed in "that white light, purged from the angry blood-like stains of action and passion."[3]

Such a bloodless vision of modern Hellenism was at once nostalgic, aware that in the "late afternoon" of the classical world, as Nietzsche had it, an irrevocable distance separated the modern from the antique, and at the same time optimistic, teasing out the possibilities of a modern art that might "burn always with this hard, gemlike flame."[4] Here the unbearable domestic nostalgia of "A Child in the House" opens to a more generalized nostalgia for the whole of history, now seen as irreconcilably separated from the present and entirely inadequate to confront or express "the modern world, with its conflicting claims, its entangled interests, distracted by so many sorrows, with so many preoccupations, so bewildering an experience."[5]

Pater found the model for this long-drawn-out death of art and culture in Hegel, tracing art's gradual giving way to "the growing revelation of the mind to itself." Only poetry, Pater found, could finally "command that width, variety, delicacy of resources, which will enable it to deal with the conditions of modern life." In this scheme architecture, the symbolic and founding art, is long lost as a force by which to express the human spirit:

The arts may thus be ranged in a series, which corresponds to a series of developments in the human mind itself. Architecture which begins in a practical need, can only express by vague hint or symbol the spirit or mind of the artist. He closes his sadness over him, or wanders in the perplexed intricacies of things, or projects his purpose from him clean-cut and sincere, or bares himself to the sunlight. But these spiritualities, felt rather than seen, can but lurk about architectural form as volatile effects, to be gathered from it by reflection.

These "volatile effects," unclearly embodied and abstractly expressed, were the result of architecture's inability fully to grasp the human form for itself. Architecture's influence on the mind was, in this sense, hardly sensuous.

As human form is not the subject with which it deals, architecture is the mode in which the artistic effort centers, when the thoughts of man concerning himself are still indistinct, when he is still little preoccupied with those harmonies, storms, victories of the unseen and the intellectual world, which, wrought out into the bodily form, give it an interest and significance communicable to it alone.

The question for Pater, caught between nostalgia for the full strength of bodily presence in Hellenic sculpture and his perception of the inevitable transience of all artistic modes, was whether the Hellenic lesson, at least, might be reclaimed in a world where philosophy dominated over art: philosophy alone, he concluded, "serves culture, not by the fancied gift of absolute or transcendental knowledge, but by suggesting questions which help one to detect the passion, and strangeness, and dramatic contrasts of life." And part of this "strangeness," as he demonstrated in *Marius the Epicurean*, resided in the fact that, despite a philosophy of history that buried the past, that past refused to remain at a proper distance. Pater's "rush of home-sickness" contemplating the death of the antique world was at once a necrophilia and a project: "It has passed away with that distant age, and we may venture to dwell upon it. What sharpness and reality it has is the sharpness and reality of suddenly arrested life."[6]

This division was expressed toward the end of *Marius* in the elaborate figures of the "Two Curious Houses," the one an emblem of the decadence and artifice of the late Roman Empire, the other an intimation of the strength of the new Christian culture. In his almost dreamlike experience of these houses, Marius tested the resources of "his old native susceptibility to the spirit, the special sympathies, of places," and their mystical significance. The houses, like that of Pater's childhood, were embodiments of life and thought; their atmospheres, as in the mystical beliefs of Swedenborg, so many garments for the soul, "only an expansion of the body; as the body . . . is but a process, an expansion, of the soul."[7] The first dwelling, a setting for the reception of the poet Apuleius in Tusculum, was already a home of latecomers, overshadowed by the haunted ruins of Cicero's villa, its blandness and daintiness effacing the otherwise sublime and terrifying rusticity of the natural surroundings. As Marius paused to enter,

he paused for a moment to glance back towards the heights above; whereupon, the numerous cascades of the precipitous garden of the villa, framed in the doorway of the hall, fell into a harmless picture, in its place among the pictures within, and scarcely more real than they—a landscape-piece, in which the power of water (plunging into what unseen depths!) done to the life, was pleasant, and without its natural terrors.[8]

Within, the aristocratic house was home both to the refinements of Greek culture, the vast library a scholar's paradise, and the roughness of Nero's Rome, with its "northern," Parisian entertainments.

The second of the houses was by contrast a model of homeliness, a house for "the orderly soul," inhabited by Saint Cecilia. "The house of Cecilia grouped itself beside that other curious house he had lately visited at Tusculum. And what a contrast was presented by the former, in its suggestions of hopeful industry, of immaculate cleanness, of responsive affection!" Without ostentation, the house was approached by a small doorway beside the Appian Way; quietly exhibiting the signs of wealth, it also displayed a sense of the past that was far from artificial: "a noble taste—a taste, indeed, chiefly evinced in the selection and juxtaposition of the material it had to deal with, consisting almost exclusively of the remains of older art, here arranged and harmonized, with effects, both as regards color and form, so delicate as to seem really derivative from some finer intelligence in these matters than lay within the resources of the ancient world."[9] A new taste, almost anticipatory of the Renaissance, had composed the fragments of the past so as to imbue it with new expressiveness, a new intellectual spirit. All cheer and peaceful industry, the house was the epitome of the *heimlich* and opposed to all the superficial attractions of the artificial sublime.

But, and Pater makes this clear, this homeliness was established firmly on its ability to encompass and overcome death. The foundations of the house were deeply embedded in the catacombs, the villa's subterranean double, that provided resting places for the ancestors of the Cecilii. The immediate spatial connection between the abode of the living and that of the dead sustained the air of authenticity, of "venerable beauty," that permeated the whole estate. Marius was comforted by the return of the family to the ancient custom of burial: a sign of "hope" concerning the body that overcame his fear of the funeral pyre. Indeed, there seemed only hope in these tombs, as if "these poignant memorials seemed also to draw him onwards" in an intimation of salvation. The *heimlich* had finally been reconciled to its apparent opposite in a spatial order that provided rest for both living and dead.

Nostalgia

If we eliminate from our hearts and minds all dead concepts in regard to the house, . . . we shall arrive at the 'House-Machine,' the mass-production house, healthy (and morally so too) and beautiful in the same way that the working tools and instruments that accompany our existence are beautiful.

Le Corbusier, Vers une architecture

It was in an attempt to free culture from what Henry James called this overburdening "sense of the past" that modernist architects, formed by futurism, attempted to erase its traces from their architecture. This urge to escape history was joined to a therapeutic program, dedicated to the erasure of nineteenth-century squalor in all its forms, that proposed an alliance between the hygienists and the architects that would be reinforced on every level by design. The destruction of the street, last trace of that "Balzacian mentality" so despised by Le Corbusier, and its replacement by expanses of verdure, the zoning of industry away from the centers of habitation, the endless biological analogies applied to functionalist mechanics, were only a few results of this polemical equation between art and health to be celebrated by modernism. At the scale of the house, too, its roof removed and replaced by a garden, its cellars filled in and its first floor open to the park, its horizontal windows and terraces encouraging the ceaseless flow of light and air, modernism proposed to consign the cluttered interiors and insalubrious living conditions of centuries to oblivion. By these means it was thought that disease, individual and social, might be eradicated once and for all, and the inhabitants of the twentieth century rendered fit for the marathon of modern life.

And if the doctors were thus served by the Ville Verte and the Maison Domino, then, by implication, so were the psychoanalysts. An open, fresh-air existence would finally address the causes of those pathologies so painstakingly treated on post-Freudian couches, purging society of its totems, taboos, and discontents. If houses were no longer haunted by the weight of tradition and the imbrications of generations of family drama, if no cranny was left for the storage of the bric-a-brac once deposited in damp cellars and musty attics, then memory would be released from its unhealthy preoccupations to live in the present. Side by side with the ubiquitous image of the modern bureaucrat as athlete, measuring his strength against a punching bag while contemplating a Léger painting, was the vision of biological functions cleanly subsuming psychological traumas: to picnic on the grass was not to recline on the couch, which, in any case, had been stripped of its layers of oriental rugs to be redesigned according to the curves of the body and sprung like a trampoline.

Yet, inevitably, this housecleaning operation produced its own ghosts, the nostalgic shadows of all the "houses" now condemned to history or the demolition site. Once reduced to its bony skeleton, transformed out of recognition into the cellular fabric of the *unité* and the *Siedlung*, the house was itself an object of memory, not now of a particular individual for a once-inhabited dwelling but of a collective population for a never-experienced space: the house had become an instrument, that is, of generalized nostalgia.

In 1947, two years after the end of the war and with Europe poised for full reconstruction, the philosopher Gaston Bachelard completed a book entitled, significantly enough in the context of this exhausted battlefield, *La Terre et les rêveries du repos,* the second volume in his study of what he called "material imagination." In this work he was concerned to examine what he called the "countermateriality" to be found in dreams of rest, of intimacy, of interiority, of involution.

We will examine images of rest, of refuge, of rootedness. . . . The house, the stomach, the cave, for example, carry the same overall theme of the return to the mother. In this realm the unconscious commands, the unconscious directs. Oneiric values are more and more stable, more and more regular. They are entirely concerned with nocturnal forces and subterranean powers.

Plumbing the depths of a terrestrial unconscious, of *la vie souterraine,* Bachelard found the topos of the birthplace, *la maison natale,* to stand at the center of his nostalgic vision: "This house is far away, it is lost, we inhabit it no more; we are, alas, certain of inhabiting it never again. It is, however, more than a memory. It is a house of dreams, our oneiric house." But such a house of dreams, a mental construct that included all houses yet inhabited and to be inhabited, was not to be found in the present, and certainly not in the present provided by modern life and modern apartments. Bachelard was clear in his rejection of urban contemporaneity:

I do not dream in Paris, in this geometric cube, in this cement cell, in this room with iron shutters so hostile to nocturnal subjects. When I dream well, I go yonder, to a house in Champagne, or to a few houses within which the mysteries of happiness are distilled.[1]

Bachelard's resistance to dreaming in his "geometric cube" might of course simply be interpreted as the antiurban stance of a *rêveur* in the long tradition established by Rousseau. But in the aftermath of the war, it might more properly be seen in the context of the anti-modern discourse that, since the early 1930s, had been gaining ground with critics skeptical of "progress" and its supposed benefits. Philosophers on both the right and left of the political spectrum contributed to this sensibility, from Theodor Adorno to Martin Heidegger, Max Horkheimer to Hans Sedlmayr, which amounted to no less than a concerted attack on the founding premises of modernism, or at least those that seemed to blame for the form of the "modern" house, its "geometric cubes" stacked up or laid out in "cement honeycombs."

Against the prismatic model of the Maison Domino, a modernist primitive hut in the line of many such structural and rationalist types since the Enlightenment, these critics advanced the complaint of uninhabitability. As Adorno wrote in 1944, "dwelling, in the proper sense, is now impossible," a sentiment that was echoed by Heidegger seven years later in his celebrated "Building Dwelling Thinking." Adorno despaired of retrieving the house of yesterday in the city of tomorrow, castigating those

functional modern habitations, designed from a *tabula rasa* . . . living-cases manufactured by experts for philistines . . . devoid of all relation to the occupant: in them even the nostalgia for independent existence, defunct in any case, is sent packing.[2]

Reduced to sleeping "close to the ground like an animal," modern man would soon be forced into a new nomadic primitivism, living in the *bidonvilles,* bungalows, and no doubt the garden huts, caravans, or even cars of the near future. Heidegger was to blame the triumph of technique, Sedlmayr the "loss of center," but the refrain was similar. Paul Claudel summed up the feeling in characterizing his Parisian apartment as a mere number, "a kind of geometrical place, a conventional hole, between its four walls." Even a detached house was no longer rooted, "fixed with asphalt on the ground so as not to be dug into the earth."[3] The house was no longer a home, ran the refrain, a burden that has since emerged as a principal leitmotiv of postmodernism.

The ensuing attempt to rebuild the home on more stable foundations, according to the specifications of countermodernists and nostalgic dreamers, complete with its cellar and its attic, its aged walls and comforting fireplace, has, however, inevitably fallen victim to a complaint inseparable from all nostalgic enterprises: that of the triumph of image over substance. In its aspiration to recover the past, postmodernism has generally substituted the signs of its absence, perhaps, in the process, engendering a house more truly haunted than that of modernism, but, for all this, hardly a more comforting or stable entity. Certainly it remains to be seen whether the mere image of "houseness" provides sufficient substitute for what has been lost, or even an effective site for oneiric play. For, like its predecessors, nostalgia for a fixed abode inevitably falls into the paradox of all nostalgia, that consciousness that, despite a yearning for a concrete place and time, the object of desire is neither here nor there, present or absent, now or then. It is, as the philosopher Vladimir Jankélévitch put it, caught in the irreversibility of time, and thus fundamentally unsettled.[4]

II
Bodies

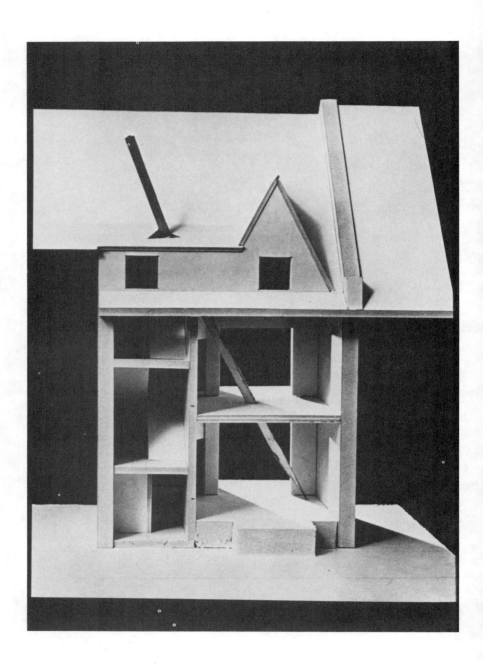

Architecture Dismembered

My body is everywhere: the bomb which destroys my house also damages my body insofar as the house was already an indication of my body.

Jean-Paul Sartre, Being and Nothingness

The idea of an architectural monument as an embodiment and abstract representation of the human body, its reliance on the anthropomorphic analogy for proportional and figurative authority, was, we are led to believe, abandoned with the collapse of the classical tradition and the birth of a technologically dependent architecture. With the isolated exception of Le Corbusier's vain attempt to establish the modulor as the basis for measurement and proportion, the long tradition of bodily reference from Vitruvius through Alberti, Filarete, Francesco di Giorgio, and Leonardo seems to have been definitively abandoned with the rise of a modernist sensibility dedicated more to the rational sheltering of the body than to its mathematical inscription or pictorial emulation.

In this context it is interesting to note a recent return to the bodily analogy by architects as diverse as Coop Himmelblau, Bernard Tschumi, and Daniel Libeskind, all concerned to propose a reinscription of the body in their work, as referent and figurative inspiration. But this renewed appeal to corporeal metaphors is evidently based on a "body" radically different from that at the center of the humanist tradition. As described in architectural form, it seems to be a body in pieces, fragmented, if not deliberately torn apart and mutilated almost beyond recognition. Further, this "body" is advanced, paradoxically enough, precisely as a sign of a radical departure from classical humanism, a fundamental break from all theories of architecture that pretend to accommodation and domestic harmony. Evoked as referent and as generator of an architecture that stands, as Coop Himmelblau has insisted since the late '60s, against "Palladian" humanism and Corbusian modernism alike, this body no longer serves to center, to fix, or to stabilize. Rather, its limits, interior or exterior, seem infinitely ambiguous and extensive; its forms, literal or metaphorical, are no longer confined to the recognizably human but embrace all biological existence from the embryonic to the monstrous; its power lies no longer in the model of unity but in the intimation of the fragmentary, the morselated, the broken.

On first inspection, this cutting of the architectural body might appear to be no more than an obvious reversal of tradition, an almost too literal transcription of the idea of "dismembering classicism." But a closer examination of the diverse sources of this new bodily analogy reveals a more complex relationship to previous "embodiments" from the Renaissance to modernism than that of simple pictorial caricature. Following the long history of the anthropomorphic analogy, these projects exhibit all the traces of their origins in classical and functional theory, while at the same time constituting an entirely different sensibility.

The history of the bodily analogy in architecture, from Vitruvius to the present, might be described in one sense as the progressive distancing of the body from the building, a gradual extension of the anthropomorphic analogy into wider and wider domains leading insensibly but inexorably to the final "loss" of the body as an authoritative foundation for architecture. Three moments in this successive transformation of bodily projection seem especially important for contemporary theory: these might be described concisely as (1) the notion that building *is* a body of some kind; (2) the idea that the building embodies states of the body or, more importantly, states of mind based on bodily sensation; and (3) the sense that the environment as a whole is endowed with bodily or at least organic characteristics. For the purposes of argument, these themes may be roughly identified with historical periods, although, as will be obvious, such a chronological "progression" is more useful for clarity than it is historically accurate.[1]

In classical theory the (idealized) body was, so to speak, directly projected onto the building, which both stood for it and represented its ideal perfection. The building derived its authority, proportional and compositional, from this body, and, in a complementary way, the building then acted to confirm and establish the body—social and individual—in the world. The principles of Vitruvius traced the origins of proportion to the Greek canons of bodily mathematics, to be incorporated by the architect-sculptor in the column and in the relations of the different parts of the order to the whole, and thence to the building; his ideal of unity was described by the celebrated figure of a man with arms outstretched inscribed within a square and a circle, navel at the center. The theorists of the Renaissance from Alberti to Francesco di Giorgio, Filarete, and Leonardo subscribed to this analogy, which determined the search for centralization in all its aspects.

Such an analogy, indeed, took on more than metaphorical meaning: in a real sense the figural expression of anthropomorphic form, from the column to the plan and facade, buildings were bodies, temples the most perfect of all, as were cities, the seat of the body social and politic. Alberti's proposition that "the building is in its entirety like a body composed of its parts"—the relations of part to whole leading to his definition of beauty as the state where nothing can be added or taken away without destroying this delicate balance— was extended to embrace all animal bodies. Francesco di Giorgio showed a figure superimposed literally on the plan of a cathedral and of a city, while Filarete compared the building's cavities and functions to those of the body, its eyes, ears, nose, mouth, veins, and viscera. Indeed, like a body, buildings and cities may fall ill: a building may, he hazarded, become sick and die, whence it needs a good doctor, the architect, to cure it. In a metaphor that established the full force of his analogy, Filarete compared the architect to a mother, carefully nurturing her child from conception to maturity.[2]

As we know, the attraction of these formulations lasted well into the eighteenth century—and even, in the sheltered enclave of the Ecole des Beaux-Arts, much longer. The body, its balance, standards of proportion, symmetry, and functioning, mingling elegance and strength, was the foundation myth of building.

But beginning in the eighteenth century, there emerged a second and more extended form of bodily projection in architecture, initially defined by the aesthetics of the sublime. Here, the building no longer simply represented a part or whole of the body but was rather seen as objectifying the various *states* of the body, physical and mental. Edmund Burke, followed by Kant and the romantics, described buildings not so much in terms of their fixed attributes of beauty but rather in their capacities to evoke emotions of terror and fear. Burke himself recognized, presciently enough, that the very definition of the sublime he was advancing, an aesthetic based on experience rather than artifice, would have the effect of rendering the premises of classical organicism null and void, if not vaguely ridiculous. Arguing against the idea that the proportions of a building should be derived from those of the human body, he made fun of the Vitruvian canon:

To make this forced analogy complete, they represent a man with his arms raised and extended at full length, and then describe a sort of square. . . . But it appears very clearly to me, that the human figure never supplied the architect with any of his ideas. For in the first place, men are very rarely seen in this strained posture; it is not natural to them; neither is it at all becoming. Secondly, the view of the human figure so disposed, does not naturally suggest the idea of a square, but rather of a cross. . . . Thirdly, several buildings are by no means of the form of that particular square. . . . And certainly nothing could be more unaccountably whimsical, than for an architect to model his performance by the human figure, since no two things can have less resemblance or analogy, than a man, and a house or a temple.[3]

In place of these specious doctrines emanating from "the patrons of proportion," Burke outlined an aesthetics founded on primary sensation. If any bodily attributes remained in the building, they were the result of projection, rather than of any innate qualities.

In architectural terms, the sensibility to the object as mirroring the states, rather than the aspect, of the body was theorized for the first time in the emerging psychology of empathy of the late nineteenth century. Thus the art historian Wölfflin, seeking to determine the change in style from the Renaissance to the baroque, following his thesis of 1886, "Prolegomena to a Psychology of Architecture," applied the new discipline of psychology to reintroduce the body into the argument, but now in an active and entirely transformed manner:

We judge every object by analogy with our own bodies. The object—even if completely dissimilar to ourselves—will not only transform itself immediately into a creature, with head and foot, back and front; and not only are we convinced that this creature must feel ill at ease if it does not stand upright and seems about to fall over, but we go so far as to experience, to a highly sensitive degree, the spiritual condition and contentment or discontent expressed by any configuration, however different from ourselves. We can comprehend the dumb, imprisoned existence of a bulky, memberless, amorphous conglomeration, heavy and immovable, as easily as the fine and clear disposition of something delicate and lightly articulated.[4]

What had previously been a foundation of classical design theory, a principle of making as well as a standard of judgment, was now entirely placed in the service of perception, and that of objects that in the classical sense were not in any way beautiful; the qualities of the architectural object, no matter what the intentions of its makers, were now those of all inanimate nature, only to be understood by a process of projection. "We always," continued Wölfflin, "project a corporeal state conforming to our own; we interpret the whole outside world according to the expressive system with which we have become familiar through our own bodies." Such a transference of bodily attributes, such as "severe strictness," "taut self-discipline," or "uncontrolled heavy relaxation," takes its place within what Wölfflin calls a "process of unconscious endowment of animation," in which architecture, as an "art of corporeal masses, relates to man as a corporeal being."

Inevitably this process is historicized in Wölfflin's scheme. There is, he claims, a "Gothic deportment" with "tense muscles and precise movements" that, together with the Gothic nose "which is sharp and thin," endows Gothic architecture with its quality of sharpness, its precisely pointed forms without relaxation or flabbiness—"everything sublimates itself completely in energy." Similarly, the Renaissance liberates these hard, frozen forms to express a state of well-being, vigorous and animated. In contrast, the baroque manifests itself in weight, the slender bodies of the Renaissance replaced "by massive bodies, large, awkward, with bulging muscles and swirling draperies." Light-heartedness has given way to heaviness, flesh is softer and flabbier, limbs are not mobile but imprisoned. Movement becomes less articulated but more agitated and faster, in dances of restless despair or wild ecstasy. And so with architecture, the violence of which is best expressed in Michelangelo's *terribilità*. Quoting Anton Springer, Wölfflin notes the combination of "mute massiveness" and unevenly distributed vitality in the sculptor's "unresisting victims of inner compulsion." Beyond this, indeed, the baroque moves away from the point at which it can even be seen in terms of the human body, or at least in terms of the articulated body invented by the Renaissance. Image, noncorporeal and atmospheric, has replaced defined plastic form, in a counterreformation dominated by yearning and spiritual ecstasy. Here Wölfflin stops; but not before he has himself projected this baroque spirit well into the eighteenth and nineteenth centuries:

Carl Justi's description of Piranesi as a "modern, passionate nature," whose "sphere is the infinite, the mystery of the sublime, of space and energy," has a more general application. One can hardly fail to recognize the affinity that our own age in particular bears to the Italian Baroque. A Richard Wagner appeals to the same emotions. . . . His conception of art shows a complete correspondence with those of the Baroque.[5]

This led Wölfflin to draw the line; for, always sensible of the lost Renaissance body, he would insist that in architecture there were limits, where in music there were not; the "restraining of the finished and rhythmic phrase, the strict systematic construction and the transparently clear articulation which may be fitting and even necessary to express a mood in music, signify in architecture that its natural limits have been transgressed." Wölfflin's message is clear: the sublime in architecture, which necessitates the "half-closed eyes" that see lines more vaguely in favor of unlimited space and the "elusive magic of light," signals the end of bodily projection in its formed and bounded character, and perhaps the end of architecture itself. For Wölfflin, the end of the Renaissance body signifies a dangerous moment from which architecture must draw back.

For the modernists, however, this moment was one of opportunity, allowing for a universalizing abstraction and a psychology of sensation and movement; embodied in architecture that mirrored all the states of a regenerated and healthy body but corresponded as well to a similarly healthy mind. Cubist and postcubist attempts to dismember the classical body in order to develop an expressive model of movement were thus dedicated not so much to its eradication but to its reformulation in modern terms. From Duchamp's *Nude Descending a Staircase,* based on Etienne-Jules Marey's careful studies of movement, to Balla's *Woman with a Dog on a Leash,* there seems to be no fear that the body is entirely lost: rather the question is one of representing a higher order of truth to perception—of movement, forces, and rest. Even in that primal scene, the "Overture" to Proust's

Remembrance of Things Past, where Marcel, on awakening, figures the parts of his body according to their "successive positions" during the night, as if seen on a bioscope—the instrument invented by Muybridge to analyze the running positions of the horse—even this fragmented body is ready at any instant to be recomposed, as Proust observes, into the "original components of the ego." Analytical science, for many avant-garde modernists, was the necessary and prophetic armature of a new awareness but not a total dispersion of the body. Le Corbusier, as we know, even tried to restate it in a newer and more fundamental way, balanced between sensation and proportion; the *promenade architecturale,* the modulor, and the very plan of the Ville Radieuse unabashedly re-create Vitruvian man for the twentieth century.

This sense of the city as a bodily organism, one still tied to the classical tradition in its modernist versions, has led more recently to a third and final extension of the body outside itself: a kind of animism, which, through an even more generalized work of projection, refuses any one-to-one ascription of body and building. The projects of Coop Himmelblau, for example, seem calculated to extend far beyond actual identification with specific body parts or whole bodies; rather they are seen like machines for the generation of a whole range of psychological responses that depend on our faculty of projecting onto objects states of mind and body. "We want . . . architecture that bleeds, that exhausts, that whirls and even breaks," claimed Himmelblau in 1980 in conjunction with the "Hot Flat Project," "cavernous, fiery, smooth, hard, angular, brutal, round, delicate, colorful, obscene, voluptuous, dreamy, alluring, repelling, wet, dry, throbbing. An architecture alive or dead. Cold—then cold as a block of ice. Hot—then hot as a blazing wing." This uncomfortable body is subsequently stretched to include the entire city, a city that "throbs like a heart" and "flies like breath."[6] "The Skin of This City" (1982, Berlin) proposed a form whose "horizontal structure is a wall of nerves from which all the layers of urban skin have been peeled away."

Such a literal biomorphism, akin to many similar but less threatening science fiction images of the Archigram era, has in recent years been extended by Coop Himmelblau's apparent desire to merge the body completely with the design and its context. In a revealing interview with Alvin Boyarsky, Himmelblau described their experiments into design as a kind of automatic writing that, operating through blind gesture translated into line and three-dimensional form, works literally to inscribe the body language of the designer onto the map of the city. Projects for Paris, Vienna, and New York emerged from their sense that "the face and body of these cities" was clearly readable; then they literally superimposed face and plan, so that "our eyes became towers, our foreheads bridges, the faces became landscapes and our shirts the plans."[7] In this way, photographic collages of Himmelblau's portraits, merged by reproductive processes into the texture of city plans, dramatically illustrate the urge to dissolve the authoritarian body of the architect into the world that receives its designs. In this procedure, in much the same way that Cindy Sherman has photographed herself almost buried amidst garbage-filled soil, Himmelblau hovers between narcissism and its opposite, in a strangely powerful celebration of the will to lose power. As they wrote in the prose poem "The Poetry of Desolation," architecture's lyrical qualities now stem not from its organically conceived life but from its evident death:

The aesthetic of the architecture of death in white sheets. Death in tiled hospital rooms. The architecture of sudden death on the pavement. Death from a rib-cage pierced by a steering shaft. The path of the bullet through a dealer's head on 42nd street. The aesthetic of the architecture of the surgeon's razor-sharp scalpel. The aesthetic of the peep-show sex in washable plastic boxes. Of the broken tongues and the dried-up eyes.[8]

Calling for an "architecture of desolation," with its own "fascinating landmarks," Himmelblau refuses all notions of a comfortable city where one might be safe and sound, while fully embracing the "solitude of squares, the desolation of the streets, the devastation of the buildings."[9]

But in this evocation of futurist and expressionist images, we sense none of the positive aspirations of the first avant-garde. For side by side with the continuity and gradual extension of the bodily metaphor, from the corporeal to the psychological, we can also detect, starting in the early nineteenth century and emerging with greatest force in the later years of the twentieth, a decided sense of loss that seems to accompany the move away from the archaic, almost tactile projection of the body in all of its biological force.

This perceived "loss" of the body began, as I have noted, with the romantic sublime; under the influence of Kant and the German romantics, it became the stimulus for a vision of a lost bodily unity fragmented by time and sense experience. The body became more an object of nostalgia than a model of harmony, manifested in art as a series of irreconcilable fragments: the "parts," for example, in Mary Shelley's story of Frankenstein, that never could be assembled into anything but a monster. Similar retellings of classical myths of the ideal body—of Pygmalion and Galatea, of Apelles and Protogenes— and new stories of the creation of the unknown "monstrous" double of man in art, exemplified in Balzac's short story "Le Chef-d'oeuvre inconnu," reinforced the romantic tragic sense of loss.

In psychoanalytical terms it was Jacques Lacan, in his classic essay of the late thirties "The Mirror Stage," who proposed the model of a pre–mirror stage body, a "corps morcelé" or "morselated body" that participated, at the moment of the mirror stage, in a sort of drama impelled toward a spatial identification of the self with regard to its reflection. In this model the mirror is construed as a lure that in Lacan's terms "machines" the fragmented phantasms of the pre-narcissistic body into what Lacan calls "a form that [is] orthopaedic of its totality." Deprived of its previous status by the reflection of the whole, this morselated body is repressed to the unconscious, where it shows up regularly in dreams or "when the movement of psycho-analysis touches a certain level of the aggressive disintegration of the individual":

It then appears in the form of disjointed limbs, or of those organs represented in exoscopy, growing wings and taking up arms for intestinal persecutions—the very same that the visionary Hieronymus Bosch has fixed, for all time, in painting, in their ascent from the fifteenth century to the imaginary zenith of modern man. But this form is even tangibly revealed at the organic level, in the lines of "fragilization" that define the anatomy of phantasy, as exhibited in the schizoid and spasmodic symptoms of hysteria.[10]

Lacan's structuralist notion of a repressed fragmentation of the body finds its poststructuralist analog in Roland Barthes's own fragmented text "Fragments of a Lover's Discourse," where Barthes describes a body that, subjected to the gaze of desire, is so to speak transformed into a corpse. For Barthes, the very gaze of a hypothetical lover projected onto the body of the sleeping beloved is as analytical and dissecting as that of a surgeon in an anatomy class. Like Proust's Marcel as he watches Albertine asleep, the watcher searches, scrutinizes; takes the body apart, as if to find out what is inside it, "as if the mechanical cause of my desire were in the adverse body." Barthes concludes, "Certain parts of the body are particularly appropriate to this observation: eyelashes, nails, roots of the hair, the incomplete objects." This process, Barthes observes, would be the opposite of desire, and rather like "fetishizing a corpse."[11]

Barthes illustrates this kind of fetishization by reference to Balzac's romantic version of the Pygmalion myth, *Sarrasine*, where the central character falls in love with the transvestite singer La Zambinella. Before seeing La Zambinella, Sarrasine loves only "fragmented woman"—"divided, anatomized, she is merely a kind of dictionary of fetish objects. This sundered dissected body (we are reminded of boys' games at school) is reassembled by the artist (and this is the meaning of his vocation) into a whole body . . . in which fetishism is abolished and by which Sarrasine is cured." A "unity" discovered in "amazement," this body will of course be returned to its previous fetishized state when Sarrasine realizes the trick that his projected desire has played on him. Barthes remarks on the list of anatomical details that make up La Zambinella's body— a "monotonous inventory of parts" that leads to the crumbling of what is being described: "language undoes the body, returns it to the fetish."[12]

This fetishization of the lost object of desire might well be extended to the interpretation of contemporary architectural fragmentation and "morselation." For behind what seem to be superficial and "pictorial" attempts literally to dismember the classical body, we sense a deliberate attempt to address the question of the status of the body in postmodern theory, not just in the outward appearance of the work but in its inner procedures.

In a first instance, the body, rather than forming the originating point of a centered projection, is itself almost literally placed in question. Confronting the architecture of Himmelblau or, less dramatically, of Tschumi, the owner of a conventional body is undeniably placed under threat as the reciprocal distortions and absences *felt* by the viewer, in response to the reflected projection of bodily empathy, operate almost viscerally on the body. *We* are contorted, racked, cut, wounded, dissected, intestinally revealed, impaled, immolated; we are suspended in a state of vertigo, or thrust into a confusion between belief and perception. It is as if the object actively participated in the subject's self-dismembering, reflecting its internal disarray or even precipitating its disaggregation. This active denegation of the body takes on, in the postmodern world, the aspect of an autocritique of a modernism that posited a quasi-scientific, propaedeutic role for architecture. The body in disintegration is in a very real sense the image of the notion of humanist progress in disarray.

But these deliberately aggressive expressions of the postmodern corporeal also operate in another register, that of the strangeness evoked—as Freud noted with regard to the feeling of the uncanny— by the apparent "return" of something presumed lost but now evidently active in the work. In this context it would be, so to speak, the return of the body into an architecture that had repressed its conscious presence that would account for our sense of disquiet.

As we have noted, Freud identified two causes of the uncanny, both founded on the movement between prior repression and unexpected return. The first stems from the return of something that was thought to be definitively repressed, such as ideas of animism, magic, totemism, and the like, which, no longer believed in as real, throw into doubt the status of material reality when they reoccur. Examples of such a form of the uncanny would be the return of the infantile belief in omnipotence of thoughts (coincidence leading to the fear that one has killed someone after speaking idly of their death); or the seeming return of magical properties to things long since divested of their magical significance, as in a story Freud recounts from *The Strand Magazine* where a house furnished with a table carved with crocodiles is the setting for a night of faint terror, when smells and forms begin to move through the rooms as if some ghostly crocodiles were haunting the place. The second cause of the uncanny stems from the return of repressed infantile complexes, those of castration or womb fantasies for example, which, on returning, throw into question not so much the status of reality—such complexes never were thought to be real—but rather the status of psychical reality. Freud gives as an example of such causes "dismembered limbs, a severed head, a hand cut off at the wrist . . . feet which dance by themselves," evidently uncanny because of their proximity to the castration complex (U 366). The temptation is strong to ascribe our sense of destabilization in the face of Himmelblau's constructions to such an uncanny, now embodied in the dancing forms of a building once a body.

Such an interpretation is in fact reinforced by Himmelblau's own consistent opposition to the domestic, the *heimlich* in any form. Their passionate appeal, expressed in explosive performances, for a deliberately nonaccommodating architecture has been tied, from the outset, to a resolute refusal of domesticity. "Our architecture is not domesticated," they stated in 1982, "it moves around in urban areas like a panther in the jungle. In a museum it is like a wild animal in a cage."[13] Thence the beam that, like a backbone and head, rises and sinks like a panther, in the exhibit "Architecture Is Now" installed at Stuttgart in 1982. This animal-like play, perhaps a recasting in terror of Alberti's benign vision of a "building like a horse," was at the same time allied to a more direct exploration of that more elusive manifestation of the antidomestic, the uncanny. Here the haunting absence of the body became as much a preoccupation as its physical presence. Speaking of the Red Angel Bar in Vienna of 1980–1981, Himmelblau asked: "Who knows what an angel's body really looks like?"[14] The bodiless object and the bodily agent, modeled in steel and wire, play together in a literally cutting fantasy. Finally, the Hot Flat (Vienna, 1978), a "permanent" monument to an architecture that burns, or the Haus Meier-Hahn (Düsseldorf, 1980), otherwise titled Vektor II, with its impaled roof, illustrates almost too directly, but uncomfortably enough, the will to destroy the house of classical architecture and the society it serves. The latter project, indeed, encapsulates didactically, if not architecturally, the twin ambitions of Himmelblau to drive a stake at once through the house and through the specifically humanist body it represents.

This didactic and dramatic example of the house impaled takes its place, in the postwar period, within that discourse concerned to reveal the existential limits of what Gaston Bachelard has termed "the coefficient of adversity." This calculus of threat was explored by Sartre in *Being and Nothingness*, itself written in the aftermath of the war, where the definition of the self and its body is described as a function of the perception of resistance that objects in the world have to the self. Thus, "the bolt is revealed as too big to be screwed into the nut; the pedestal too fragile to support the weight which I want to hold up, the stone too heavy to be lifted up to the top of the wall." In other cases, objects will be threatening to an already established instrumental complex—the storm to the harvest, the fire to the house. Step by step, these threats will gradually extend to the body, the center or reference indicated by all these instruments; this center will in turn indicate the center of reference to them. Thence Sartre's proposition with regard to the body: the body is indicated firstly by an instrumental complex, and secondarily by a threat posed within this context:

I live my body in danger as regards menacing machines as well as manageable instruments. *My body is everywhere: the bomb which destroys my house also damages my body insofar as the house was already an indication of my body* [my emphasis]. This is why my body always extends across the tool which it utilizes: it is at the end of the cane on which I lean against the earth; it is at the end of the telescope which shows me the stars; it is on the chair, in the whole house; for it is my adaptation to these tools.

In this way Sartre rejects a classical notion of embodiment that then projects itself into the world as a mode of apprehension or control of the external environment. Instead, he poses our original relation to the world as the foundation of the revelation of the body; "far from the body being first for us and revealing things to us, it is the instrumental-things which in their original appearance indicate our body to us." "The body," he concludes, "is not a screen between things and ourselves; it manifests only the individuality and the contingency of our original relation to instrumental-things."[15]

In this context, any initial interpretation of Sartre's formulation of the "body in the house" as resonating with all the power of a long classical tradition, a tradition that posed the body as the essential model for all other created instruments, the body as a priori a foundation for the recognition and apprehension of all other objects, suffers a defeat. Sartre's body participates in a world within which it has to be immersed and to which it has to be subjected even before it can recognize itself as a body. It knows itself precisely because it is defined in relation to instrumental complexes that themselves are threatened by other instruments, understood as "destructive devices." The body knows itself to be by experiencing a "coefficient of adversity." Thus where, in classical theory since Alberti, the house is a good house only insofar as it is constituted analogically to the body, and the city a good city for the same reasons, in Sartrean terms the body is only seen to exist by virtue of the existence of the house: "it is only in a world that there can be a body." The bomb that destroys the house does not destroy a model of the body, but the body itself, because the house is needed for the body to project it. We are at once precipitated into a world of absolute danger and at the same time made to understand that this threat exists only insofar as we *are* in this world. It is, no doubt, the shiver of this world that Coop Himmelblau wishes us to experience.

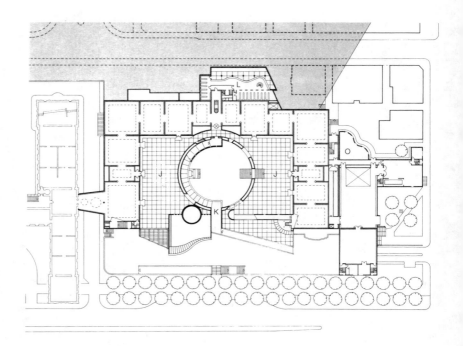

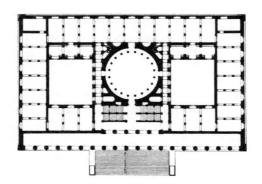

Losing Face

The museum is the colossal mirror in which man contemplates himself finally in all his faces, finds himself literally admirable, and abandons himself to the ecstasies expressed in all the art journals.
Georges Bataille, "Musée"

In a recent article on the architecture of James Stirling, Colin Rowe observed, not uncritically, that the new Staatsgalerie in Stuttgart was to all intents and purposes comparable to Schinkel's Altes Museum, but "without a facade." This lack of facade Rowe found troubling; there was "something slightly crumbly" about the result, a "presence too casually disclosed." Against such a lack of facade, Rowe posed the necessity for walls, the thicker the better; dense and opaque vertical surfaces that would present the building to the eye, not, as with the plan, intellectually and conceptually, but perceptually. A building without such a facade, frontally posed to the approaching viewer, lacked, in Rowe's terms, an essential ingredient of representation. Like the face, the facade operated for Rowe as "a metaphorical plane of intersection between the eyes of the observer and what one may dare to call the 'soul' of the building." For Rowe, indeed, the face/facade, "the existential interface between eye and idea," was necessary for *any* interaction between building and observer to take place: "when considering intercourse with a building," Rowe concluded, "its *face*, however veiled, must always be a desirable and provocative item."[1]

This lack of interest in the face, Rowe has consistently argued, has been a continuous failing of modern architecture. Once the horizontal slab on columns, permeable to light, air, and space, had technically and polemically replaced the vertical load-bearing wall, the facade was inevitably at risk. As expressed in the prototype of Le Corbusier's Maison Domino, the emphasis on the horizontal, on the interpenetration of inside and outside, had created the means for a "free facade"; and this, for all intents and purposes, was no facade, in the traditional sense, at all. The loss of facade would thus simply be the direct result of the loss of the bearing wall, a necessary precondition to the "free facade," which allows the long window to be inserted in what becomes no more than a thin skin stretched across the edges of the horizontal slabs. The bearing wall, the construction of which was simply a preliminary to the marking of its vertical surface as a premonition or intimation of the inside, had, to all intents and purposes, been done away with. The free plan destroyed the fixed facade. "Face," concluded Rowe, "was never a preoccupation of modern architecture."

How might we then interpret Rowe's objection to modernist effacement now raised with regard to Stirling's museum, a building that seems monumental enough and seems to have overcome many of the deficiencies of the Domino model and its stylistic consequences? On one level, we might infer that Rowe, a humanist by predilection, was simply calling for the erasure of any trace of modernist program, and especially so in a building that in other respects seemed to reply successfully to his general criticism of modernism, especially with regard to its replication of a fragmented urban discourse that to all intents and purposes echoes the formal project of Rowe's own "collage city."

On another, more visceral level, Rowe's objection to a lack of face might be an extension of that understanding, derived from Wölfflin and sustained by Geoffrey Scott, that Renaissance building owed its special qualities as an "architecture of humanism" to its direct analogies, in theory and physical presence, to the human body. A confessed Wölfflinian himself, Rowe would seem to agree with the ascription of a corporeal psychology to the experience of architecture, a response of the human body to a building that, for the building to be successful, would have, so to speak, to be matched and instigated by the building itself. We sense an echo of Wölfflin's conclusion that "we judge every object by analogy with our own bodies." Wölfflin wrote of the "creature"-like nature of the building, "with head and foot, back and front": "we can comprehend the dumb imprisoned existence of a bulky, memberless, amorphous conglomeration, heavy and immoveable, as easily as the fine and clear disposition of something delicate and lightly articulated."[2]

For Geoffrey Scott, the building's "body" acted as a referent for "the body's favorable states," the "moods of the spirit . . . power and laughter, strength and terror and calm." Translating the long tradition of Renaissance bodily analogy into psychological terms, Scott identified two complementary principles at work: the one, founded on the response we have to the appearance of stability or instability in a building, is our identification with the building itself: "we have transcribed ourselves into terms of architecture." The other was founded on the fact that with this initial transcription we unconsciously invest the building itself with human movement and human moods: "we transcribe architecture into terms of ourselves." Together, these two principles formed, he asserted, "the humanism of architecture." On the one hand, the "tendency to project the image of our functions into concrete forms" provided the basis for design; on the other, "the tendency to recognize, in concrete forms, the image of these functions" was the basis of all criticism. Thence Scott's impassioned plea for the body in architecture: "architecture, to communicate the vital values of the spirit must appear organic, like the body."[3] It might well be assumed that Rowe, following Scott and more directly Adrian Stokes, subscribes to such notions, at least in so far as they prove useful for criticism.

In Rowe's criticism of Stirling's museum, however, the demand was not necessarily for a body but rather for a face, which, with its direct appeal to the notion of a facade, implies a more figurative and mimetic correspondence than one based simply on abstract qualities of height, weight, stability, instability, and the like. Looking for a more direct understanding of the face/facade analogy, we might find it in the more precise physiognomical analyses of the late eighteenth century that compared, sometimes all too literally, a building's front to a human face. We might think of the theories of writers from Le Camus de Mézières to Humbert de Superville, the projects of Ledoux and Lequeu, and, in the later nineteenth century, of Charles Blanc and his disturbing comparison of racial physiognomies with regional styles.[4]

But this tradition would not explain Rowe's reference to the question of a building's *soul;* physiognomy as a guide to the inner states of the soul was, after all, largely discredited, save for its survival in Balzac's characterological mythology, following Hegel's devastating attack on physiognomy and phrenology in the *Phenomenology* of 1807. Yet Rowe insists on the face as an indication of the "internal animation" of a building, at once "both opaque and revealing." Evidently he is implying a less religious and more aestheticized notion of "soul" than was present in eighteenth-century physiognomical theory—perhaps something closer to that sketched by Georg Simmel in 1901, in an essay entitled "The Aesthetic Significance of the Human Face," where he explored the nature of the face as an index of modern spirituality.[5]

Simmel, struck by the adage "The face is the mirror of the soul," observed that this was no doubt the result of its unity in repose, a symmetry that rendered all the more expressive the even slight distortion of one of its parts. Further, he noted that the structure of the face makes any too-exaggerated transformation in any one of its parts impossible without positively unaesthetic, almost inhuman results. Simmel equated such "centrifugal movement"—characteristic of baroque figures—to "despiritualization," the weakening of the domination of the mind over the extremities of the being. Beyond this, the face is an index not simply of "mind" in the abstract but of individuality in the concrete: "the face strikes us as the symbol, not only of the spirit, but also of an unmistakable personality." Rowe's distaste for faceless architecture would, in these terms, simply be a dislike of the lack of "personality" implicit in the generalist and anti-individualist program of modernism.

This conclusion would be reinforced by Simmel's insistence on the face as a bearer of meaning that far surpasses the body in expressiveness. Indeed, he argued, the very capacity of the body for expression is limited:

Bodies differ to the trained eye just as faces do; but unlike faces, bodies do not at the same time *interpret* these differences. A definite spiritual personality is indeed connected with a definite, unmistakable body, and can at any time be identified in it. Under no circumstances, however, can the body, in contrast to the face, signify the *kind* of personality.

Nor is the body able to display psychological processes; its movements are crude when compared to those of the face: "in the face alone, emotion first expressed in movement is deposited as the expression of permanent character." These individual qualities of the face are balanced by its perfect symmetry, by virtue of which either of its two halves can be inferred from the other, each pointing to a higher principle that governs both; "as a whole it realizes individuation; but it does so in the form of symmetry, which controls the relation among the parts."[6] The correlates to such qualities in architecture have been theorized since Alberti, and Rowe certainly makes reference to them.

For Simmel the essential characteristic of the face, sealing its position as the most complete model of the relations demanded by the work of art, was then this "task of creating a maximum change of total expression by a minimum change of detail." And of all the parts of the face contributing to this effect of dynamic economy, the eye was, for him, the most subtle and powerful, through its mobility and through the importance of the gaze, which, in painting for example, interprets and structures space itself.

The eye epitomizes the face in mirroring the soul. At the same time, it accomplishes its finest, purely formal end as the interpreter of mere appearance, which knows no going back to any pure intellectuality behind the appearance. It is precisely this achievement with which the eye, like the face generally, gives us the intimation, indeed the guarantee, that the artistic problems of pure perception and of the pure sensory image of things—if perfectly solved—would lead to the solution of those other problems which involve soul and appearance. Appearance would then become the veiling and unveiling of the soul.[7]

To follow here the implications of such a statement with respect to the openings in a facade—doors and windows—would lead us too far from our argument, but it is clear that Rowe's comment on the soul of the building revealed or at least intimated by its face gains substance in comparison to Simmel's proposition. To strip away the face from the soul would be in some sense to denature the soul itself, or at least to deprive it of that content it received from the face as its expression and representation. The absence of a face would then imply the lack of a soul, for without visibility, nothing may be inferred to exist.

We are thus presented with an apparently clear set of oppositions, between classical humanism and modernist antihumanism, between faced buildings and faceless ones. But evidently Rowe is not indiscriminately opposed to all modern buildings: Le Corbusier is cited alongside Renaissance and baroque architects as ("sometimes") a master of the vertical surface. Certainly we have more than ample evidence that Le Corbusier's very notion of architecture was itself founded, like that of Alberti, on the body, and indeed, the principles of the free plan, as I described them above, reside on a concept of the body that Le Corbusier never tired of repeating. From the house to the city, the body, for Le Corbusier, acted as the central referent: its shape informed the layout of the Ville Radieuse; its analogy infused biology into the mechanics of the city and the building; its proportions were embedded into every measure through the operation of the *tracés régulateurs* or the modulor. Despite the rhetoric of the free plan and the free facade, there would seem to be a countertendency at work in Le Corbusier's work emphasizing the continuity of the humanist position, an ever-present body reflected in and projected into a bodily architecture.

Rowe himself admires the facades of the villas Schwob and Garches that exploit the tension between horizontal floors and vertical walls with considerable skill. The facade of Garches, certainly, seems caught between a representation of its non-load-bearing status and its frontal, entry condition. And this example could be multiplied in Le Corbusier's work—I mention only the Maison Plainex, with its witty symmetry that implies facial characteristics. There are many others. If we need reminding of Le Corbusier's own love of walls, as opposed to "skins," we would only have to turn to an early notebook (c. 1910) to read:

A wall is beautiful, not only because of its plastic form, but because of the impressions it may evoke. It speaks of comfort, it speaks of refinement; it speaks of power and of brutality; it is forbidding or it is hospitable;—it is mysterious. A wall calls forth emotions.[8]

Similar passages in *Vers une architecture,* as well as many self-explanatory sketches, reinforce our sense that Le Corbusier's love of walls is hardly less than Rowe's. Certainly Rowe's long exegesis of the qualities of the side wall of the chapel at La Tourette would suffice to confirm that Le Corbusier fills at least some of the critic's criteria with regard to walls.[9]

What seems to be at stake, then, is not so much the simple opposition humanism/modernism. In the first place, given Stirling's deliberately ambiguous mingling of modernist and classicist codes, his formation of a heterogeneous language that otherwise fascinates Rowe, we cannot easily charge the critic with any form of literalist nostalgia. Secondly, if there is an implied critique of modernism in his question, it is, in the context of Stirling's reformulation of the architectural problem, hardly to be taken in the same spirit as, for example, the same question addressed to Gropius's Bauhaus building.

Rowe's observation gains depth when it is remembered that the precise formulation of Stirling's facelessness was rendered by an implied parallel between Schinkel's Berlin Altes Museum and the new Stuttgart Staatsgalerie. This parallel, indeed, is suggested by a comparison made by Rowe much earlier, in a note appended to his essay on "The Mathematics of the Ideal Villa," that brought side by side for the purposes of tracing the traditional roots of modernism the two monuments of Schinkel's Altes Museum and its (formal) reconstitution in Le Corbusier's Assembly Building at Chandigarh.[10] Implicitly, then, Stirling's building completes a series begun with Schinkel and continued with Le Corbusier, operating adeptly with both in order to produce what, for Rowe, must appear as a witty, if not "mannerist," transformation of the classical prototype into the postmodern assemblage, with traces of its modernist typology preserved for dialectical good measure.

And yet, although Rowe does not note the fact, we recognize that Schinkel's museum had itself already begun to suppress what, traditionally at least, might be termed a face. The facade of the Altes Museum was after all formed by the equal colonnade of a "stoa" set into the block of the building. And such a stoa, with no formal indication of symmetry save for applied motifs such as steps or the sight of the attic of the central space, and with a permeability hardly indicative of the thick and vertical wall plane demanded by Rowe, offers little of the kind of "face" presented by other museums of the epoch, such as the temple fronts of London or Munich. The true face of Schinkel's building, indeed, is set behind the colonnade, a wall paneled to receive a narrative history of culture, pierced in the center to provide access to the museum and the stair to the second floor. A facade hidden, then, behind a screen; the "face," however veiled, of Simmel's analogy. Stirling has, in this sense, stripped away not one but two faces, in order to reveal the drum of the central space not now as interior but as exterior surface.

This again leads to a peculiar reversal. For Schinkel, as is well known, built up his model museum from a number of architectural elements each meaningful in its own origin and again in combination with the other elements. These may be identified as the overall block, similar in its courtyard parti to the royal palace that faced the museum across the square; then the inset entry stoa that, on approach, screened the panoramic vision of the historical development of culture on the wall behind, and on the upper floor screened and framed the equally panoramic view of the city of Berlin, with the royal palace and Schinkel's own architecture school building prominent to left and to right; finally, inset into the composition, the central rotunda, a miniature Pantheon, with dome and internal colonnade. Such a combination of type forms taken from historical architecture brought together the Greek ideal of civic accessibility embodied in the stoa, a type of the agora rather than the acropolis; the sequence of rooms en suite characteristic of the palace turned museum and responding to the chronological exposition of the objects; and the temple of memory or Pantheon, emblem of Rome but also of the absolute suprahistorical nature of aesthetic quality, a reminder of the nature of "art" in the historical work of art.

When, as in Stirling's museum, such an assemblage is dismantled, the effect is immediately to alter the meaning of each element and thereby of the whole. Thus Stirling takes away not only the facade of the Altes Museum but also its front sequence of rooms, turning the original palace plan into a U-shaped block reminiscent of the old gallery to one side. The site of the original stoa is marked by a terrace, reached by a ramp from street level. Then the stair, once set behind the stoa, is turned into a second ramp that rises from this terrace to the entrance and gives access to the courtyard in the rotunda. This rotunda, without dome and open to the sky, presenting interior and exterior volumes by virtue of the high surrounding wall, is no more than the "shell" of the Pantheon, blasted open and left to stand as an absent presence, a space returned to the city by an act of violence to a monument. Another ramp curving along the inside wall of the rotunda leads to the upper level of the site. The effect of defacing has been, so to speak, to disembowel, to reveal the inner organs without protection or representation. The rotunda offers its curved wall as if turning its back on the visitor, who is left without even a porch, that usual manner of entering a Pantheon-like rotunda.

Rather there is the entrance lobby, a glass-faced curvilinear pavilion standing in front of the line implied by the front ends of the U-block. The message seems to be one of deracination, of indeterminacy, of discomfort with the monumental face of past institutions; of a tentative reconciliation of architecture and the city, revealing the elements of architecture in order in a second moment to facilitate their dispersion into the city fabric.

But the type of Schinkel's Altes Museum was not available for Stirling, for all the appropriateness of the model for his German audience, without having been submitted to considerable transformations during the modern period. Indeed, a glance at the ground plan of Le Corbusier's Musée Mondial immediately reveals the debt owed to its German predecessor; the square plan, framed by a U to the rear, and the central, cylindrical volume of the Sacrarium both refer back to Schinkel and anticipate Stirling's version.

Following Rowe's own lead, in his comparison of the Altes Museum and Le Corbusier's Palace of Assembly at Chandigarh, such an analysis would reveal "a conventional classical *parti* equipped with traditional *poché* and much the same *parti* distorted and made to present a competitive variety of local gestures—perhaps to be understood as compensations for traditional *poché*." If this comparison were to be systematically developed one might notice, for example, the transformation of the original stoa into a kind of propylaeum or gigantic umbrella porch, almost freestanding in front of an uneven and broken wall that screens the first row of interior columns; the formation of the U-shaped block framing the interior hall by the joining of three separately conceived blocks, each with its independent columnar grids and exterior sun breakers; finally the displacement from the center of the central circular volume, one equally independent as an element, surrounded by its own interior-exterior wall and reinforced by its own circle of columns that neatly intersect with those of the interior hall in order to bring its spinning form to (provisional) rest. The ramp, finally, turned at right angles from the original position of Schinkel's central stair, balances the offset site of the council chamber, and the entry itself is displaced one bay to the right of center.

In view of this preliminary transformation, the Stirling Staatsgalerie might be said to be already a second-degree version of the Schinkel prototype, operating on Schinkel by way of his modernist re-interpretation. One might extend Rowe's comment logically to read "a Palace of Assembly without a facade." Thus Stirling's central circular volume would be at once a memory of the Pantheon rotunda and of an empty assembly hall; the ramp would already be included in the elements of the project; the three-sided U of offices already substituted for the courtyard parti; the entrance already off center, and, most importantly, the rear wall of the "stoa" already eroded into a screen.

Such a formal transformation was, as we have noted, however, already present in the Musée Mondial where Le Corbusier retained a reference to Schinkel in plan while entirely reformulating the type in section. The first-floor plan of the Corbusian museum is, indeed, uncannily similar to Stirling's own reformulation of Schinkel. In both, a U-shaped block frames a central circle; in both, the original dome of the Pantheon has been lifted: in the case of the Musée Mondial, Le Corbusier has substituted the inner space of a high pyramid; in that of the Staatsgalerie, Stirling has completed its ruination, opening it to the sky. Le Corbusier himself made the point that, with the entire monument raised up on pilotis, the distinction between front and back had been erased, thus beginning the process that Stirling accomplishes by means of the continuous public route through the site from top to bottom. In this sense, Stirling would not simply be destroying the Pantheon, or attacking Schinkel's monumental version of history, but also gently criticizing the idealistic and quasi-mystical aspirations of Corbusian modernism.

With the results of this "Wölfflinian" analysis of formal techniques in mind, we might enquire, by way of conclusion, as to the specific causes of Stirling's apparently ambivalent attitude toward monumentality. In the first place, of course, this would be attributable to the modernist rejection of what Sigfried Giedion called the pseudomonumentality of the nineteenth century, the routine "misuse" of shapes from the past, the devaluation of traditional language, a loss of monumentality attributable to no "special political or economic system."[11]

In the second place, and in the context of postwar Germany, Stirling's resistance to traditional monumentality stemmed evidently from his opposition to a specific variety of pseudomonumentality, that of the Third Reich. The memory of Nazi "misuse" of Schinkel's neoclassic forms rendered a direct and "postmodern" quotation of

Schinkel, or any other classic image, immediately suspect. Thus we might well read Stirling's "empty center," with its ruined columns, as an ironic gesture that explodes the monumental focus of the building to the city, to imply the inhabitation of an already ruined monument or at least the establishment of a cemetery at its heart. And with the heart exposed and dead, the dismantling of all the other organs followed, culminating in the loss of face. It is as if Stirling were commenting on the reuse of an already ruined nineteenth-century monument, following Giedion's pathology—"the so-called monuments of recent date have . . . become empty shells"—to the ironic letter.

And yet, of course, the very citation of Schinkel, however ruined, was in itself suspect, and especially in the context of a new museum dedicated to memory, and one that, despite the fragmentation of its parts, evidently aspired to and attained a form of monumentality of its own. This has inevitably led to charges of a kind of "fascism" leveled against Stirling himself. Peter Bürger recently commented on what he called the "fascist" overtones of the Stuttgart museum, a design that has been assailed by traditional modernists and traditionalists alike.[12] Frei Otto and other neomodernists committed to a "democratic" architecture of flexibility, indeterminacy, and technocratic "lightness" found Stirling's walls, terraces, and monumental cylinder "inhuman"; Professor Benisch, winner of the third prize in the competition, saw distinct echoes of "totalitarian" architecture, one dedicated, he stated, to an autonomous and formalistic (and therefore socially meaningless) play of quotations. Even the building workers, not to be outdone, spoke of the architect wishing to rival Speer at the Zeppelinfield at Nuremburg.

Certainly, the building of a "ruin" by a British architect in the center of a city itself devastated by war seems to have overdetermined its negative reception, especially as the ruin refers to a museum that was indeed ruined by the bombing. Stirling's "best of intentions" have been canceled by a context that no merely formal irony could expect to overcome.

In these respects, then, the notion of an escape from or effacement of monumentality would seem to turn back on itself, implying the immediate absorption of the most "critical" vocabulary of references and the monumentalization of any institutional form, however veiled its "soul." The very eradication of the face that veils representation becomes symbolic in its own right, monumentalizing, despite itself, the most difficult contradictions in the debate over monumentality.

We might now better understand Stirling's attempt to invent a form of monumentality that weaves the museum back into the city once more, dispersing its architectural contents as so many half-ruined elements that resist any reintegration into a classical unity. Stirling's decomposition of Schinkel, via Le Corbusier, seems in the light of this brief history of representation somehow inevitable, an unwitting paradigm of what the German philosopher Arnold Gehlen has termed (in French) *posthistoire*.

But this said, and with all respect paid to the brilliant formal gestures that result, we might also recognize one further characteristic of Stirling's building that marks it out as entirely different from either its nineteenth- or its twentieth-century predecessors. In both Schinkel and Le Corbusier, as we have noted, architecture is indissolubly bound to the contents, real and ideological, of the museum. In the Altes Museum, the sequence of rooms that assemble the schools of western painting in chronological order is posed against the calm Pantheon at the center that establishes the notion of ahistorical permanence; the public, semipermeable face of the stoa confirms the museum's connection to the city. Architecture operates as both representation and instrument for the display of a nation's history and its artistic heritage as the active ingredient of continuing cultural development. It is at once sign and agent of a living history.

Similarly, in Le Corbusier's Musée Mondial, the grand route of time is extended back to prehistory and forward to the ever-expanding present, working to insert temporality and spatiality across cultures and peoples into a universalizing frame that, again, proposes history (enlarged in its scope by the sciences of anthropology, ethnology, and geology) as the foundation of the future. The central volume, or "Sacrarium," universalizes the western Pantheon and acts again as a center of atemporality. Here too the architecture operates as a symbol and mechanism and is tied to its contents.

But with Stirling's museum, as with so many other contemporary museums, this "content" is now dispersed into a generalized notion of flexibility. The brief no doubt called for a series of well-lit and well-ventilated rooms of certain sizes; but their structure, sequence, and scale are in the event subordinated to the debate among the architectural fragments at the center of the museum. The consequence of this withdrawal from program is to place all the burden of signification on the architecture itself, freed entirely of any contemporary obligations, speaking only of its relationship to the past. But we have seen that while this "speech" relies on a set of carefully selected precedents, museum paradigms, these are used to indicate the presence of a museum without the inconvenience of their former significations. Theodor Adorno characterizes this condition in his essay on the "Valéry Proust Museum": "Once tradition is no longer animated by a comprehensive substantial force, but has to be conjured up by means of citations because 'It's important to have tradition,' then whatever happens to be left of it is dissolved into a means to an end."[13]

Posthistoire, we might then assume, would privilege the internal discourse of an architecture turned on itself, an architecture disassociated from its cultural obligations, at least insofar as this culture has lost any secure belief in its own history. Perhaps this is what disturbed Colin Rowe the most, as he contemplated the lost face of history at Stuttgart.

To leave the critic-historian adrift, as it were, before the shards of history at Stuttgart, however, would be to ignore the peculiar nature of that history. For the fragments of architectural types all too neatly exploded by Stirling are, in the end, pieces of a history itself constructed artificially. The desire of the historian and thence the architect to make architecture speak has forced its fragmentation into allegorical units, made up from pieces of the past. In this sense it might be said that what Rowe experienced at Stuttgart was the product of the history he himself had elaborated with post-Wölfflinian expertise, one that deliberately tore the fragment loose from one context in order to press meaning on it in another.

Taken to its extreme, such a history would result in the endless circulation of signs, the foreclosure of history itself, a fate that does not dismay the neoconservative adherents of *posthistoire*. As Habermas has noted, Gehlen's "sigh of relief" in the face of what he sees as the "crystallization" of culture and the death of Enlightenment leads all too quickly to the cheerless admonition favored by Gottfried Benn, "Count up your supplies":

The possibilities implanted in [modern culture] have all been developed in their basic elements. Even the counterpossibilities and antitheses have been uncovered and assimilated, so that henceforth changes in the premises have become increasingly unlikely. . . . If you have this impression you will perceive crystallization.[14]

Against such a bleak future of endless repetition, one easily imagined within the premises of "collage architecture" and certainly practiced by exponents of postmodernist allegory, the history of the modern museum offers at least one alternative understanding of architectural representation: the recognition that the construction of a contemporary architecture has to remain entirely distinct from the history that it shelters. Architecture would here be denied a representative and allegorical role in order for it to take on a spatial and structural existence independent of its contents.

Certain historical museums have demonstrated this form of architectural autonomy. One might cite the rear gallery of John Soane's house, where historical fragments are attached to a geometrical and almost aclassical structure, or the more comprehensive exploration of abstract classicism at the Dulwich Art Gallery, where structure, lighting, and spatial definition come together to form additive units that present (rather than represent) the museum's exhibits. Schinkel himself, perhaps following Wilhelm von Humboldt's concept of historical objectivity, approached such a separation in the private museums of the Prince Regent at Kleinglienicke and at the home of von Humboldt at Tegel. In both buildings, the historical fragment is clearly distinguished from its architectural frame. Contemporary equivalents that might offer some resistance to the excesses of "cultural crystallization" might be, for example, Louis Kahn's Kimbell Art Museum at Fort Worth, where the studied relationship between structure and lighting seems to extend the lessons of Soane's Dulwich; or, finally, Raphael Moneo's museum of Roman artifacts at Mérida, where a simple repetitive wall and arch structure creates a haunting ambience that, without citation or mimicry, is entirely appropriate to its contents. In all these examples, the refusal to dismember architecture allows for a provisional contract with the present, and thus escapes, for a moment at least, the contradictions of historical representation.

For it is perhaps not an accident that all these examples are truly faceless: the interiority of Soane's museums, with even Dulwich awkwardly entered through a private mausoleum, is echoed by Schinkel's homes for collectors, while the structural logic of Kahn and Moneo resists any application of a representational facade. Against the dramatic "call for a lost facade," acted out by Stirling and so elegantly analyzed by Rowe, these quiet structures have preserved a space for architecture in a modern museum where, as Bataille noted, "one must take account of the fact that the rooms and objects of art are only a container the content of which is formed by the visitors."[15]

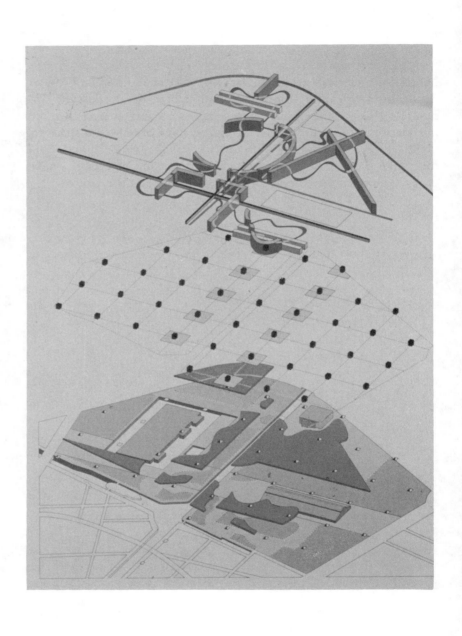

Trick/Track

"I don't think they play at all fairly," Alice began in rather a complaining tone, "and they all quarrel so dreadfully one can't hear oneself speak—and they don't seem to have any rules in particular; at least, if there are, nobody attends to them."

Lewis Carroll, Alice's Adventures in Wonderland

Contemporary architecture, in the most general sense of an art after modernism, seems increasingly to be caught in the dilemma of Alice playing croquet with the Queen: she knew what the game was called, but there did not seem to be any fixed rules, and, to complicate matters, the equipment was in continuous and random movement, from the flamingo-mallets to the hedgehog-balls and the soldier-hoops. What had previously been understood as being played according to categorical rules that fairly divided up loss and gain, chance and skill, victory and defeat, was now entirely open to chance, deprived of the security of articulated moves and their known consequences.

Some such game is no doubt to be played on and between *les cases vides* of Bernard Tschumi's Villette-board: "*case,* in backgammon, each of the places marked with a kind of arrow, in chess and in draughts, each of the white or black squares that divide up the board" (Littré). Here empty and awaiting the play, these once-meaningful places in a well-regulated partition of "chance and calculation," of loss or gain, are reduced to the status of markers, somewhat like the trestles of Mallarmé's mime theater. As punctuation, innocent of all meaning, they work not so much to define the events that take place around them but to identify and situate actions that are not necessarily events. Their regular dispersal across an undifferentiated field substitutes for a traditional kind of representation, of scenic and narrative unities, a theater of repetition where instead of "acts" and "actors" a dynamic play of forces inserts itself over time.

Both the "event" and "time" have, in this context, been reconceived. In a historicist vision of the past, present, and future, time moved inexorably toward a goal; events, like little works of art, followed each other in quick or slow succession and derived their contours, limits, meaning, and relative importance from this unbreakable flow of time. In historicist terms, art itself sought to imitate both this flow and these events, embedding them in the grand master narratives of progress or decline. Neither modernism nor indeed postmodernism has sought radically to change this sense of temporality directly; they have simply tried to endow it with different significance and new ends, apocalyptic or nostalgic as the case may be. But Tschumi's poststructuralist sensibility would deny this thrust of historical force, as well as depriving events of both their form and their meaning in the historicist context. This denial leads not simply to a void but logically to a *case vide*, with all the traces of a once-played game still in place. Here the *case* becomes not just a square space but also a compartment, a pigeonhole, a drawer within a drawer, ready to be filled with new contents at any moment. The activity of the architect, as Littré explains the procedure for drawing up *cases* in ledgers and logbooks, is then to construct spaces by means of lines that "transversely cut the vertical columns."

Tschumi's *cases are vides*, necessarily emptied of nostalgia in order to prepare for another kind of inhabitation, one not predicted by functionalist taylorization or cozy family myths. It is for this reason that Tschumi builds *cases* and not *maisons*: "*case,* a poor and wretched house, a hovel, as in 'the hovels of natives in the colonies,'" from the Latin *casa* or cottage, as opposed to the *maison,* manse or mansion, from the Latin *manere,* to dwell in. Tschumi's *cases vides* echo, but from a long way off and with little desire to return, the forgotten huts of numberless peoples, displaced by war, famine, or agrarian depression. Their red frames stand not as signs of some romantic ruined cottage but as open structures for the nomadic *banlieue.*

Their formal structures are as "empty," in a traditional, formalist sense, as their implied content with respect to function; or rather the procedures for their subdivision and assemblage prescribe no fixed contents. A transparent cube of space is internally crossed and cut by points, which turn into lines, and by planes, which turn into surfaces, which in turn define volumes. Occasionally the points widen into cones, the lines assemble into lines and lattices, and the planes fold into contours; often, all fall out of the cube in random fashion. In this formal method, there are echoes of modernism's techniques: Le Corbusier's Five Compositions, Van Doesburg's Neoplasticist experiments, constructivist formalisms. Where abstraction was conceived in modernism, however, as a replacement of one set of rules for another, as a response to a new and re-formed social content it was to house and shape, Tschumi's forms are different: they lack both the rules and the content of modernism's utopian design. Unlike the series of house types invented by the moderns, limited in form and number by a controlling, empirical determination, there are no limits to Tschumi's series or to their permutations. Nor does the series refer to any origin; its cubes are not established by the four posts of Laugier or the four walls of Goethe, or the anthropological elements of Semper, or the primal symbolism of Loos. They start where they start and finish equally arbitrarily.

In this sense, as the counters in an elaborate and arbitrary architectural game, they must be understood to refer, if not to the reality principle of function, then to the pleasure principle of their architect. And here Tschumi breaks radically with tradition. Once entirely fulfilled, as depicted in Filarete's graphic image of Renaissance organicism, by an aesthetic enactment of conception, birth, and post-partum nurture, the architect's pleasure has been vouchsafed little or no place in contemporary theory. The traditional objects of such pleasure have been dispersed with the demise of the anthropomorphic analogy and its very exercise has been rendered suspect by an apparently hedonistic search for consumerist images.

Against this, Tschumi has defined his own version: "My pleasure," he writes, "has never surfaced in looking at buildings, at the 'great works' of the history or present of architecture, but rather in dismantling them."[1] For an architect deliberately *not* to take pleasure in the contemplation of great works, past or present, or even in their competitive emulation, but rather in their "dismantling," would certainly be to divert pleasure to apparently perverse ends.

And yet Tschumi's pleasure principle is consistent enough. As he describes it, it resides in the calculated transgression of traditional canons: in questioning the idea of order, reexamining the concept of unity, departing from the orthodoxies of formalism and functionalism, that is, in testing the very limits of architecture. Substituting for the traditional terminology of "form and function, space and event, structure and meaning" a vocabulary of transformation and operation, Tschumi allies himself firmly with a present condition characterized by fragmentation and dissociation. Such terms as disjunction, displacement, dislocation, decentering indicate strategies that, for him, seem appropriate for the historical moment. These themes have been consistently present in Tschumi's designs and writings from the early seventies, recalling those advanced by Roland Barthes and Jacques Derrida for literature and philosophy. Indeed, with inevitable lags and necessary mediations, his architectural projects, from *The Manhattan Transcripts* through La Villette to the more recent designs for the Tokyo National Theater, provide an interesting conceptual and visual commentary on the emergence of poststructuralist models of analysis over the last decade.

Thus, his pleasure in "dismantling" would be, to use a distinction drawn by Roland Barthes in 1971, a pleasure not of the "work" but of the "text."[2] Against the traditional idea of a work, defined as a concrete, finite object, closed within its aesthetic limits, single, authored, institutionalized, and ready for explication, interpretation, and consumption, Barthes poses the conditions of the text, seen as a methodological field. The text, in Barthes's terms, would not be, like the work, "displayed" and ready for consumption, but would have to be demonstrated. Impossible to subsume within the traditional artistic genres, the text would be potentially unlimited. Open to the play of associations, contiguities, dislocations, overlappings, it would be a plural condition, set in an intertextual matrix that denied any secure individuality. In this sense the text would not be an object to be passively "read" or appreciated but an object of play, to be written. Whereas the pleasure of the work, undeniably present in reading a great author or looking at a great building, would remain circumscribed by its nature as an object of consumption, the pleasure of the text would be a full enjoyment, a *jouissance,* of writing as well as reading.

Tschumi's lack of pleasure in the "great works" of architecture might be explained in similar terms. On the one hand, an architectural "work" that is theorized, created, and interpreted according to all the monumental ideals of the classical tradition is closed, a suitable object for nostalgia or consumption but nothing more. It does not enter into play. In Barthes's terms it is something already distant from us, an object that can never be recreated. This recognition is an essential mark of our modernity: "for what is 'being modern' but the full realization that one cannot begin to write the same works once again?" On the other hand, Tschumi's pleasure in dismantling these works would be to create something that, in architecture, had the status of what Barthes has called a "text" in literature. His operation would perhaps be the architectural equivalent of a philosophical or literary deconstruction.

This said, however, the conditions of such a "textuality," one that was not reducible to a forced linguistic analogy or a literal caricature of "deconstructed" structural and formal elements, would be, as Tschumi realizes, difficult to determine. In the terms posed by *The Manhattan Transcripts,* it would be derived not by the simple manipulation of the internal codes of traditional or modern architecture, but rather by their confrontation with concepts drawn from outside architecture, from literature and philosophy, film and music.[3] In this often violent encounter, the limits of the discipline would be tested, its margins disclosed, and its most fundamental premises subjected to radical criticism. Thus the deeply rooted ideals of transparency between form and function, sign and signifier, space and activity, structure and meaning would be forced into dissociation, induced to collide rather than coincide. Play of this kind would celebrate dissonance over harmony, difference over identity.

It is significant, with respect to the Barthesian notion of text, that Tschumi proposes, as the instrument of this play, a work on *notation.* Notation, in this sense, refers to the marks or graphic signs used to denote certain operations, not all architectural, that are central to the dismantling procedure, and, with some reservations, to the process of reassembly as well. Notation is used to build a system of forms that include the recognizable elements of architecture but also embrace movements, events, actors, even states of mind, translated into graphic conventions. Thus the *Manhattan Transcripts* assays the transcription of events and buildings conceived as filmically linked forms; the three parallel and superposed *bandes dessinées* form a visual field that at once zones activities and stories—the horizontal function— and explodes them by juxtaposition—the vertical implied connections. In La Villette, these notational realms, expressed as superposed fields defined by points, lines, and surfaces, similarly come into conflictual conjunction. The banded "zoning" of the Tokyo Theater transforms the sequences of the *Manhattan Transcripts* into spatial domains, each with repercussions on the next, horizontally and vertically.

In the development of the notational language itself, Tschumi has had recourse to a number of already partially defined codes. First and most obvious is the filmic, the diagrammatic, frame-by-frame analysis of montage, taken in the explosive sense developed by Eisenstein. These banded diagrams are transformed into a form of static "animation" implying the movement of the film, as if emulating the late nineteenth-century flicker books. The implications of the *Manhattan Transcripts* for architecture are, with this method, explored in the transformational drawings of the La Villette follies. Supplementing these graphic conventions, Tschumi relies on two additional languages drawn from architecture itself. Both are derived from the experience of the modernist avant-gardes, and both, as we shall see, are deeply implicated in Tschumi's complex stance toward the "modern." The first is that set of conventions developed in order to express movements and forces, and the implicit movement and force of forms in particular, expressed literally by arrows and lines and more implicitly by the balance and weight of forms on the page. Here the Russian suprematists and constructivists and German expressionists, from Malevich and Lissitzky to Kandinsky and Klee, have provided means for "writing" the dynamics of form in space, fully exploited in the exploded, elementarist drawings of the follies. The dynamic flow of activities and forms implied by the juxtapositions of the Tokyo Theater are likewise indicated, denoted, by lines and arrows of varying types. A second "language" is provided by the conventions of architectural representation explored by the constructivists, the dynamic implications of plans and sections and, notably, of the axonometric, twisted, broken, and shattered on the page. Tschumi, of course, does not leave any of these codes untouched; in bringing them together and using them to speak of a dismantled architecture, he develops a convention that is plural but not eclectic; one code is always used to put another into play. thus the exploded axonometric acts on the perspective, itself inserted into the bands of a plan, and the whole is often, as in the case of the rapid-fire "scenes" of the

Tokyo Theater, turned at ninety degrees. These scenes are in turn transformed by their refusal to be framed, in the same way that the "shot" of Eisenstein, carefully prepared in order to montage with the next, is already subverted and intersected with the effects of such montage.

Such notations, like those of music or, more graphically, dance, do not in themselves, of course, imply an architecture; but in double play, at once withdrawing from and entering into the conventions of architectural representation, they suggest a realm that is neither architecture nor (for example) film. Following Rosalind Krauss's characterization of Barthes's "texts" as "paraliterary," reflecting their ambiguous status somewhere between criticism and literature, we might call this realm *paraarchitectural*.

Paraarchitecture might be defined in terms similar to those developed by David Carroll in his explanation of the neologism *paraesthetics*, coined to refer to the realm of aesthetic speculation described in the work of Nietzsche, Lyotard, Foucault, and Derrida. Carroll cites the Oxford English Dictionary description of the sense of *para* in its original Greek usage: from its locational sense in "by the side of," "alongside of," "past," and "beyond" to its compositional sense of "to one side, amiss, faulty, irregular, disordered, improper, wrong," the prefix came to denote subsidiary relations, alteration, perversion, and simulation. Carroll concludes, "Paraesthetics indicates something like an aesthetics turned against itself, or pushed beyond or beside itself, a faulty, irregular, disordered, improper aesthetics—one not content to remain within the area defined by the aesthetic."[4] It is important to note that this "paraesthetics" would not be an aesthetics *of* the irregular, the disordered, the improper; nor an aesthetics that simply broke the boundaries of convention, in the sense meant by much romantic aesthetic theory; but rather a truly improper aesthetics. The effort to describe a paraarchitecture would similarly refuse the picturesque and the fragmentary for their own sakes, the aestheticization of disorder, in favor of a faulty and disorderly architecture.

Confined to the domain of theory, even to that of the "analytical diagram," Tschumi's paraarchitectural "transcripts" would no doubt seem entirely benign. The difference between the traditional work of formal analysis and a paraarchitectural work of dismantling is, on the level of the drawing, imperceptible enough. It does not necessar-

ily threaten the certainties of architecture. But with the commitment
to reassemble and to build, to create an experiential *paraarchitectural*
realm, the threat to "architecture" becomes palpable, much in the
same way that the paraliterary texts of Barthes and Derrida have
threatened the conventions of the literary work. Thus in the realization of La Villette, when the drawn superpositions and fragmentary
exploded diagrams are translated into buildings and spaces, Tschumi's new pleasure principle may indeed pose problems for architecture. Against the eternal principles ruling the occupation of territory
and the construction of shelter, and the historical conventions gov-
erning the identity of parks, *fabriques* are thrown into question by
follies that demand no functions, arcades are confused by routes that
meander with no goals, empty spaces pose riddles that ought to be
solved by contents.

The tension emerges at the point of transition between the drawn
and the built. For Tschumi has evidently refused the traditional
mediations that allow an easy and idealized passage from theory to
practice and from drawing to building. In a traditional practice, the
notations of the plan, elevation, section, geometrical and perspectival
projection are accepted *as* notations; they refer to something else,
concrete and tangible in the realm of the building. In Tschumi,
however, what were, in one frame of reference, recognizable as
merely notations become, indeed, built notations. The result is that
the work on notation is, quite literally, constructed. And here the
confrontation with well-worn criteria becomes sharpened. For "to
build the diagram" has always marked the failure of the architect;
and, further, Tschumi's "diagrams" are not "architectural" to any
recognizable degree. Thus, from the standpoint of the architect,
Tschumi has not only broken the rules, he has broken the rules
doubly, and the result must only be "bad architecture." Such a
transgression of professional codes, however, despite the shock value
it implies, has little interest for Tschumi. His project would only be
successful if he had managed to invent a realm where such rules
simply do not apply, managed not only to theorize the paraarchitectural but to establish it in the city.

Here, however, the paraarchitect is confronted with a double problem, operating on the level of language. In order for the notational
play to imply a type of constructed entity that will convey, if not reify,
the sense of transformation, infinite sequence, overturning of con-

ventions, and endlessly subversive activity of the dismantler, it has to contain within its heterogeneous codes the elements of a signifying practice. That is to say, the codes of notation have to imply both an architectural language and its subversion. The problem is complicated by the fact that at the very moment when deprived by disjunctive operations of a signified, the signifier must stand for itself. For this task Tschumi has selected a "ready-made" language—the elemental and structural signs of constructivism—and, in testing its limits, has transformed it into something else. What at first glance might seem to refer to the post-Revolutionary avant-garde, in both style and substance, is, on consideration, revealed to say nothing of the kind. Tschumi's stance toward the languages of modernism is in this sense both affectionate and critical, without nostalgia or a real desire to register anything but the most general allusion to the Red years. Here notation is used not for the purpose of denotation, the indication of carefully selected sources, but precisely for the purposes of connotation, to suggest one of many possible meanings. For Tschumi, understanding that the avant-gardes were but one manifestation of the many faces of the "modern" would go beyond a purely historicist reference to develop a thoroughly modern language, necessarily composed of recognizable elements from previous modernisms but at the same time agile enough to criticize them.

The point may be made by a comparison of that paradigmatic emblem of the Russian avant-garde, the Tatlin Tower project of 1917–1922, and one of the La Villette follies. The Tatlin Tower certainly set out to challenge the limits of classical architecture. Relying on the structural innovations of Eiffel's own construction, it mimicked the Tower of Babel, only to press the conventions of stability and verticality into question. The slanted, open structure was then put to use in order to house the dynamically rotating chambers of the new political order. Themselves formed according to "eternally" true solids—the cube, the pyramid, the sphere—their movement and transparency were equally indicative of transformation from static to dynamic. The whole structure, then, together with its parts, acted as a symbolic form of the new, even as it criticized the old. It relied on this "old," indeed, for the denoted sense of each of its gestures; deprived of architectural tradition, the tipped, spiral, open structure, with its motivated contents, could not begin to mean. Now, in the case of the folly built at La Villette, Tschumi has made obvious reference to the *vocabulary* of this first, revolutionary, avant-garde gesture; he has even with evident pleasure adopted the "red" color, originally so evocative of political as well as architectural revolution. Certainly the spiral, diagonal, circular, and stepped elements so brutally inserted into the openwork structure of the cube are reminiscent if not directly imitative of constructivist style. And yet, of course, every aspect of its political, social, and urban context, as well as the aesthetic program, render this folly a veritable study in difference to its apparent referent.

The necessity of repetition for the statement of difference has been argued in philosophical terms by Derrida. In aesthetic terms it is even more essential. For without the accompanying text, without a word-play that reinforces and reinstates difference in similarity, the silent object is forced to rely on a system that at once exploits overt visual references and subverts their apparent destination and closure in their "source." Knowingly, Tschumi does not fall into the fallacy, hopefully propounded by the avant-gardes, of a language that speaks with entirely new words; rather he selects a range of elemental forms, already stated in this avant-garde project, and submits them to an almost contemptuous disassembling and reassembling. The gaze of the dismantler fractures and reconstrues, and the resulting meaning is hardly a repetition of origins. On examination, the folly is, on one level, genuinely a meaningless object, a reassemblage of once-meaningful terms to make a nonsense out of them. With no hidden political agenda, no revolutionary aesthetic or social aim, and no historicist nostalgia, the allusion to constructivism becomes a mad shot in the dark that at once cherishes avant-gardism but comprehends its madness. On another level, the folly is precisely calculated for its own purposes: an object fully expressed without a function to express. Empty or full of one activity or another, it is still full of architectural meaning; or rather, paraarchitectural significance. Its cubic skeleton, exploded elements, lack of classical "knowledge," and refusal of romantic formulas betray a sign of architecture denatured. Without origin, and with no certain end, the folly stands on its own, so to speak.

It would be simple to describe such an object, repeated with infinite transformation in the grid of the park, as sculptural rather than architectural. Such a "criticism" has been leveled at other conceptual works in the recent past. But this would be to ignore the evidently "architectural" intent of the work, from the primitive structure of the cubic grid to the naming of the objects as *cases,* however empty. And here, perhaps, we may find a clue to the peculiar nature of Tschumi's linguistics that, on at least two distinct levels, radically departs from that of modernism. In the first place, while the Tatlin Tower, together with all other works in the constructivist canon, were in some way symbolic of a new socioaesthetic order, their very language of struts and mechanical forms, their dynamic relations and deliberate transformations of tradition an expression of their didactic and manifestolike identity, Tschumi's designs hold no such symbolic connotations. They are, as he has himself insisted, signifiers without signifieds, pure traces without meaning. In the second place, while each notational system developed by the avant-garde was dedicated to the reinscription of the (modernist) body in architecture, with every arrow, moving form, or architectural element disposed to promulgate *health,* the notations of Tschumi eschew such utopian ends. Where the upward-spiraling ramps of the Tatlin Tower stood, at one level, for the endless and regenerative calisthenics of the new society, the follies of La Villette presuppose no therapeutic ends. Analogically, the folly stands for a body already conditioned to the terms of dissemination, fragmentation, and interior collapse. Implied in every one of his notations of a space or an object is a body in a state of self-acknowledged dispersion, without a center and unable to respond to any prosthetic center fabricated artificially by architecture. The body is not, as in modernist utopia, to be made whole through healthy activity; no avant-garde aerobics can save it from decay. Rather it has finally recognized itself as a text, not a work, whose finitude is ever in question and whose powers are in doubtful play, always to be tested by the infiltration of other discourses, other texts. Thus the fragmented bodies in movement of the *Manhattan Transcripts* would find their always provisional resolution in La Villette or Tokyo: the filmic fragmentation of bodily unity finds its paraarchitectural complement in the textual fragmentation of architectural unity. In this ascription, the architect's pleasure would be turned to more perverse ends yet than the simple dismantling of architecture; it would aspire to the exhaustion of corporeality itself. For while inhabitation of some kind or another is expressed in every element, ramp, stair, or balcony, the potentially occupying body receives no comforting organic referent but is every moment experienced through antibodily states, such as vertigo, sudden vertical and sideways movements, and even potential dissection. The functional analogies of modernism theorized the building as a "machine for living in," with the implication that a smoothly running machine, tailored to the body's needs, was modernity's answer to the proportional and spatial analogies of humanism. Tschumi's machinelike structures have rejected their assumed contents and have been exploded so that all questions of maintenance, repair, or even working are suspended. With no need to run smoothly any more, and without the necessity to respond to real bodies, they are complete in themselves, free to play endlessly in space, the texts of previously encoded works.

This spatial play, further, takes place in a landscape itself shaped by the concerns that produced the follies. Here transformation takes place similar to that between building and notation, now between the traditional space of an urban park and the site of Tschumi's game plan. For Tschumi has not, as many critics have asserted, abandoned the characteristics of traditional parks, but rather put them in motion, utilizing their recognizable elements and shattering their former compositional unities.

Such reencoding, of course, has had a respectable history in the development of the modern public park itself. In the blissful but short life of the park, bound to the redevelopment of London, Paris, and Vienna in the nineteenth century, all the motifs of the aristocratic landscapes of the previous epoch were pressed into service by the new public gardeners as they drew up an easily repeatable lexicon of elements. What had taken centuries to develop, from the enclosed hortus of classical and medieval times, to the allegorical gardens of the Renaissance and baroque, to the narrative and playfully symbolic landscapes of Pope and Girardin, were now collapsed into handy guides for a mass-gardening public, and imitated at every scale from the suburban villa to the city. Alphand, Haussmann's gardener, marked Paris with the traces of Le Nôtre in its avenues and of Kent in its parks, where he created a new genre, the artificial imitation of nature, including the prefabrication of wooden fences in concrete. By the mid-twentieth century, a park had become so removed from nature that the promise of verdure throughout the city, offered by the Ville Verte, had no chance of being mistaken for anything but a carefully orchestrated cover for parking lots.

Tschumi's park retains at least two formal aspects of these historical precedents, however abstracted to dissimilarity and transformed entirely in significance: the axis and the *parcours,* the straight line and the undulating line, the one characteristic of classicism and the other of romanticism. Neither of Tschumi's lines attempts to refer to its patron except in form; both are reused as empty signs of their patrimony. The "three routes" of La Villette, the aerial (the covered, intersecting axes of the raised bridge), the terrestrial (the winding path joining the philosophic gardens of the meandering twentieth-century flaneur), and the aqueous (the old commercial canal), are no longer symbolic or evocative of initiation. They are simply three routes through and out of the park. Thus the axis, unlike that of Versailles, pretends to control no territory but its own, linking in no necessarily significant sequence a series of views, objects, and functions; as a physical line it stands, like the *cases,* as a marker, a *point de repère* for the distracted visitor. Similarly, the undulating *parcours,* unlike the carefully staged routes of the literary landscape garden, stands for no narrative, joins no symbolic *fabriques* in cumulative succession; it simply serves as an alternative to the axis, another way in or out. In this sense, Tschumi has bound the park to the city, acknowledging its fundamentally urban character and fabricating it out of bits that might also be found elsewhere; not a privileged realm, but another one.

This refusal of a preconceived narrative, despite the apparent similarity of Tschumi's framed and montaged representation to that of filmic discourse, in fact goes much beyond the *bandes dessinées* of the *Manhattan Transcripts.* There, the complex and random relations between objects, movements, and events were filmic and staged; a calculated breaking down of functionalist and formalist logic, a manifesto for the assimilation of architecture into life. Here, there is no obvious staging precisely because there is yet no movement, not event. The vision of the contemporary park dweller is well enough trained in frames for each visit to be lived as a movie.

Considered as a park, then, Tschumi's *cage-rouge* game ostensibly evokes none of the aura of Alphand, Kent, or Le Nôtre. It systematically detaches itself from such consoling origins, preferring its random game of chance against the powerful geometries of Versailles, the pleasurable aristocratic rambles of Ermenonville, and the pretty picnic spots of Les Buttes Chaumont. We are reminded of Gilles Deleuze's comparison of an empty space to a still life:

Between an empty space or landscape and a still life properly speaking there are certainly many resemblances. But . . . an empty space is distinguished above all by the absence of a possible content, while the still life is defined by the presence and the composition of objects that are wrapped up in themselves or become their own container.[5]

If La Villette is a landscape at all, it is one deliberately emptied out; if it is a fragment of nature, it is more a still life, a *nature morte*, than any attempted imitation of the real thing.

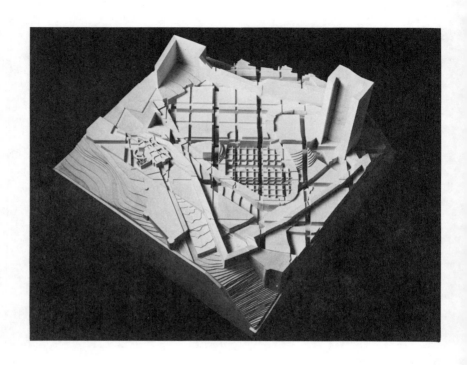

Shifting Ground

There is a common urge, namely, to visualize a thing in its beginnings, because the beginning is the simplest mode in which the thing is to be seen. . . . But the simple beginning is something so insignificant in itself, so far as its content goes, that for philosophical thinking it must appear as entirely accidental.

Hegel, Aesthetics

A poststructuralist sensibility has for some time felt uncomfortable with the positive versions of architectural origins advanced by the classical tradition from Vitruvius, and refabricated in terms of abstract form by modernism. What Hegel contemptuously dismissed as the "charming tales" invented by the Greeks to explain beginnings in art and social life have been increasingly subjected to a criticism that finds even the rationalization of such myths in "models" or "types" specious.[1]

In much the same way as linguists have long discarded the search for language origins, architects have by and large rejected a theoretical foundation for their art that relied on the empirical, accidental, or purely imaginary origin. One by one, from the end of the eighteenth century to the present, the cave, the hut, the tent, the temple, either in their supposed historical beginnings or in their hypothetical typical forms, have been relegated to the status of historicist fictions, useful for their time but without resonance in the present.

And if beginnings have been rendered suspect, replaced or rather displaced by more dispersive concepts such as source, trace, and difference, endings have become equally difficult to resolve. Where once, as Hegel again noted, it was possible to believe in the idea of origins as explaining all future developments—"the dim idea that this simple mode [of beginnings] reveals the thing in its essential nature and origin, and then that the development of this beginning up to the stage really in question is to be understood, equally easily, by the trivial reasoning that this progress has *gradually* brought art up to this stage"[2]—now a disbelief in progress and the logical inevitability of historical chronology has rendered any ending provisional and illusory.

In such an intellectual context any semblance of unity in beginnings and endings, or in chronological sequence, must be regarded with especial alertness to lapses, fault lines, irreconcilable propositions, and eruptions of asystematic contents into apparently smooth and uninterrupted processes of transformation and development. This would seem especially pertinent to a reading of the projects and texts of Peter Eisenman, which seem deliberately to avoid, sidestep, or efface questions of origin and development, beginnings and ends, forms and contents, as a way of rejecting the inscribed history of the architectural tradition. Posed self-consciously against anthropo-morphic analogies, closed formal systems, and functionalist deriva-tions, these designs implicitly overturn the classical system of representation, while denying any authenticity to the grand master narratives of architectural history.

Nevertheless, despite authorial and critical injunctions to the con-trary, it is tempting, now the series seems finished, to regard the projects entitled House I through the Fin d'Ou T Hou S as an exercise in the rational exploration of certain preestablished formal constructs; a self-conscious, logical sequence with a beginning and an end.[3] This is, after all, what appears to be implied by the numbering, by the chronology, by the internal transformations from one scheme to another, and by the possibility of relating a first design to a last, a first house to a Fin[al] house. What makes this ascription even more compelling, in terms of classical form, is the postulation of a final coda to the series, a kind of resumé, or grand finale, in the two postseries projects, House El Even Odd and the Fin d'Ou T Hou S, that accompany a shift in the professional life of their architect. These schemes, tightly related in scale, vocabulary, and syntax, also then seem to comprise a biographical unity. Neatly, they appear to sum up an era, a period style, an investigation begun in an open-ended search for an alternative architecture and concluding with its complete description. Certainly their ostensible and often repeated intention to destabilize their apparent object—the house, nucleus and origin of architecture—by attacking all its elements of structure and signification systematically, from the roof to the basement, leaving no functional or mental assumptions untouched and stripping, finally, the house of "houseness" and nostalgia, would seem to propose an unassailable unity of purpose.

But another look might reveal a very different pattern, entirely opposed to any neat trajectory of beginning, development, and end. That works were composed in chronological order, as artists from Breton to Duchamp have noted, is no guarantee of their logical relationship in such a chronology. That they bear a superficial relationship to a biographical event or events is, as Freud pointed out, often a ruse of narrative rather than an index of meaning. That they seem to operate according to rational laws of transformation and system is, finally, not a verification of their actual systematic contents. A different kind of reading, one that emphasized discontinuity, and indeed one that has already been provided by their author, would see these works as dividing among themselves, around, say, House VI, as between a predeconstructive and a postdeconstructive stance.[4]

Ostensibly conceived at the end of this line, and seeming to mark a moment of pause, a caesura in its architect's development, a culmination or closure before a new period and form of exploration, the Fin d'Ou T Hou S might be expected to undo or confirm such analyses based on continuity or its opposite. But the house frustratingly resists any single interpretation. Its L figures are readily assimilated to previous schemes, as are the processes of form generation, the vocabulary, and even the representational play. On another level, one might be inclined to follow the authorial clues and to read the Hou S as a developed exercise in decompositional moves, a complex play on origins that successively destabilize each other, a project that begins a new phase of design rather than ends an old. Between such interpretations one is placed as between minimal differences, such as that between black and black, or, in this case, white and white, gray and gray. Similarly, when the Fin d'Ou T Hou S is juxtaposed with any others in the series of Houses, or, more disturbingly, with, say, House I, the "beginning" of the line, one is faced with a difference that nevertheless poses as the same.

In a recent essay entitled "The End of the Line," the critic Neil Hertz identified a series of problematic moments in literature or art that resist interpretation by virtue of their deliberate obfuscation between differences of a similar kind.[5] As examples of such moments, he cites Courbet's paintings of *La Source de la Loüe* and *La Grotte de la Loüe,* both of which center on an invisible line between the blackness of the cave and that of the water, "an axis along which the residual tension of minimal difference, of black against black, is felt." A poetic version would be the moment in Wordsworth's *Prelude* when the narrator, moving through a London crowd, comes to rest before a blind man: here the "difference" in similarity is given by the fact that the figure carries a label on his chest describing his plight that seems to the viewer to strangely double the effect of his sightless visage. The "emblem" of the text stands in for the face, duplicates it, and yet in the distinction between similarities—text/face—a tension is established. Hertz, borrowing a term from Kenneth Burke, terms this condition "an end-of-the-line mode."[6] This condition, in literature, occurs when, at the end of a line, a figurative turn is introduced that occludes its antecedents and renders them resistant to interpretation because framed by the minimal difference that is now seen to operate between beginning and ending. Such tension may be, Hertz argues, emblematic of the similar tensions that separate and join viewer and painter, standing outside the frame, from their identifiable surrogates inside the frame, as well as from the scene depicted. They seem to go beyond any clear code of representation and are precipitated by "an engagement with the act and with the medium of painting or writing condensed almost to the point of non-reflective opacity." They may be interpreted, Hertz argues, as complex treaties between author and reader that seem at once to introduce a possibility of autobiographical reading, but then quickly move to deny any overdirect relationship between author and surrogate. Another of the peculiarities of "the end of the line" would seem to be its aftermath: De Man and Hertz insist on the violence of what happens "after" the end of the line, a violence especially aggressive as it seeks to reassert a subject's stability at the expense of another subject. After the end of the line one might expect a sacrifice, "a field littered with the remains of acts of mutilation."

Along these lines, one might reexamine the house El Even Odd and the Fin d'Ou T Hou S as two interrelated end-of-the-line turns that inevitably render opaque what precedes them; an autobiographical reading would not be precluded, but neither would it be privileged over a consideration of the formal "differences" that might be discerned between apparently similar "white" and "gray" structures.[7] Thus, such a reading would discriminate between elements that seem directly derived from an abstraction and commentary on classical architecture (Houses I through VI) and geometrical permutations that, while superficially similar to earlier projects, in fact, in these "last" two projects, disturb representation itself. An end-of-the-line reading would also leave open the possibility that the final turn (the Fin d'Ou T Hou S) places all the earlier constructions in doubt at the same time as implying future violence; in this case, not only to an architectural discourse but also to the discourse of the line itself, now viewed in retrospect through the frame provided by the equivocal figure at its "end." In this sense, the Hou S would appear not simply as a traditional Janus looking neatly both ways, but rather as a deliberately opaque moment in a narrative that is thereby forced to double back on itself while precipitating a scene of unprecedented rupture.

The anticipation of the violence that the Fin d'Ou T Hou S dissimulates, or rather encloses with calm, is to be found in the scheme for Cannareggio. Here another end-of-the-line project, that odd El Even Odd, is reduced in scale (or else enormously enlarged) in order to become a monument. This monument, exorcised of its contents as house, yet bearing the traces of its own, elided, origin, is then repeated according to a grid that is placed over the city of Venice. Sometimes buried, sometimes standing in a piazza, sometimes forming a fragment within another structure, these repetitive punctuations, colored red, find their place in the city fabric wherever the grid comes to rest. Like the silent megaliths of some prehistoric memory system of which the key has been lost, these red stones resist interpretation on a number of levels.

They seem not to be houses, or at least habitable; their emptiness suggests that the civilization that once inhabited their strangely configured rooms has long disappeared. Thus abandoned, they take on the air of ready-made tombs, in much the same way as the houses of Pompeii or Herculaneum: the house become tomb simply by virtue of a catastrophic event, for which, paradoxically, it seemed ready. The dividing line between the house of the living and the house of the dead in form and in function, has always been perilously thin.

Further, as tombs, they are then, wittingly or not, monuments: the distinction made by Hegel and then by Loos, between the house as conserving life—a proper activity of the builder—and the tomb as memorial or monument—a proper activity of the symbol-making architect—has been developed into a principle of transformation. The house has become tomb which has become monument. But, immediately, the ascription "monument" fails to adhere to these inserted forms in a fabric. For the very definition of monument or memorial implies a singularity, a particularity that encloses the meaning of a single event or individual, that carries a symbolic memory of a once-unique presence, one thereby worthy of memorializing. These repeated, serial objects lose, in their repetition, any such signification; if they are tombs, then they are the graves of anonymous persons; if they are monuments, they are to unknown heroes. But then again, this would imply that the city of Venice has been construed as an immense graveyard, or at best a site for the memorialization of the world's unknown soldiers.

Certainly Venice has been joined many times in the recent past to the idea of death; its own fabric has, since Ruskin, seemed perilously near to collapse; it was, after all, his self-appointed task to "draw till it falls." But, with the Fin d'Ou T Hou S in mind, it would not seem that so obvious a pun as "Death in Venice" was in the mind of this architect. What then might have died, in this elaborate allegory of trans-formation, would seem to be architecture itself: no longer house, no longer tomb, no longer memorial. This said, the question remains to what code of signification the resulting structures may be joined; do such structures have a meaning in themselves, and, if so, what might be the nature of their "signs"?

The nature of an architectural semiology that presupposed and contained the seeds of its own death was first explored by Hegel in the context of a general theory of art's own inevitable death. His final judgment on art's inadequacy to the highest needs of contemporary religion and philosophy, his certitude as to the dissolution of art in the modern world, was embedded in the notion of a grand progression of the arts as vehicles for the expression of human consciousness, from architecture at the beginning to poetry at the end, a progression that finally led to the abandonment of art altogether as a proper vehicle to express the highest truths:

Each art has its time of efflorescence, of its perfect development as an art, and a history preceding and following this moment of perfection. For the products of all the arts are works of the spirit and therefore are not, like natural productions, complete all at once within their specific sphere; on the contrary, they have a beginning, a progress, a perfection, and an end; a growth, blossoming, and decay. (HA 2:614)

In this scheme, architecture, as the founding art, holding a privileged place as the essential manifestation of the symbolic mode, not only came first but also, deservedly and inevitably, died first. The section on architecture in the aesthetic ends abruptly with the architecture of the Middle Ages, the full flowering of the "Romantic" mode and spiritual counter to the "Classical." After this, architecture seems to find no place in the descent of art (or the ascent of the spirit) through sculpture, painting, music, and poetry. Tied irredeemably to the "Symbolic" or "Independent" form, it must pay the price for all the inadequacies of its primitive manner. Bound to the essential non-spiritual nature of its materials and the abstract quality of its signs, it cannot express either spiritual individuality (as sculpture) or spiritual interiority (as the other arts with varying degrees of success).

In defining the complex inner reasons for architecture's fallibility, Hegel confronted the fundamental question as to how architecture signified, and in so doing revealed the internal paradoxes of the art as art. This paradox, or rather fatal division, starts at the beginning of art; for Hegel, art consists in an act that prefigures its dissolution:

The first task of art consists in giving shape to what is objective in itself, i.e. the physical world of nature, the external environment of the spirit, and so to build into what has no inner life of its own a meaning and a form *which remain external to it* because this meaning and form are not immanent in the objective world itself. (HA 2:631; emphasis added)

The very act of impressing meaning on meaningless material, the fact that, however embedded in form, this meaning will remain always external to the material, gives a particular instability to the artistic process. And architecture, as the beginning of all art, partakes in this instability in a direct way. In the first place it is an art whose repertory of signification is essentially limited. Unlike sculpture, painting, and the other arts, architecture's forms are abstract, generalized, and vague, in comparison to words or visual signs, and suitable thereby only to convey ideas of a similar generality and vagueness.

To be purely architectural, however, and not painterly or literary, such a "wordless" language should signify completely *by itself*: "the productions of this architecture should stimulate thought by themselves, and arouse general ideas without being purely a cover and environment for meanings already independently shaped in other ways" (HA 2:636). Architecture is thereby bound from the start to a fate that denies it the possibility of expressing any but the most general ideas of a culture, and these in a fundamentally inflexible and often ambiguous way. Inevitably, with the development of sculpture, an art that realizes the representation of the individual figure, and subsequently with the other arts, architecture will quickly reveal itself inadequate to the task of spiritual expression. A period of the subordination of meaning to use (the classical) will be followed by a momentary unity of symbolic and classic form in the Gothic cathedral (the romantic), after which there will be no use, at least as a culturally *expressive art*, for architecture.[8] It will have anticipated by its death the dissolution of each of the arts in turn.

In this context the red "standing stones" of Cannareggio might be read as the posthumous traces of such a death. These are not symbolic monuments of the order of lingam pillars, obelisks, memnons; nor are they approaching the useful, as the labyrinth, once a riddle but serving as habitable space, or the pyramid, once a symbol but then a tomb, occupied by a body. They neither symbolize nor may they be used. Indeed, it is the mark of their posthumous existence that they have *already symbolized*, have *already been occupied*. The entire history of architecture is implied in absentia, so to speak, in their resistance to meaning. Which does not lead to the conclusion that they therefore mean *nothing;* for precisely in the rejection of history, and the defined moments in history rejected, signification is retrieved, but not now in its attempted fullness. The striving to achieve an expression of the absolute, doomed to ultimate failure; the mythical survival of this attempt in the Renaissance revival of classicism; the final discrediting of any search for illusory origins, all endow these totems of post-structural absence with some form of meaning, without, however, turning them into signs.

A final rift with classicism, which at the same time relies on all the conventions of classical representation for its effect, is displayed in Eisenman's Romeo and Juliet project. Here the commonplaces of Albertian perspective are put into deliberate question by means of a

direct interpenetration of the forms of representation and their subject matter, accomplished by a manipulation of the notion and the
literal presence of the "screens" through which in classical theory we
see the world.

In a celebrated modification of Alberti's comparison of a painting
to a view through the window, Emile Zola, writing to a friend in
1864, defined the work of art as like

a window open to creation; there is, set into the frame of the window, a sort
of transparent screen, through which one sees the objects, more or less
deformed, submitted to changes more or less perceptible in their lines and
in their colors. These changes correspond to the nature of the Screen.[9]

Following this essentially classical analogy, now given problematic
form by the relative qualities of what, for Alberti, was ideally a perfect
transparency, Zola then typified the "screens" that seemed to him to
correspond to the differences between classical, romantic, and realist
vision; differences articulated by the characteristics of the screens
each set before nature. Thus the classical screen was something like
a "fine sheet of chalk . . . of a milky whiteness," its images appearing
in sharp, black lines; the romantic screen, by contrast, "let all the
colors through," together with "large spots of light and shade," like
a prism, or perhaps, "a mirror without stain." The realist screen,
finally, had all the pretensions to being a "simple windowpane, very
thin and clear . . . so perfectly transparent that the images come
through and reproduce themselves afterward in all their reality." But
even this pristine glass, Zola noted, possessed a thickness that served
like any other screen to refract its objects and transform them, however slightly. He compared this refraction to "a fine gray dust" on
the surface, troubling its limpidity. In this way, Zola returns all defi-
nitions of painting to their relative nature as projections of a viewer,
rather than, as classical theory held, mirrors of nature.

Zola's image of a dusty screen, critical of realism's aspirations,
anticipates another dust-laden glass, that on which Duchamp "raised
dust" (élever, in the sense of cultivating), and which might be taken
as the fourth in Zola's implied sequence: a modernist screen. The
Large Glass, Duchamp insisted, was not a painting, or even a painting
on glass; it was something that he explained by the notion of "delay"
(retard), which meant nothing but a means "of ensuring that the object
in question was no longer to be considered a painting." All the shades

of meaning contained by the word *retard* were here brought together in "their indecisive union."[10] Confronted with textual appellation and glass object, the viewer was caught in a matrix of conceptual ambivalence, anxiety, and indecision; no traditional reading was possible, yet no certain alternative emerged. Indeed, such was the explosive nature of Duchamp's strategy that error and misreading seemed to be privileged over any single truth.

Something like Duchamp's technique, embedded in the avant-garde tradition of creating impossible oxymorons and exploiting the equally well-known trick of affirmation by negation (Diderot's "Ceci n'est pas un conte," Magritte's "Ceci n'est pas une pipe") seems to be operating in the Romeo and Juliet project, as exhibited in Venice and later at the Architectural Association and subsequently boxed (Eisenman's Plexi-Glass Box to Duchamp's Green Box) by the same institution.[11] In exhibition, the scene was carefully staged, seeming to represent one of those Renaissance drawing lessons staged by Dürer: a series of vertical, transparent planes held up to nature as if to allow the faithful transcription of the image thus presented and framed. But this apparent transparency posed a problem of focus for the viewer. For while the vertical planes were indeed clearly transparent, the images that spotted and lined their surfaces were evidently *not* representations of the scene beyond. Further, these images themselves were partially obscured by the added complication of successive planes held at short distances one in front of the other, effectively blocking both the view through and an unambiguous reading of any single plane.

A similar condition was created in the subsequently published Box, where the drawings, now etched onto sheets of transparent acetate, as if conventional overlays, were superimposed in order to prevent meaningful readings of any single sheet, and to produce a complicated multiple image when all the sheets together were held up to the light. In both exhibition and Box, the problem resolved itself as one of focus, rendered impossible by the laminated format of the presentation. In both, what might have been destined to evoke focused clarity—a condition of transparency—seemed calculated instead to generate obscurity. It is as if Eisenman has literalized Lacan's tantalizing formulation: "And if I am anything in the picture, it is always in the form of the screen, which I earlier called the stain, the spot."[12]

A comparison with Duchamp's Glass is revealing on a number of levels. First, Duchamp, despite his efforts to destabilize all positive contents for art, remains largely faithful to the conditions posited by modernist transparency, literal and phenomenal. His work stands as a technical artifact, playing with all the optical structures of engineering projection, collapsed, so to speak, into the thin membrane between the two pieces of glass. As such it exploits the techniques of representation in the same way as its analog in poetry, Mallarmé's *Un coup de dés*, similarly critical, incomplete, and transgressive in representational form. In the same way as the poet called for the reader to make something of the "white spaces" normally residual between words, but now rendered positive because of the particular layout of the page,[13] so the artist noted that before the Large Glass "the spectator makes the picture," thus completing the slow drift of subjective representations traced by Zola. In the Romeo and Juliet project, however, there is no such polemic of contents: the planes are inscribed with their lines and tones as if mechanically transcribing a geographical reality. The opacity is rendered by their conflation, not by any warping in any single image. Certainly the spectator does not make the picture: indeed, there seems to be little need for a spectator, or rather, the superimposition of transparent planes takes no heed of a spectator's needs, does not, in fact, imply the existence of a subject demanding to make sense of the work. Here, in this suppression of a knowing subject, we are returned to the idea of a work independent in itself, existing for itself and by itself. The continuous referent, the landscape of the surroundings of Verona and Verona itself treated as landscape, at varying interposed scales, only reinforces this geological muteness.

Secondly, both Duchamp's Large Glass and Eisenman's Romeo and Juliet project apparently share a similar if not common text: *The Bride Stripped Bare by Her Bachelors, Even* and Romeo and Juliet are versions of marriage, and both play with the ambiguities inhering in the double play of Eros, masculine and feminine. But there the resemblance stops. Duchamp's ironic and critical machine, which makes of marriage a ceremony of modernist desire, technological striptease, and mechanical wizardry, has little in common with the postromanticism of a story that has three versions, each one tied to a myth of love and death, reconciliation and happy endings, and each one allowed to play itself out on the screens in scaled interaction. And while these overt references to love stories evoking blushing Eros opposed to the Sadean machines of Duchamp's desire might propose the simple thesis of a postmodern atavism critical of modernism's implacable psychologism, the message of Eisenman's screens is notably lacking in comfort.

For there is in this triple narrative no consolation, no cathartic moment of the triumph of love; the spectator remains shut out of the process whereby the three levels interact, even as the assumed "subjects" Romeo and Juliet are replaced by inanimate forms, their "castles," rocky surrogates for dramatic players. Gazing through these glacial screens one is reminded of Derrida's characterization of writing as "a system of relations between strata. . . . Within that scene, on that stage, the punctual simplicity of the classical subject is not to be found."[14] Derrida is here explaining the "Mystic Writing Pad" whose mechanism of erasure and conservation of trace so fascinated Freud. This apparatus was for Freud a more or less simple analogy for the functioning of the mind as it receives perceptual stimuli that form no permanent traces behind which an unconscious operates; for Derrida it represented, together with Freud's own essay, a mechanism devoted to the production of the *trace* and its potential erasure, a veritable scene of writing devoted to the eradication of the metaphysics of presence.

In the context of the Large Glass and the Romeo and Juliet project, such an analogy might intimate another difference between the two. The Large Glass would then stand in for Freud's wax pad, with its "permanent trace of what was written . . . legible in suitable lights," while the Romeo and Juliet project would manifest the erasure of even the slightest impression of a once-full presence: "the trace," as Derrida concluded, "is the erasure of one's own selfhood, of one's own presence, and is constituted by the threat or anguish of its irremediable disappearance, of the disappearance of its disappearance."[15]

In Derrida's characterization of Freud's discourse as a "scene of writing" and the Mystic Pad "as the psyche, society, the world," the question of the screen is transformed into that of the stage, or rather the pro-scenium, the changing nature of which, not unnaturally, may be paralleled to that of the painterly screen itself. If the analogy of the mirror might call up the fullness of classical theatricality, its space dedicated to framing the actions of human subjects, central figures in a representational drama, then a stage with an absent subject would perhaps resemble that reversed mirror-theater described by Philippe Sollers in *Nombres,* a three-sided scene with its proscenium formed by a mirror, but now turned with its back to the observer, its stain alone manifesting the action enclosed and self-reflected behind. Sollers describes the proscenium as a surface:

This fourth surface is easily forgotten, and therein doubtless lies the illusion or the error. In effect, what one takes too easily for the opening of a scene is no less than a deforming panel, an invisible and impalpable opaque veil that plays toward the three other sides the function of a mirror or reflector, and toward the exterior (that is to say toward the possible but consequently always repelled and multiple spectator) the role of a negative informer.[16]

This opaque mirror resembles, in position and function, the parallel planes of the Romeo and Juliet project, while the unrevealed interior drama is silently mimed in the spots or stains that, as if Plato's cave were turned inside out, create a shadowy landscape of geological formations, the trace of an origin always concealed from view. At the end of this line, violence no doubt also awaits, for the irrepressible subject finds such sleepwalking, such opacity, against the grain: "And so all was modified by fragments, arrows . . . and I was obliged to tear the veil again, and once more attack the plane of sleeps, tearing the screen anew, breaking the mirror, the error."[17]

Perhaps it is worth remembering the "foundations" or "origins" of the Romeo and Juliet stories, so many variations on a theme of betrayal, artificial sleeps, and false deaths. In each version, an apothecary or his surrogate is called upon to supply a poison which in turn plays surrogate for a sleeping draft, and which in the end leads to death. In the oldest known narrative, told by Xenophon of Ephesus, this poison/remedy is termed, naturally enough, a *pharmakon,* which in its two Greek meanings might signify either or both.[18] Eisenman's architectural *pharmakon,* like that described by Socrates in relation to the invention of writing, would be at once poison and remedy, a salutary medicine for the mirage of a full return to classical values.

A curious feature of the Romeo and Juliet project is the absence of identifiable buildings; this might be expected, of course, as a natural result of the demand to erase a traditional ascription of architecture—an absorption of architecture into something else, so to speak, or a deliberate suppression of the signifying elements of architecture in order to imply the emergence of its opposite. Yet the play of forms, however opaquely revealed, does not seem to harbor such a clear and dialectical logic; there is no reference, for example, to a discourse of "architecture as city" or "architecture without architects," even as there is no trace of the suppression of conventional architectural elements. A system of form seems to be at work that does not rely on such immediate referents for its existence, and, indeed, does not refer to them at all.

Rather, the image is one of a formal process developed out of the whole cloth of what might be termed, provisionally, the landscape; in this one would include what were once rocks and hills, fields and forests, rivers and pools, as well as buildings (individual, such as castles, churches, and Roman remains, and collective, as in the city of Verona itself). This "landscape" is not treated in the manner of a seventeenth-century formal garden, with its geometries uniting man-made and natural objects; nor is it conceived like an eighteenth-century landscape garden, with its deliberate obscuring of the lines between nature and art in order to provide a self-conscious and picturesque "imitation" of nature.

In the complex process by which the Romeo and Juliet landscape is generated, there is no sense of an aesthetic or even a natural "origin" that gives it meaning. Rather, the forms are produced in a seemingly implacable autogeneration of grids, surfaces, and their punctuation that stems from an equally autonomous procedure called by the author "scaling." Referring to the random and fractal geometries of Mandelbrot, this method applies a notion of continuum to all scales and all intervals between scales that represent objects in nature, and produces new objects by virtue of their superpositioning, here achieved by transparent overlays.[19] The result is nothing stable, nor anything preconceived; it exists as a complex artifact marked by the traces of the procedures that generated it. Neither city nor country, building nor nature, it is a landscape in itself; what was once architecture has been entirely subsumed into a continuous surface inside which habitation cannot be predicted. Duchamp, it might be remembered, spoke of "geographic 'landscapism'" but also of "geological landscapism."[20]

On this scene, if one were to ascribe functions to any of the forms, one would risk, perhaps, plunging fireplaces in water, carving shelters out of solid rock, or equally, finding forests where there seemed to be houses; nothing reveals the code to the presence or absence of subjects that would give the form meaning. In this posthistoric geology, the only constant is the systematic nature of the *random,* a quality well known in the mathematics of topology and topography but less so in architecture. Its entrance onto the architectural scene provides the essential vehicle for the abandonment of those dualities that have plagued the art for centuries; it allows, in fact, for an architecture without meaning applied from without, for what Hegel would have recognized as a truly "independent" architecture. The sole recourse of any trespassing subject would be to begin at the beginning, naming arbitrarily according to a random experience of a landscape yet to be mapped or explored. Here the etymology of "random," from the old French *randon,* gives a clue as to the mode by which the territory might be incorporated into the known: a *randonnée* would be a long and extended promenade, with unexpected twists and turns, or, in terms of the hunt (a vocabulary pertinent to this land yet to be populated with gods), the anguished and impetuous movement of a trapped beast just before the kill.[21]

Perhaps the correct description of this mapped form would be "buried transparency," a term that would not so much refer to a preconceived architecture ensconced underground but to a kind of architecture embedded in ground zero, operating according to all the counterrules of an underground existence. The inevitable association with the cave and the tomb might not be out of place here, referring to what Boullée termed *architecture ensevelie,* illustrated by fantasies of the Egyptian sublime.

Hegel, likewise, reflected on subterranean architecture as the prefiguring of the classical house or temple. But Hegel went further than his preromantic predecessor, deriving from the idea of buried architecture a postulate of signification especially useful in understanding what he himself meant by architecture's death. For Hegel, these hollowed-out caves, with their "colonnades, sphinxes, Memnons, elephants, colossal idols, hewn from the rock and left growing out of the unworked mass of stone," seemed to anticipate a later architecture above the ground, the prototypes of the classical:

In comparison with the buildings on the surface such excavations seem to be earlier, so that the enormous erections above ground may be regarded as imitations and above-ground blossomings of the subterranean. For *in exca-*

132
Bodies

vating there is no question of positive building but rather the removal of a negative.
(HA 2:649, emphasis added)

This idea of a once-buried architecture, brought above ground by
means of the removal of a negative, would seem in a literal way to
predispose architecture once more toward its own burial. But Hegel,
in his complex but paradoxical definition of the architectural sign,
endows this positive pyramid, poised over a negative void that indeed
it imitates, with more significance than might be inferred from such
an obvious reversal.

For Hegel, in fact, is not only concerned to explain the nature of
the architectural sign, as symbol, but more generally to understand
the nature of signs themselves, by means of an architectural metaphor
that itself images the problematic nature of the sign: in an interesting
transposition, he sees the relationship between the signified and its
signifier in terms of a "*pyramid* into which a foreign soul has been
conveyed." As in the pyramids, a sign would be closed on the outside
while on the inside it would conceal an inner meaning (the body)
foreign to and imported into the outer shell. Such a sign might be
distinguished, Hegel argues, from a symbol; the sign, an arbitrary
signifier, and the symbol, which in some way partook of the qualities
of its signified.

But this explanation, however elegant, raises implicit questions for
architecture in Hegel's use of the metaphor of the pyramid. For how
might we read the pyramid at once as the metaphor of an arbitrary
sign and as the starting point for a theory of symbolic architecture;
or, in other words, what might be the implications of a building that
at once signifies the arbitrariness of the sign and is itself a symbolic
building? This sign of a sign is therefore doubled, a property reflected in its architectonics:

Here we have before us a double architecture, one above ground, the other
subterranean: labyrinth under the soil, magnificent vast excavations, passages
half a mile long, chambers adorned with hieroglyphics, everything worked
out with the maximum of care; then above ground there are built in addition
those amazing constructions amongst which the *Pyramids* are to be counted
the chief. (HA 1:355)

Yet this very double architecture, previously characterized as a shell
housing a foreign body, an alterious meaning, is also posed as the
foundation stone of the symbolic, essential condition of architecture:

In this way the pyramids put before our eyes the prototype of symbolical art itself; they are prodigious crystals which conceal in themselves an inner meaning and, as external shapes produced by art, they so envelop that meaning that it is obvious that they are there for this inner meaning separated from pure nature and only in relation to this meaning. (HA 1:356)

The nature of this *meaning* was, of course, part of the problem; for Hegel makes it clear that the pyramid was a symbol of death, a death that was concealed within it, invisible and sealed. The pyramid therefore was properly symbolic *only* of this "realm of Hades" and thereby it was entirely inadequate to the expression of life itself in any form. A symbol of death could never stand for anything that was liberated and free in spirit. The pyramid therefore is at once pure symbol, trapped in the boundaries of its limited form, and symbol of the inadequacy of the symbol, an arbitrary sign, "just an external form and veil for the definite content of meaning."

In this sense we might see how Hegel's "half-buried," half-positive, half-negative architecture of death was both the essential beginning of all architecture and inevitably a predisposition toward architecture's death, a death that is in no way illustrated by any literal correspondence between the pyramid as symbol of death and the pyramid, but by the problematic nature of the architectural sign itself. Which, put in other terms, meant simply the problematic nature of architecture considered as a sign at all; as long as architecture remained symbolic, with its meaning bound up in its outer form and understood by a society that saw its built symbols participate in their struggle toward consciousness, then architecture was alive. Once it was forced to subject itself to uses, to subordinate form to use, turned, that is, into a representation of coded as opposed to symbolic meaning, architecture inevitably started to "die." What Hegel could not say, and what we begin dimly to perceive, is of course the inevitability of his conclusions given their starting point: architecture, when considered primarily as sign, is bound to die from the very moment it is considered *to be* sign and thereby inauthentic in comparison with its imagined symbolic past.

For Eisenman to return architecture to the ground, therefore, would seem on one level to return it to an origin; but, as Hegel noted, this would be an origin already revealed as problematic in that the cave, as such, cannot be freely symbolical, but already presupposes the house or the temple. At the same time, to bring a once-buried architecture above ground would imply replacing the "original" excavation by its negative, removed but not filled in. One might imagine, beneath the apparent bedrock of Romeo and Juliet's landscape, a vast subterranean void, sealed up and never to be reinhabited, like the pyramids themselves.

The notion of the sealing of the void, the closing of the crypt, is of especial interest in Eisenman's last projects, from Romeo and Juliet through Tokyo to Cleveland, for it is here that the problem of burial, half intimated in the two last houses by the cubic excavations in which they sit, half in and half out, is confronted as a problem of the (false) origins of signification. Where, in the House El Even Odd and the Fin d'Ou T Hou S, the ground line signifies in an almost traditional sense a division between earth and sky, such a ground line no longer exists in the recent projects, as it has been entirely subsumed into an ambiguity of top and bottom. Which would be, indeed, an exit from the trap noted by Hegel in his complex but paradoxical definition of the sign.

In upsetting these doubled terms, the buried architecture of Eisenman's later works attempts to leap a divide, which Hegel might have called a *pit,* and to constitute a sign without need for a signified; to configure without figure. That the meaning of such configurations may be deciphered only with reference to that initial semiotic schism is only one pitfall of the end-of-the-line mode, a mode for which contemporary criticism has coined the term *mise en abîme,* and which, as Derrida has pointed out, establishes the necessary relation between semiotics and psychology:

This requisite discontinuity between the signified and the signifier coincides with the systematic necessity that includes semiology in a psychology. . . . Psychology—in a Hegelian sense—is the science of the spirit determining itself in itself, as a subject for itself. . . . This is why it was indispensable to assert the architectonic articulation between psychology and semiology. This allows us better to comprehend the meaning of arbitrariness: the production of arbitrary signs manifests the freedom of the spirit.[22]

This might suggest a fundamental reason for architecture's inadequacy: as a symbolic art, it could in no way signify, arbitrarily, a free psychology. At best it would conceal any potential arbitrariness within an outer shell, burying knowledge of self in a preconscious crypt. But when such concealed prehistories are brought into the light, uncovered by the analyst's archaeological dig, long after the triumph of the spirit over its dark primal dreams, the condition for the "uncanny" is established. The threat of absence raised by Eisenman's unburied buildings participates in this complex psychology, which Freud further linked to the sense of something that was once homely (*heimlich*) turning, suddenly, at the end of the line, unhomely (*unheimlich*). Only perhaps through such a reading would the autobiographical moment implicit in all Eisenman's refusal of autobiography, and the formal turn that resists all but violent interpretation, converge. But such a convergence, once located, might best be left unanalyzed, even as Freud himself, shying away from the full interpretation of a dream, wished to reserve one place to "be left in the dark"; this would be, Freud conceded, the "navel" of the dream, "the place where it straddles the unknown." A buried architecture, brought to light, would be an analog of this dark bridge, suspended halfway between an abyss of concealed meanings and a field of chattering signs.

In this process the characteristics of traditional monumentality have inevitably been jettisoned; Eisenman has searched for a "counter-" or at least an "a-" monumentality that might seem a more appropriate expression for what Lewis Mumford described as "an age that has deflated its values and lost sight of its purposes" and can no longer "produce convincing monuments."[23] In Eisenman's more recent work, this question has been explored directly in the context of programs that have, in the past, demanded expressly monumental solutions, notably in the Wexner Center at Ohio State University.

Discussing the competition for this project, Kurt Forster intimated that the quandary of contemporary architecture may be measured according to architects' responses to institutional building, and especially to that of the museum. Forced to choose between "an idolatrous re-creation of the past 'temple of the arts' on the one side; an amusement park of cultural recreation on the other," architects were in neither case able to respond to a condition of flux. Forster concluded in favor of the solution by Eisenman and Robertson that, in his words, was "all process rather than product," as against other solutions that attempted a more traditional monumentality.[24]

But if this opposition was evident in the competition designs, and reinforced by the distinctly different discourses of the entering architects, the built realization of a scheme founded on indeterminacy and process raises the question of monumentality once again and in a more paradoxical way. A project established according to premises of the impermanent has become permanent; a form developed out of a criticism of monumentality has been, so to speak, instantly monumentalized.

Such a dilemma poses special problems for the finished building, now unsupported by helpful text and bound to categories of empirical experience. In the context of Peter Eisenman's designs this question is rendered the more acute as the theoretical and specifically antimonumental parti pris of the work has been imposed from the outset. If monuments, classically speaking, might be defined as "human landmarks which men have created as symbols for their ideals, for their aims, and for their actions," then Eisenman has consistently worked against such a concept.[25] But if, as Hegel insisted, the work of art is defined by the meaning attached to formed material by culture, then what is to prevent the process being reversed, so that a building not intended to be a monument, once deprived of its author, might be interpreted by society as monumental? How might the critical premises of countermonumentality survive in the face of the human will to force meaning onto objects whatever the objections of their makers?

Georges Bataille attempted to account for the power of monuments, tracing their effect to the very architectonic structure of power in society and comparing their character to the physiognomies of hieratic officials: "Thus the great monuments are raised up like dikes, opposing the logic of majesty and authority to every troubled element." For Bataille, it was the presence of architectural composition itself, underlying all the traditional arts, that signaled authority, whether exhibited in physiognomy, costume, music, or painting: "the grand compositions of certain painters express the will to constrain the spirit with an official ideal." Monuments, he argued, were "the true masters of the entire earth, grouping in their shadow the servile masses": "it is under the form of cathedrals and palaces that the Church or the State address and impose silence on the masses. It is evident, in effect, that monuments inspire social wisdom and often even a veritable fear."[26] To be condemned to such authority was, indeed, like being condemned to the galleys. The taking of the Bastille in the French Revolution could be explained, in this way, as an expression of "the animosity of the people against the monuments that are its true masters."

Monuments, indeed, took their place quite naturally in the ordered development of society, by virtue of the fact that their origin—the imposition of mathematical order on stone—was accomplished by evolution itself, by the passage from the "simian form to the human form, which latter already presented all the elements of architecture." Here Bataille gives a new twist to the anthropomorphic dependence of architecture on the body. Architecture is now seen as an organic part of the biological development, the "morphological process," in which man is forlornly stranded as a mere intermediate stage between monkeys and great buildings. Architectural order, developed out of human order, is of a higher kind; thence the power of monuments.

Such a characterization of monumentality, as the very definition of the role and nature of architecture, succinctly summarized the classical monumental tradition at a moment when such monumentality was under attack from technocratic and idealist modernists alike. Bataille himself noted that with the disappearance of the architectonic substructure of the art work, that "kind of dissimulated architectural skeleton," the way was opened to the expression of psychological processes, profoundly incompatible with social stability. Only the movement away from the elegance of the human figure, architectural in essence and therefore dominated *by* architecture, and toward a form of "bestial monstrosity," Bataille concluded, might provide a chance of escaping the architectural penitentiary.

Writing in 1929, Bataille was of course intervening in a continuing debate that had pitted modernists, calling for a "new monumentality" as opposed to the "pseudomonumentality" of eclectic historicism (to use Sigfried Giedion's terms), against nostalgics and traditionalists who mourned the passing of the grand epochs of monumental splendor and saw little hope in the cultural forms of the declining West. In this debate, Bataille deliberately confused the terms, ascribing to all monumentality the architectural will to power and finding the only remedy in the complete rejection of architecture, at least as traditionally defined. Tristan Tzara and Salvador Dalí, among others, were to advance this position in articles published in *Minotaure*, outlining the possibilities of a psychoanalytically theorized architecture of hysteria, of digestion, or of the uncanny, intrauterine, cave. In each case the tradition of geometry was opposed by a psychoformal sensibility that once more assimilated architecture to the natural. The monstrous, half-natural, half-cultural was posed as a counter to the abstract and the rational.

In retrospect, Bataille's gently ironic attack on monumentality, which called for the dissolution of architectural order and the irruption of the monstrous as the only defense against the virtually Darwinian law of the monuments, takes on a new cast in the context of a quarter-century of attempts to revive a perceived "lost monumentality." This revival, which has seen the pseudomonumental proliferate to a degree unimagined even by Giedion, has once more raised the question of the architectural monument as dissimulated power, but in a strangely attenuated form. In this context, it has become evident that a simple argument against, say, historical quotation, or stylistic revival, and for a vague "modernity" easily falls into the trap anticipated by Bataille; both postmodern and late modern evince a nostalgia of form, both seek a lost architecture, both attempt to achieve monumentality and thereby domination. To pose the question in other terms, however, would, as Bataille intimated, involve an absolute rupture with the architectonic tradition, and, by implication, the "body" on which that tradition was based and that it dominated.

Certain architects have advanced possible forms of this countermonumental argument. Some, like Coop Himmelblau, have preferred a textual mode, illustrating the idea of the nonmonumental, the grotesque, the uncanny, in graphic and arresting images; others, like Hejduk, have explored the surrealist legacy, attempting to configure a "monstrous" double for architecture that would privilege the victim over the victor. Others again, like Libeskind, have turned to other formal models—impossible machines, decomposed bodies—as the emblems of an abyss no architecture can finally bridge. Some, like Gehry, have embraced a bricolage populism that attempts to underplay the monumental in favor of the apparently accidental.

In this field of possibilities, that proposed by Peter Eisenman has been especially tantalizing. Founded on a discourse of rupture with the classical-humanist past, a postapocalyptic vision of a world inhabited by absence and uncertainty, his projects have progressively explored the dimensions of the counterarchitectural. Rejecting the authority drawn by classicism from fixed and stable origins—origins in need, in use, in anthropomorphism, in aesthetic formulae—Eisenman's work has moved from an initial reliance on the vocabulary of modernism in the House series to a more radical assumption of architecture's demise, as exemplified in the excavations and almost geological mappings of later projects like the Romeo and Juliet box, or the Cleveland, Ohio, Progressive Corporation development.

Exemplified in projects, however, and presented in complicated self-analytical graphics and models, such designs have remained hypotheses in the fabrication of a countermonumental myth, untested by being built, comfortably surrounded by a textual discourse that, by metonymy, implies their radicality and assimilates them to the cause.

In the case of the Ohio State University Wexner Center for the Visual Arts, this fragile compact between text and project, between criticism and design, has been definitively broken. The almost completed building rises from the ground, ready for inhabitation, taking its place among a series of monuments around the formal periphery of the campus center, standing for and set in the institutional structure of the university. Sited between two already existing monuments, themselves clothed in the stripped classical style of Giedion's "pseudomonumentality," how could such a building, if only by its sheer physical bulk and presence, *not* participate in the monumentality that surrounds it and, institutionally at least, defines the reason for its existence?

At first glance, indeed, the building seems to aspire to and achieve a monumentality of impeccable proportions. With its brick-faced castellated frontispiece, its arched recesses mimicking the original armory, its majestically rhythmic three-dimensional grids forming closed and open arcades, and its sensitive interstitial connections to the existing auditoria, the center takes on the aspect of a carefully contextualized institutional complex. Whether viewed from the oval or from the entrances to the campus, the building sits elegant and pristine, its brilliant white matrices and deep red brick surfaces scaled perfectly to its environs. Its presence is undeniable.

Yet, immediately, this image of certain stability, of monumental power, is undermined in a number of increasingly unsettling ways. First, the "entrance" through the reconstructed armory tower is revealed on closer inspection not to be an entrance at all; its huge arch is blocked and sunken, as if some ancient fortification had been closed off as unsafe. Further, the brick mass of this ostensibly historical "restoration" is peeled back in layers, as if sliced by a surgical scalpel, to reveal a sequence of shifting surfaces that effectively break any illusion of security. The once-stable historical fragment emerges, in fact, as an elaborate commentary on temporal destabilization, on the ruinating work of time replicated in simulacrum in a complex play between the restored and the de-restored.

Secondly, the grids that form the body of the building itself, calibrated on three measures, 12, 24, and 48 feet, seem to operate independently of and entirely distinctly from either structure or spatial enclosure. They quite evidently work against any resolution, even one of a dialectic between, say, support and enclosure as in the free plan, explicitly refusing any comfortable reconciliation of the two. Indeed, at times, as in the open "arcade" (which itself performs no sheltering function) that runs between the existing auditorium and the new structure, or in the intersection of the largest grid with uses such as internal stairs, the grids clash with deliberate abruptness with any intimation of occupation and use, and sometimes with each other.

The "monument" here gradually dissolves into a series of discrete fragments—of replicated history, of grids and structures—that uncomfortably touch, intersect, or break into each other, with no overall unity save that of metonymic resonance.

Such fragmentation has recently been compared to the structural expressionism and aclassical composition of Russian constructivism, based on superficial resemblances of clashing axes and grids. But there is little affinity between the Russian examples, deliberately distorting and scrambling the codes of classicism while exalting the potentials of steel and reinforced concrete structure, and the abstract and distanced grids of the Wexner Center. In the first place Eisenman's grids do not in fact stand for structure nor symbolize any structural potential of architecture; they are simply built grids that are their own structure but that do not coincide at every point with the real structure of the building. They are not, in this sense, images of the "origins" of architecture conceived of as essentially structural, nor are they signs of the absence of this origin. Rather they stand for another, less stable origin, one that lies in the geometrization of territory.

For each grid is itself shifted according to a different axial direction taken from already existing mappings on the site or its context. Clues are drawn from at least two mapped directions latent in the site: that of the city of Columbus, and that of the campus itself. A further reference to mapping lies in the "fault" line cutting through the building, an echo of the Greenville line cutting through Ohio itself. Each built grid is then envisaged in three-dimensional space, so to speak, and built up from the ground as a realization of the virtual. The conflicts between grids, then, are not *compositionally* generated, they are latent in their hypothetical occupation of the same site and are explicitly brought to light only by the constructed attempt to occupy the same site with three different contents.

In this sense, the nature of the grids deployed in the Wexner Center departs radically from the traditional use of grids in architecture. Grids, in the classical tradition, have generally been utilized for two complementary purposes: for the composition, layout, and arrangement of elements of architecture in space—the instrumental grid—such as that employed in drafting or in surveying; and for the manifestation of structure in modeled or real space, as in a column grid. Modernism altered this dualism very little: the instrumental grid became more pervasive with the introduction of graph paper and the mass production of architectural elements, and the structural grid became revealed as an integral part of the abstract "essence" of architecture, but the double representational status of the grid remained. Generally, the two kinds of grids were virtually synonymous in practice, especially in the work of Mies van der Rohe where instrumental and structural grids coincided as the basis for an abstract language of structure. Even in more overtly metaphysical projects, such as those of the de Stijl architects, the grid was seen, in Rosalind Krauss's words, as mediating between a necessary "coordinate system for mapping the real" and a "staircase to the Universal."[27] Whether physically or metaphysically instrumental, modernist grids were utilized precisely because of this dualism and, even more importantly, for the implied correspondence between the grid and the essentially architectonic.

In Eisenman's work, however, the grid seems to signal none of these connotations. Tied neither to instrumental reason nor to a transcendental other world, the Wexner grid stands as the merciless demonstration, as it were, of conflict in the mapping of the real, while it definitively rejects any essentialist message with regard to the structural or spatial nature of architecture. On the one hand manifested in the form of a set of apparently arbitrarily located fragments pre-

cipitated out of a potentially unlimited field, and on the other defining the physical limits of the structure, the grid seems to hover
between the infinite and the bounded, ambiguous and refusing all
single-origin narratives.

In her seminal essay "Grids," first published in *October* in 1979,
Rosalind Krauss has remarked on this dualistic nature of the grid, at
once centrifugal and centripetal in implication. The grid, she argues,
makes the work of art a *fragment* by virtue of its extensions in all
directions to infinity, from the work of art out; the art work thus
becomes "a tiny piece arbitrarily cropped from an infinitely larger
fabric." At the same time, as a definer of the outer limits of the
aesthetic object, the grid appears as "an introjection of the boundaries
of the world into the interior of the work"; here the grid appears as
"a mapping of the space inside the frame onto itself . . . a mode of
repetition."[28] In the three-dimensional realm of the architectural
grid, these two conditions have generally oscillated: a traditional
humanism, such as that evinced by Palladio, has taken the grid metaphysically as a fragment of infinity and physically as a container
and centralizing property; modernism simply broke this defined oscillation to provoke ambiguity so that, for example, in the case of a
composition by Theo van Doesburg, the conceptual grid is infinite
and the realized grid is both centripetal and centrifugal, the one
pointing to the potential of the other.

In Eisenman's case this dualistic condition of the modernist grid
still seems to operate—the fragmentary grids reach out to infinity
and their edges limit the object's boundaries—but any clear dialectical
reading, such as that enabled by the paintings of Mondrian, has been
thwarted. First, the conceptual field—that of the infinite grid—has
been a priori disrupted by the intrusion of more than one grid. The
calm and pristine state of the "universal" has been transformed into
an abyssal conflict among a potentially infinite number of grids, all
struggling for primacy. The regular and geometrical prison of Bataille's "architecture" has been reformulated as a field of battle of
infinite difference that refuses repetition or similarity from the outset. The conceptual field is thus composed of so many possible human
errors of mapping, and is no longer a "universal" in the transcendental sense offered by classicism or modernism.

Secondly, nothing in the conflicted play of these fragments of the
nonuniversal indicates that the boundaries of the object logically and

centripetally work their way toward a meaningful center. There is indeed no such center, each axis once started on the interior dissolving into or broken by another. Reinforcing this impression, the "rooms" or "spaces" in the building repeat the confusion and conflict of fragment and grid while at every moment resisting a centralizing reading. If, as Rosalind Krauss asserts, "behind every twentieth-century grid there lies—like a trauma that must be repressed—a symbolist window parading in the guise of a treatise on optics,"[29] behind Eisenman's grids there lie the ruins of modernist grids, ruins that are by no means suppressed like a trauma but are brought into the light of their own contradictions.

As Krauss notes, the very conditions of the grid itself reinforce these ambiguities: "Because of its bivalent structure (and history) the grid is fully, even cheerfully, schizophrenic."[30] In Eisenman, this cheerful splitting is developed out of traumatic repression into expression. Jacques Lacan wrote of such expressions, valuable for psychoanalytical practice "not only as symptoms of profound troubles in thought, but also as revelations of their evolving stage and of their interior mechanism."[31] The manifestation of these "more or less incoherent forms of language" was named "schizophasia"; their written counterparts Lacan termed "schizography." Akin to that "automatic writing" studied with so much care by nineteenth-century mystics, schizography, as defined by Lacan, would be the study of disturbances, written or spoken, in words, names, grammar, syntax, and semantics; all referred to formal disruptions in normal writing or speech. Lacan analyzes cases of elision, denegation, neologism, displacement, and the like in order to demonstrate that rather than ascribing such disorders to the "inspirational" or mystical category, one should see in them the demonstration on a linguistic level of the disorder itself.

Reading Eisenman's schizophrenic grids in this light, we might be tempted to see in the conflation of conflicting fragments evidence of a deliberate evocation of a schizographic condition—inherent in the world more than in the author—a condition that works with all the "methods" of the paranoiac in order to reveal a "real" disturbingly disturbed. Here we might follow Lacan himself, as he compared the schizographies of his patients—in which, "depending on the intellectual and cultural level of the patient, happy conjunctions of images could be produced episodically giving a highly expressive result"—

to those more self-conscious experiments in automatism conducted by the "sur-realists" that exploited play as a state of oscillation between intention and automatism.[32] But more revealing still was Lacan's conclusion that the most common characteristic of schizographic disturbance was a heterogeneous conjuncture of the "waste products [*les scories*] of consciousness, words, syllables, obsessive sonorities, catchphrases, assonances, different automatisms: everything that a thought in a state of activity, that is, which identifies the real, repulses and annuls by a judgment of value."

Placed on the level of the intentional blurring of the planned and the automatic, we might now be able to read Eisenman's insistence on the automatic nature of his grid generation—an automatic transcription of previous geometrical mappings—together with his evident pleasure in manipulating the conflicts in this "real," as a conscious schizography. Further, in his use of simulated fragments of history, at once marking previous sites of architectural and institutional occupation and fabricating shifted and cut-apart versions of this history, Eisenman seems to be utilizing the *scoria*—literally the "slag"—of architectural tradition in order to fabricate a counter, necessarily schizophrenic, architecture.

Here we are returned to Bataille's initial desire to counter architecture with the monstrous, form with the formless. By rupturing architecture's link with anthropomorphic imitation, Eisenman has broken with its tradition of form, has indeed produced something that in existing cultural terms has no recognizable form, and moreover has worked insistently to counter any idea of "form" wherever it might arise.

In his note on the word "formless," Bataille advanced the philosophical explanation for his position on architecture: "formless" was a word, he noted, that was normally employed to denote a will to form, a loss of status in a universe where everything ought to have form: "In effect, in order for academic men to be content, the universe ought to have form. Philosophy in its entirety has no other aim: it is concerned with giving a frock coat to what is, in itself, the frock coat of mathematics." "Formless" in this context would be something base, like a spider or an earthworm. Substituting the words "architecture" and "geometry" for "philosophy" and "mathematics," we might infer that in Bataille's terms an architecture that, like a formless universe, resembled nothing on earth "was something like a spider or a pool of spittle."[33] Perhaps it is in this sense that we might identify the "grotesque" and the "monstrous" in Eisenman's oeuvre: no longer content to dress up a frock coat in a frock coat, he prefers to reveal the inherently formless in all attempts at fixed and closed form, the schizographic nature of an architecture that refuses its monumental duties by writing out its pathological condition. Where, in classical terms, a monster might be fabricated out of the untoward mingling of genres, in this quasi-automatic mode the monstrous is no longer to be repressed by a preconceived code, but rather explored as the necessary precondition of postapocalyptic society. Architecture might then become once more, in Bataille's formulation, "the expression of the very being of society," and the architect might work like Bataille's modernist painters who opened the way "toward bestial monstrosity; as if there was no other chance of escaping from the architectural chain gang."[34]

Homes for Cyborgs

The cyborg is resolutely committed to partiality, irony, intimacy, and perversity. It is oppositional, utopian, and completely without innocence. No longer structured by the polarity of public and private, the cyborg defines a technological polis based partly on a revolution of social relations in the *oikos,* the household. Nature and culture are reworked; the one can no longer be the resource for appropriation or incorporation by the other.

Donna Haraway, "A Manifesto for Cyborgs"

If, for the first machine age, the preferred metaphor for the house was industrial, a "machine for living in," the second machine age would perhaps privilege the medical: the house as at once prosthesis and prophylactic. In the Corbusian "home of man" technology took the form of more or less benign "object-types" and perfectly controlled environments that allowed for the full play of the natural body in nature. The line between nature and the machine, between the organic and the inorganic, seemed crystal clear; organicism was a metaphor, not a reality. Now, the boundaries between organic and inorganic, blurred by cybernetic and bio-technologies, seem less sharp; the body, itself invaded and reshaped by technology, invades and permeates the space outside, even as this space takes on dimensions that themselves confuse the inner and the outer, visually, mentally, and physically. "L'homme-type," the modulor muscleman, has through a combination of prosthetic devices, drugs, and body sculpture emerged as Cyborg, a potentially gender-free mutant, and its home is no longer a house. As Walter Benjamin presciently observed, "The work of Le Corbusier seems to arise when the 'house' as mythological configuration approaches its end."[1]

In the terms introduced by Donna Haraway, cyborg culture, a product of late capitalist technology, is at once an all-embracing and controlling reality and a utopia full of promise. The totalizing and hegemonic power of "modern production seems," in Haraway's words, "like a dream of cyborg colonization of work, a dream that makes the nightmare of Taylorism seem idyllic." But it also, she argues, opens up the possibility of a political struggle over the different boundaries it cuts through: the boundaries between the human and the animal, the animal-human organism and the machine, the physical and the nonphysical. "Late twentieth-century machines have made thoroughly ambiguous the difference between natural and artificial, mind and body, self-developing and externally designed. . . . Our machines are disturbingly lively, and we ourselves frighteningly inert."[2] For Haraway, it is precisely in the interstices of these differences, in "the simultaneity of breakdowns," that the "matrices of domination" might be cracked open and, in the "pollution" that results, a new political and social practice opened up. Such a practice, she hopes, will create the conditions of a gender independence through the construction of what Alice Jardine has dubbed "Technobodies" by means of medicotechnologies of reproduction, transplants, and the like.[3]

The implications of this metamorphosis for architecture are more radical than even Reyner Banham would have envisaged. No longer are we fooled by the promise of the house as a bubble-container that frees its human contents from the vicissitudes of external environment: neither the Dymaxion dome nor the spacesuit reflects the infinite permeability assumed by the contemporary skin, the interchangeability of body part and technical replacement, or the spatiomental reconstruction implied by the cyberspace. This complex and impure system of existence, indeed, offers neither the luminous promise of technological utopia nor the dark hell of its opposite. The sleeper in *When the Sleeper Wakes,* H. G. Wells's turn-of-the-century dystopia, was faced with a clear confrontation between the scientific and the social; the hacker in William Gibson's *Neuromancer* no longer knows the difference between waking and sleeping.

In such a context, architectural exploration, as Elizabeth Diller and Ricardo Scofidio have understood it, might best be limited to the precise dimensions of a controlled experiment. In a world of infinitely disseminated power—of surveillance, of the image, of the technological—the stylistic metaphor is as suspect as the functional solution. In their place, the minute and exactly calibrated interrelations of body and machine are subjected to a dispassionate scrutiny, transcribed as the automatic writing of a generation of readymades. These calculations take as their starting point the clearly distinguished systems identified by modernist technique: the system of the object, of the body, of the optical, and finally of the home. Each of these is carefully unwrapped, disassembled, and confronted, as it were, defenseless, to the next. The sites of these strategic deployments emerge as so many battlefields, strewn with the disemboweled residues of yesterday's biotechnical encounters: "no-man's-lands" or homes for cyborgs.

Cyborgs and their homes, of course, have a respectable prehistory in the modern period, in the monstrous merging of animal and human so characteristic of surrealist imagery. As Haraway writes, "The cyborg appears in myth precisely where the boundary between human and animal is transgressed. Far from signalling a walling off of people from other living beings, cyborgs signal a disturbingly tight coupling."[4]

Such coupling has its own history. Thus the gentle horse-headed women and boys that populate Leonora Carrington's *House of Fear* and its illustrations by Max Ernst seem deliberately to transpose the attributes of the centaur and the unicorn in gender and implication. As Carrington herself remarked, "A horse gets mixed up with one's body . . . it gives energy and power. I used to think I could turn myself into a horse."[5] From the figure of Fear, in the Castle of Fear, who "looked slightly like a horse," in Carrington's text and Ernst's collage, through the Oval Lady, who holds the secret of turning herself into a living version of her rocking horse, to little Francis, a mask for Carrington herself, who grows a horse's head, these equine presences play on the register of sexual and mental ambiguities with evident autobiographical reference. It was, after all, Father who burned the rocking horse to punish the Oval Lady for even desiring to be a horse, and Francis whose horse's shape at once displayed his shame at failing to be woman and his androgynous desire. Carrington's horse-people seem to prefigure Haraway's separatist cyborgs.

Carrington's homes for androgynes are equally filled with a mixture of organic and inorganic objects: thus Uncle Ubriaco's workroom in "Little Francis" was "a spacious apartment on the ground floor filled with half-constructed constructions and wholly demolished bicycles. The walls were lined with bookshelves that held books, spare tires, bottles of oil, chipped figureheads, spanners, hammers, and reels of thread."[6] A series of books—*Man and Bicycle, Intricacies of Pedals, Tobson's Essays on Spokes and Bells, Free Wheels and Ball Bearings*—was piled beside a heterogeneous collection that included starved cockroaches in a small cage, a string of artificial onions, a spinning wheel, ladies' corsets of a complicated pattern, and a great many cogwheels.

For Carrington and the surrealists in general, these semiorganic and dream objects were arrayed to counter the implacable rationalism of purely technological modernism, epitomized in the shape of the Father, who, in the "Oval Lady," seemed "more like a geometric figure than anything else," and who achieved grotesque proportions in the character of Egres Lepereff, "The Great Architect," in "Little Francis." Based on Serge Chermayeff, appointed a surrogate parent during Carrington's stay in London, this designer of guillotines for the execution of boys like Francis espoused "good machinery and efficient planning," which "are always artistically moving." "My platform . . . was pleasing," purred the Architect, "though utterly devoid of anything save the merest mechanical necessities. It was a symphony of pure form." Francis himself was less certain that "architecture . . . in modern art is the nearest form to pure abstraction," observing innocently, "But if you build abstract houses, the more abstract you make them the less there'll be there, and if you get abstraction itself there won't be anything at all."[7]

Surrealism's antipathy to modernism, reflected in the well-known quarrels between André Breton and Le Corbusier, was, on the surface, based on this suspicion of abstraction. For Breton, modernist functionalism was "the most unhappy dream of the collective unconscious," a "solidification of desire in a most violent and cruel automatism." The argument was elaborated by other surrealists: Dalí in his exaltation of the art nouveau, with its "terrifying and edible beauty"; Hans Arp's championing of the "elephant style" against the "bidet style"; Tristan Tzara's indictment of modern architecture as "the complete negation of the image of the dwelling." All posed a volatile and elusive sensibility of mental-physical life against what was seen as a sterile and overrationalized technological realism: the life of the interior psyche against the externalizing ratio.

Le Corbusier himself summarized the opposing positions succinctly in his only contribution to a quasi-surrealist journal—a note on the work of the psychologically troubled artist Louis Soutter, in an article published in *Minotaure* in 1936. To Soutter's remark, "The minimum house or future cell should be in translucent glass. No more windows, these useless eyes. Why look outside?," Corbusier replied,"This affirmation of Louis Soutter . . . is the very antithesis of my own ideas, but it manifests the intense interior life of the thinker."[8] For Le Corbusier, looking always, as Beatriz Colomina has observed, toward a universally transparent exteriority, the attempt to reenvision the objects of daily life metaphorically was misguided, leading to a dangerous imbalance in the human "technico-cerebral-emotional equation," the creation of a "sentiment-object" rather than an object of use. As Benjamin noted, it was in this debate that the essence of modernity might be summarized: "To embrace Breton and Le Corbusier—that would be to draw the spirit of contemporary France like a bow which strikes with knowledge to the heart of the present."[9]

Against the cold rationalism of the modernists, the surrealists called for an architecture more responsive to psychological needs: what Tristan Tzara termed an "intrauterine architecture" was thus conceived as a radical criticism of the house of Corbusian and Miesian rationalism. "Modern architecture," Tzara argued, "as hygienic and stripped of ornaments as it wants to appear, has no chance of living." Against the horizontal extensions and the dissolution of the barriers between public and private implied by the Domino model, Tzara posed the maternal and sheltering images of "uterine" constructions which, from the cave to the grotto and the tent, comprised the fundamental forms of human habitation:

From the cave (for man inhabits the earth, "the mother"), through the Eskimo yurt, the intermediary form between the grotto and the tent (remarkable example of uterine construction which one enters through cavities with vaginal forms), through to the conical or half-spherical hut furnished at its entrance with a post of sacred character, the dwelling symbolizes prenatal comfort.

Entered through "cavities of vaginal form," these conical or half-spherical houses were dark, tactile, and soft. They imitated the play-constructed shelters of childhood.

When one returns what was torn away during adolescence and childhood, man could possess those realms of "luxe, calme et volupté" that he constructed for himself beneath the bed covers, under tables, crouching in cavities of earth, above all at the narrow entry; when it is seen that well-being resides in the *clair-obscur* of the tactile and soft depths of the only hygiene possible, that of prenatal desires, it will be possible to reconstruct the circular, spherical, and irregular houses that mankind has conserved from the time of the caves to the cradle and the grave, in his vision of intrauterine life which knows nothing of that aesthetics of castration called modern. This will not, in valorizing these arrangements with the acquisitions of actual life, be a return to the past, but a real progress, based on the potentiality of our most strong desires, strong because latent and eternal, the possibility of being liberated normally. The intensity of these desires has not changed much since the stage of man's savagery; only the forms and satisfactions have been broken up and dispersed over a larger mass, and, enfeebled to the point of being lost, with their acuity, the sense of true reality and quietude, they have, by their very degeneration, prepared the way for that autopunitive aggressivity that characterizes modern times.[10]

In Tzara's mingling of popular psychology and primitivism—his observations on architecture were published in *Minotaure* following Michel Leiris's illustrations of Dogon huts in 1933—we can identify a double nostalgia. On the one hand, the return to archetypal forms marks an identification with the origins of civilization and an explicit critique of its technological results, human and material; on the other, the notion of womb *as* origin displays a familiarity with Freudian explanations of desire and the repressed or displaced routes of homesickness: "There is a joking saying that 'Love is homesickness,'" Freud had written in 1919, "and whenever a man dreams of a place or a country and says to himself while he is still dreaming: 'This place is familiar to me, I've been there before,' we may interpret the place as being his mother's genitals or her body" (U 368). It is no doubt in this light that we may interpret Tzara's desire that "the architecture of the future will be intrauterine if it has resolved the problems of comfort and material and sentimental well-being, if it renounces its role of interpreter-servant of the bourgeoisie whose coercive will can only separate mankind from the ways of its destiny."[11]

Such nostalgia, however, hardly evoked the comforting images of hearth and home that were, during the same period, being raised by philosophers of the *Heimat* from Tessenow to Heidegger. For the apparently warm and all-enclosing interiors of intrauterine existence were, as Freud pointed out, at the same time the very centers of the uncanny. At once the refuge of inevitably unfulfilled desire and the potential crypt of living burial, the womb-house offered little solace to daily life.[12]

Thus, Matta Echaurren's "intrauterine" design for an apartment dedicated to the senses, published in *Minotaure* 11, in 1938, was a deliberate attack on the commonplaces of the bourgeois home. The perspective view shows materials and forms that merge nature and the inorganic, the mathematical and the tactile. It was, Matta noted, "a space that will bring into consciousness human verticality." A true vertigo machine, composed of "different levels, a stair without a handrail to overcome the void," it was also a space of psychological interaction. Its columns were "psychological Ionic"; its furnishings "supple, pneumatic." Matta specified inflatable rubber, cork, paper, and plaster for the soft areas, all for better contrast, framed in an "armature of rational architecture." The whole space simulated a kind of artificial womb.

Man looks back at the dark pulsions of his origin which enveloped him with humid/dank walls where the blood pulsed close to the eye with the noise of the mother . . . we must have walls like damp sheets which deform themselves and join with our psychological fears . . . the body insinuated as into a mold, as into a matrix based on our movements.[13]

It was the task of the architect, Matta concluded, "to find for each individual those umbilical cords that put us in communication with other suns, objects in total freedom that would be like plastic psychoanalytical mirrors." Frederick Kiesler's "Endless House," designed in multiple versions between 1924 and 1965, was similarly conceived. Hans Arp spoke of this "egg"-like form as if it were the egg of Columbus: "In his egg, in these spheroid egg-shaped structures, a human being can now take shelter and live as in his mother's womb."[14]

This blurring of lines between the mental and physical, the organic and inorganic, was, for the surrealists, one of the characteristic pleasures of art nouveau. Dalí's celebrated eulogy to Gaudí's "edible" architecture had stressed its images of metamorphosis, of all historical styles merging into each other, of the intersection of the biological and the constructional, building and psychoanalysis, architecture and hysteria, in order to produce the ultimate object of desire, or at least its reification. Characterized by its mimesis of the digestible—gates with panels like pieces of calves' liver, columns with bases that seemed to say "eat me!," buildings that as a whole might be assimilated to cakes—it was an architecture that, in Dalí's words "verified that urgent 'function,' so necessary for the amorous imagination: to be able in the most literal way possible to eat the object of desire."[15] Opposed to modern functionalism in every way, the Style 1900 discovered its real functions in the appetites and desires.

A "traumatism" for art, this style equally modeled itself on the postures of human trauma and psychosis. Using Charcot's photographs of female hysterics at the Salpêtrière, Dalí drew a "psychopathological parallel" between these images of "ecstasy" and the carving of the art nouveau.

Invention of "hysterical sculpture."—Continuous erotic ecstasy.—Contractions and attitudes without antecedents in the history of statuary (I refer to the women discovered and understood after Charcot and the School of the Salpêtrière).—Confusion and ornamental exacerbation in relation to pathological communications; precocious dementia.—Close relations to the dream; reveries, day dreams.—Presence of characteristic oneiric elements: condensation, displacement, etc.—Blossoming of the sado-anal complex.—Flagrant ornamental coprophagy. Very slow, exhausting onanism, accompanied by a huge feeling of guilt.[16]

The well-known theory of surrealist-inspired ecstasy that followed, summarized in Dalí's collage "Le phénomène de l'exstase," with its focalization of ears ("always in ecstasy") and juxtaposition of Charcot's photographs with art nouveau sculpture, also included a telling image of a tipped chair, empty as if having thrown its contents out of the picture.

This uncanny property of objects to adopt the characteristic behavior of their owners, thence to take revenge, the habit of the inanimate to take on the characteristics of the animate, and vice versa, had already been recognized by Freud. In a passage that seems to anticipate Ernst's collages, he speaks of the naive story of the haunted table from the *Strand Magazine*:

I read a story about a young married couple who move into a furnished house in which there is a curiously shaped table with carvings of crocodiles on it. Towards evening an intolerable and very specific smell begins to pervade the house; they stumble over something in the dark; they seem to see a vague form gliding over the stairs—in short, we are given to understand that the presence of the table causes ghostly crocodiles to haunt the place, or that the wooden monsters come to life in the dark, or something of the sort. It was a naive enough story, but the uncanny feeling it produced was quite remarkable. (U 367)

This sensation, evoked, Freud explains, by an "over-accentuation of physical reality in comparison with material reality," was the precise equivalent of Dalí's architecture of "hyper-materialism." Le Corbusier characterized the sensibility, accurately enough, as a disturbance in the balance of "our tehnico-cerebro-emotional equation," an overinvestment of "sentiment" in objects, to the extent that "the feeling for cause and effect falters. We are seized by disquiet because we no longer feel well-adapted; we revolt against our enforced servitude to the *abnormal*."[17]

And yet, of course, modernism's own object imaginary was hardly less disquieting. Walter Benjamin, indeed, went beyond Dalí's simple opposition to make the conceptual link between the technical visions of modernism and the apparent antitechnical stance of art noveau. Benjamin, who cited Dalí on the "delirious and cold buildings" of art nouveau, formulated a vision of the Jugendstil that was, in reality, an "attempt of art to take the measure of technique."[18] Precisely because, Benjamin argued, the Jugendstil considered itself no longer "menaced" by technique, it could identify itself with technique. Thus he noted the correspondence between the curving lines of art nouveau and their modern counterparts, electric wires, which in turn paralleled the nerves of the modern city dweller: "In the characteristic line of the art nouveau are brought together—united in a montage of imagination—the nerve and the electric wire (and which in particular brings into contact the world of organism and of technique by means of the intermediary form of the neurovegetal system)."[19] For Benjamin, this intersection of technology and nature was represented by the displacement of symbols from romanticism to modernism.

Here we may begin to trace the affiliations of surrealism and modernism on the level of technique, affinities that were announced by Benjamin himself in the aphorism: "The reactionary attempt that seeks to detach the forms imposed by technique from their functional context and to make natural constants out of them—that is to say, to stylize them—is found sometime after art nouveau, in a similar form, in futurism." The structure that united the two, in Benjamin's terms, was fetishism. For it was fetishism that, in its multiple displacements, "suppresses the barriers that separate the organic from the inorganic world," that is "at home in the world of the inert as in the world of the flesh."[20] Such confusions of identity were, as Sigfried Giedion noted, the inevitable product of the modern mechanization of the dwelling in its mission of repression against the bric-a-brac of the nineteenth century.[21] Giedion observes of the interiors of Ernst's *Une semaine de bonté*,

Of the billowing drapes, of the murky atmosphere, Ernst's scissors make a submarine cave. Are these living creatures, plaster statues or models of the academic brush found reclining here or rotting? To this question no answer can or should be given. The room, as nearly always, is oppressive with assassination and non-escape.[22]

Surrealism and purism, indeed, fetishized precisely the same *types* of objects: what for surrealists were "objets trouvés" or vehicles of oneiric desire and for Le Corbusier were "objets-membres-humains," or the physical extensions of the body. As Le Corbusier himself recognized,

The new "Surrealists" (formerly Dadaists) claim to lift themselves above the brute nature of the object and are ready to recognize only relationships which belong to the invisible and subconscious world of the dream. Nevertheless they compare themselves to radio antennae; thus they raise radio onto their own pedestal . . . the supremely elegant relationships of their metaphors . . . are all the time very clearly dependent on the products of straightforward conscious effort . . . the finality necessary to polished steel.

To prove the point Le Corbusier cited De Chirico, writing in the first number of *La Révolution Surréaliste*, December 1924: "They are like levers, as irresistible as those all-powerful machines, those gigantic cranes which raise high over the teeming building sites sections of floating fortresses with heavy towers like the breasts of ante-diluvian mammals."[23]

In this dependency of surrealist fantasy on the real objects of the machine world, "type objects" and "sentiment objects" met in their common aim to overcome technique in its banal manifestations in favor of a technological imaginary that would transform technology into the human and vice versa, into the prosthetic and potentially critical devices of the cyborg. It was not by chance that Walter Benjamin identified Olympia, the automat doll of E. T. A. Hoffmann's "Sandman" and subject of Freud's analysis of the uncanny, as the ideal woman of the art nouveau. "The extreme point of the technical organization of the world," concluded Benjamin, "consists in the liquidation of fertility."

The modern cyborg was, in this way, anticipated by the automat, with its long tradition in romantic thought, from Hoffmann's Olympia to Mary Shelley's monster, from Villiers de L'Isle-Adam's *Eve future* to Duchamp's "Bride." These "celibate machines" were, as Lyotard has observed, all ruses, fabricated to obscure the essential impossibility of mechanically dominating nature, to blur the distinctions between the biological and the technical; the first such contraption was constructed by Hephaistos for Zeus and named Pandora.[24] Indeed, following Diller and Scofidio's experiments with the staging of Duchamp's Large Glass, we might hazard that their project includes a careful opening of the box belonging to that first "automate," as Alice Jardine has redubbed her, in order to expose the ruse of modernism.[25]

Conceived of in these terms, the objects of architecture become so many prostheses, extensions of the body tied to it in almost organic ways; instruments that, as Michel de Certeau has characterized them, might be defined according to their functions:

Two main operations characterize their activities. The first seeks primarily to *remove* something excessive, diseased, or unaesthetic from the body, or else to *add* to the body what it lacks. Instruments are thus distinguished by the action they perform: cutting, tearing out, extracting, removing, etc., or else inserting, installing, attaching, covering up, assembling, sewing together, articulating etc.—without mentioning those substituted for missing or deteriorated organs, such as heart valves and regulators, prosthetic joints, pins implanted in the femur, artificial irises, substitute ear bones, etc.[26]

Of course, most of the object types conceived by modernism were prosthetic to one degree or another: Le Corbusier never tired of vaunting the claims of "objets-membres-humains," those type objects responding to type needs and type functions and operating as liberating extensions of our limbs—"chairs to sit on, tables to work at, devices to give light, machines to write with (ah! yes), racks to file things in." a "human limb object," properly designed to harmonize with the body, would act for all the world like "a docile servant. A good servant is discreet and self-effacing in order to leave his master free."[27]

The modernist prosthetic object was equally a master: the etiquette machines fabricated by Schreber for his children—to construct correct posture while lying, sitting, and standing—as well as the taylorized furniture of the Gilbreths were all so many devices to control the body for its own good, chastity belts for the machine age, bringing the organic into line with the social and economic systems of industrial production.

Against this, the object types of Diller and Scofidio neither serve nor dictate; they simply reveal. Peeling back the layers of consumer coverings, Bauhaus black or suburban veneer, they show the form of the guts inside. Televisions are transformed into biological analog through disemboweling, their tubes, wires, and connections left bare, as if to demonstrate their temporary, makeshift nature. On the one hand enfeebled and weak, cut open and wounded, these machines are at the same time threatening, as they parade the enormous power of the technologically constructed microorganism invading the house.

But these operations are not entirely neutral: beginning as a ready-made, the unmade object is itself subjected to a subtle transformation and mutation that points not only to its internal nature but also to its expanded field of operation, its relation to the body. Thus the television screen, shifted from vertical to horizontal, is no longer the focus of a conventional view but now reflected in a mirror that takes its place. The screen, simulacrum of the real, is literally displaced through a simulacrum of itself, at the same time as its controlling (picture-frame) position has been unfixed and refracted through the action of the mirror. Similarly, chairs, which normally would image as well as serve comfort, are cut through in order to threaten the (sitting) body at its most vulnerable point.

Such objects are no longer subject to subjects; they counterattack. As in the collages of Max Ernst, they unionize in revolt, but now in the form of critical machines that pose new identities for their subjects. As apparatuses that both work on and fuse with once-separate bodies, they, like the cyborgs that "use" them, scramble all the recognized codes. Such objects fight back, they machine us as much as we machine them. Indeed, the only resistance, as many of the visitors to Diller and Scofidio's 1990 installation at the Museum of Modern Art realized, was to fall back on the commonplace reading of the objects, using the mirror for making up and envisioning the chair in the air as a misplaced seat. The network of relations established among objects becomes itself a phenomenal prosthetic for the body, to be refused by normalcy.

If, at one level, the body can be interpreted as a construction determined by the discursive practices of its surveillance and punishment, in the literal constructions of Diller and Scofidio the body both transcribes itself and is written on. The chair that leaves a message impressed on the buttocks—the right way round for another to read—is a machine for transcription. But, unlike Kafka's writing machine that inscribed the name of the punishment in the flesh of the victim, these architectural "magic writing pads" leave only temporary marks. In this way, the states of the modern body are mirrored in reactive structures. Cybernetic and biotechnical operations—hacking, probing—are given material life through the physical exploration of inside and out and the optical scanning of a myriad blind eyes that observe without knowing.

Here the optical networks set up by screen and camera, observer and observed, stage a voyeuristic space in which objects and subjects alike are trapped *en abîme*. But while the apparent trajectories of the eye, marked by the intersecting visual cones of so many lenses, seem to replicate the laws of true vision, in fact the space is traversed by the lines of a "pseudo-optics" established not so much by the geometries of real optical systems as by the psychology of the viewers. And viewers are equally absent in this simulated science where objects take their place, describing an optical scene that both includes and excludes subjects, or rather includes them in the form of a system of virtual signs. In this way an empty chair will "stand in" for its user, closing the system from the outside, as if obligingly supplying itself in the position of the hypothetical spectator of Goya's *Las Meninas*, no longer a technical instrument but a psychological contrivance.

No-body, then, can place itself at the central projection point in this optical system, which operates as a kind of literalization of post-Lacanian space. We who have become used to the diagram of our historically relative, rapidly changing perceptual structures, from Alberti's perspectival window to Nietzsche's labyrinth, are now presented with their archaeological reconstructions, each in conflict with the next, literalized by means of objects that project each system's sinister implications.

The gaze intimated by these layered and fractured cones of vision is, of course, no longer panoptical. In Alice Jardine's words, "We are no longer in the system of the panopticon described so accurately by Foucault . . . we are rather in a mode of self-surveillance: we watch ourselves as someone else."[28] From panoptical gaze to cyborgian gaze, Diller and Scofidio's intricately intersecting watchers shift attention from the written inscription of surveillance to the disseminated, three-dimensional network of glances and reflections. The carefully calibrated glances of the Dutch group portrait as described by Alois Riegl, the culturally precise meanings of perspective as symbolic form explicated by Panofsky, give way to three-dimensional hyperspatial constructions, in which fault lines figure as importantly as any completed sight lines. Where, in a pure cybernetic system as modeled by de Certeau, the privilege is given to writing, now boundaries are broken down and confused by their very inspection in three dimensions.

By the simple but critical act of "realizing" the model in practice, Diller and Scofidio establish a host of half-completed, half-broken refracted lines between mechanical objects and organic subjects; this network *is* in a real sense the cyborgian construction. Emulating at the same time as provoking both inner "hacker" or "cyber" space and outer or body space, the apparatus acts for all intents and purposes as a complicated and imaginary prophylactic among its subjects. The machine-age bachelor mechanism was forced to construct a real barrier, as in the hymenal wall of Alfred Jarry's "island of lubricious glass," which took on the form of any sexual organ when touched.[29] The contemporary cyborg, in contrast, is already insulated by a deflected gaze of a constructed gender and needs no traditional home.

But the home of a cyborg is by no means a site of technological utopia. Describing "home" as a social location, Donna Haraway confronts the breakdown of the bourgeois domestic myth in the face of cybernetic industry:

Home: Women-headed households, serial monogamy, flight of men, old women alone, technology of domestic work, paid homework, reemergence of home sweat shops, home-based businesses and telecommuting, electronic cottage, urban homelessness, migration, module architecture, reinforced (simulated) nuclear family, intense domestic violence.[30]

What for the postwar generation of architectural technotopias, from Archigram to high tech, simply signified burgeoning social oppor-

tunity—the unlikely communitarianism of the "global village"—
emerges in reality as a suburban battlefield strewn with the dismembered nuclei of imaginary families and the wreckage of their "homes."
In such settings, for better or for worse, there is, Haraway claims,
"no 'place' for women." In their place, there are "only geometrics of
difference and contradiction crucial to women's cyborg identities."
Where, in the taylorized settings of the twenties and thirties, the
home was to be retooled to produce a generation of engineers and
technocrats, the woman smoothly integrating time and motion into
the carefully calculated spaces of a "kitchen-house-factory," now the
space of technological competency is reduced to the flat surface of
the monitor, the breadth of two hands on the keyboard. In this
context the spatial order of the home carries less and less meaning,
and its traditional "rooms" and their furnishings even less. A "machine for living in" has been transformed into a potentially dangerous
psychopathological space populated by half-natural, half-prosthetic
individuals, where walls reflect the sight of their viewers, where the
house surveys its occupants with silent menace.

In the Capp Street project constructed by Diller and Scofidio, all
these dimensions are explored: the space of each object is remapped
as dining table and chairs are lifted in the air, beds and chairs are
split in two, all following the vectors established by their (traditional)
uses exaggerated to cutting effect. Objects now act out beyond their
proper domains: chairs are attached to tables by locks and swings
that emulate the presence of human arms; chairs are bisected by the
locks of doors—all connected in ways they should not be, in order to
reveal their sinister interdependence in the domestic system. Domestic objects are now set free to map their own space of instrumentality;
human agency is supplied by surrogate objects, themselves prostheses
of objects in their dangerous extensions.[31] Like the dust traces falling
on Duchamp's Large Glass, the phantom operations of absent inhabitants and living objects are also mapped in their deposits. The moving bed is tracked by films of dust beneath it; the presence of former
drinkers marked by the rings of glasses on the table. The house is
left as if an obsolete and already abandoned technological space—
like the inside of an old radio—a readymade, found again to be
reused at will, dust and all; the traces of nonoccupation as well as of
occupation seem to provide a schematic archaeology by which to
begin again.

Such an assemblage no longer prefigures a robotic future of unified and gleaming technology; rather it is composed in a present of uneven development, filled with the detritus of past systems of technical order. As described by Michel de Certeau, this present takes on the characteristics of an open-cast mine, still operative in a terrain layered by the fragments of already obsolescent systems:

Epistemological configurations are never replaced by the appearance of new orders; they compose strata that form the bedrock of a present. Relics and pockets of the instrumental systems continue to exist everywhere. . . . Tools take on a folkloric appearance. They nevertheless make up a discharged corps left behind by the defunct empire of mechanics. These populations of instruments oscillate between the status of memorable ruins and an intense everyday activity.[32]

Despite the apparent homogeneity of the cybernetic system, it operates in the interstices, and with the help of every previous system of bodily and textual inscription. Thus the readymades found by Diller and Scofidio are neither pure types, as imagined by Le Corbusier, nor ironic countertypes, as re-represented by Marcel Duchamp. They are nothing more than junk, throw-away objects found in the street or at the local dump. Already useless to the system of technological utopia, they nevertheless have been recuperated by precise operations for another system, the cyborgian.

In this way, Diller and Scofidio construct environments that have all the air of those transitional wastelands described in contemporary science fiction: the "Night city" of William Gibson's *Neuromancer,* at once "a kind of historical park: reminding the most advanced Japanese technology of its humbler origins," and an "outlaw zone," "a deliberately unsupervised playground for technology itself."[33] More specifically, Diller and Scofidio's Capp Street project resembles in microcosm that other "Nighttown" depicted by Gibson in the short story "Johnny Mnemonic":

The mall runs forty kilometers from end to end, a ragged overlap of Fuller domes roofing what was once a suburban artery. If they turn off the arcs on a clear day, a gray approximation of sunlight filters through layers of acrylic, a view like the prison sketches of Giovanni Piranesi. The three southernmost kilometers roof Nighttown. . . . The neon arcs are dead, and the geodesics have been smoked black by decades of cooking fires.[34]

In the trusses of these abandoned domes lives a community of LO TEKS, dedicated to a reversal of progress into primitivism, transformed biologically into cyborgs of Darwinian regression, half-dog, half-human. Their city is a bricolage of junk held together by rough epoxy joints, taped to the rafters of this technotropia, "jury-rigged and jerry-built from scraps that even Nighttown didn't want." But where Gibson seems to celebrate, however savagely, a "neuromanticism" that points to a cybernetic sublime in these technological ruinscapes, Diller and Scofidio remain analytical and dedicated to the didactic dissection of the processes that construct this new world.

In this project, the selection of the everyday and well-used object—the old chair, the worn-out television—is deliberately calculated to lull suspicion. Old friends, thrown away after years of service, these objects are nothing but familiar—so familiar indeed as to become banal. But in their recuperation and necessary deconstruction they take on more sinister overtones. Returned from their proper burial, discovered in the wrong place, invested with an uncanny life of their own, they break the long process of deterioration and degradation that leads from the familiar, the ordinary, to the banal, returning once more to the status of the unhomely.[35] In the event, their effect is neither uncanny nor familiar, but rather a demonstration of the potential uncanny, an unveiling of the secret but ever-present reciprocities that bind people to objects in posttechnological domesticity.

What Gibson calls "the consensual hallucination" of cyberspace, occupied by the disembodied consciousness of a hacker jacked into a matrix of spatially represented information—the public realm of the cybernetic—is now brought home. What Adorno epitomized as the dilemma of homesickness—the result of "distancing"—is now solved. The illusionistic virtuosity needed in order, as Adorno dreamed, to experience homesickness at the same time as staying at home is now technologically supplied.[36]

Private space is revealed as infinitely public, private rituals publicized to their subjects and these in turn connected to the public matrix. No longer sheltered from public surveillance by a well-defended private realm, the space of the domestic will now become, as Alice Jardine has hazarded, an agent of self-surveillance: "A lot of these ethical and political regimes will come together in self-surveillance; not all of it will be imposed from the outside . . . self tests . . . in the privacy of your own home . . . soon no-one will be able to touch anyone else, and I think it's going to be everyone."[37]

In this sense, Haraway's cyborgian myth operates as much on the level of dystopia as of utopia; it is, as she explains, built out of irony, "the attempt to build an ironic political myth faithful to feminism, socialism, materialism."

Irony is about contradictions that do not resolve into larger wholes, even dialectically, about the tension of holding incompatible things together because both or all are necessary and true. Irony is about humor and serious play. It is also a rhetorical strategy and a political method.[38]

Her attempt to pose the cyborg as "a creature of social reality as well as of fiction" that emblematizes the contemporary state of "lived social relations, our most important political construction," is a valiant effort to hold the unthinkable and the possible in the same frame, a counter to the gender divisions and relations that construct the (traditional) present.[39] Such irony, of course, can only be sustained in the active play of political and social experience; its difficult dialectic can rarely be incorporated in the positive spaces and aesthetic constructions of a material shelter. Thus the "house" implied by Diller and Scofidio demands continuous consciousness of physical and psychological discomfort from its para-inhabitants; it converts the pabulum of Heideggerian nostalgia into a *Hausangst* that reveals the banal and everyday nature of the *unheimlich;* the dream of *Heimat* founders on the reality of the coffin-hotel in the zone.

III

Spaces

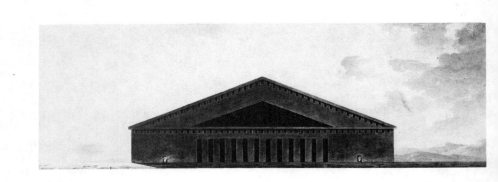

Dark Space

A whole history remains to be written of *spaces*—which would at the same time be the history of *powers* (both these terms in the plural)—from the great strategies of geo-politics to the little tactics of the habitat, institutional architecture from the classroom to the design of hospitals, passing via economic and political installations.

Michel Foucault, "The Eye of Power"

Space, in contemporary discourse, as in lived experience, has taken on an almost palpable existence. Its contours, boundaries, and geographies are called upon to stand in for all the contested realms of identity, from the national to the ethnic; its hollows and voids are occupied by bodies that replicate internally the external conditions of political and social struggle, and are likewise assumed to stand for, and identify, the sites of such struggle. Techniques of spatial occupation, of territorial mapping, of invasion and surveillance are seen as the instruments of social and individual control.

Equally, space is assumed to hide, in its darkest recesses and forgotten margins, all the objects of fear and phobia that have returned with such insistency to haunt the imaginations of those who have tried to stake out spaces to protect their health and happiness. Indeed, space as threat, as harbinger of the unseen, operates as medical and psychical metaphor for all the possible erosions of bourgeois bodily and social well being. The body, indeed, has become its own exterior, as its cell structure has become the object of spatial modeling that maps its own sites of immunological battle and describes the forms of its antibodies. "Outside," even as the spaces of exile, asylum, confinement, and quarantine of the early modern period were continuously spilling over into the "normal" space of the city, so the "pathological" spaces of today menace the clearly marked out limits of the social order. In every case "light space" is invaded by the figure of "dark space," on the level of the body in the form of epidemic and uncontrollable disease, and on the level of the city in the person of the homeless. In other words, the realms of the organic space of the body and the social space in which that body lives and works, domains clearly enough distinguished in the nineteenth century, as François Delaporte has shown, no longer can be identified as separate.[1]

In what follows I want to examine only one aspect of this new condition, one that touches on its implications for monumental architecture and more generally on the theorization of spatial conditions after Foucault. I will, that is, analyze the visual construction of images and objects that refer to this dark side of space in the modern period, as a way of approaching a more complex and (I hope) more politically subtle interpretation of subject-space relations than that offered by the conventional wisdom of modern urbanism (flood dark space with light) or architecture (open up all space to vision and occupation).

In the elaboration of the complex history of modern space following the initiatives of Foucault, historians and theorists have largely concentrated their attention on the overtly political role of *transparent* space—that paradigm of total control championed by Jeremy Bentham and recuperated under the guise of "hygienic space" by modernists led by Le Corbusier in the twentieth century. Transparency, it was thought, would eradicate the domain of myth, suspicion, tyranny, and above all the irrational. The rational grids and hermetic enclosures of institutions from hospitals to prisons; the surgical opening up of cities to circulation, light, and air; the therapeutic design of dwellings and settlements; these have all been subjected to analysis for their hidden contents, their capacity to instrumentalize the politics of surveillance through what Bentham termed "universal transparency." Historians have preferred to study this myth of "power through transparency," especially in its evident complicity with the technologies of the modern movement and their "utopian" applications to architecture and urbanism.

Yet such a spatial paradigm was, as Foucault pointed out, constructed out of an initial fear, the fear of Enlightenment in the face of "darkened spaces, of the pall of gloom which prevents the full visibility of things, men and truths." It was this very fear of the dark that led, in the late eighteenth century, to the fascination with those same shadowy areas—the "fantasy-world of stone walls, darkness, hideouts and dungeons"—the precise "negative of the transparency and visibility which it is aimed to establish."[2] The moment that saw the creation of the first "considered politics of spaces" based on scientific concepts of light and infinity also saw, and within the same epistemology, the invention of a spatial phenomenology of darkness.

Late eighteenth-century architects were entirely aware of this double vision. Etienne-Louis Boullée, who was among the first to apply the newly outlined precepts of the Burkean sublime to the design of public institutions, exploited all the visual and sensational powers of what Burke had called "absolute light" to characterize his projects for metropolitan cathedrals and halls of justice. He was equally obsessed with absolute darkness as the most powerful instrument to induce that state of fundamental terror claimed by Burke as the instigator of the sublime. His design for a Palace of Justice confronted the two worlds, light and dark, in a telling allegory of enlightenment; the cubiform justice halls, lit from above, are set on top of a half-buried podium containing the prisons. "It seemed to me," Boullée wrote, "that in presenting this august palace raised on the shadowy lair of crime, I would not only be able to ennoble architecture by means of the oppositions that resulted, but further present in a metaphorical way the imposing picture of vice crushed beneath the feet of justice."[3]

It was perhaps not by chance that Boullée's reflections on the dark were elaborated during the period of his enforced withdrawal from public life under the real Terror—one that Robespierre himself had described as predicated on the necessities of the "political sublime." During this internal exile, sometime in the mid-1790s, Boullée recounted his "experiments" in light and shade as he walked by night in the woods surrounding his home:

Finding myself in the countryside, I skirted a wood by the light of the moon. My effigy produced by its light excited my attention (assuredly this was not a novelty for me). By a particular disposition of the mind, the effect of this simulacrum seemed to me to be of an extreme sadness. The trees drawn on the ground by their shadows made the most profound impression on me. This picture grew in my imagination. I then saw everything that was the most somber in nature. What did I see? The mass of objects detached in black against a light of extreme pallor. Nature seemed to offer itself, in mourning, to my sight. Struck by the sentiments I felt, I occupied myself, from this moment on, in making its particular application to architecture.

Out of his experiences, Boullée formed a notion of an architecture that would speak of death. It should be low and compressed in proportions—a "buried architecture" that literally embodied the burial it symbolized. It should express the extreme melancholy of mourning by means of its stripped and naked walls, "deprived of all ornament." It should, finally, following the model of the architect's shadow, be articulated to the sight by means of shadows:

One must, as I have tried to do in funerary monuments, present the skeleton of architecture by means of an absolutely naked wall, presenting the image of buried architecture by employing only low and compressed proportions, sinking into the earth, forming, finally, by means of materials absorbent to the light, the black picture of an architecture of shadows depicted by the effect of even blacker shadows.

Boullée gave the example of a Temple of Death, a temple front etched, so to speak, in shadow form on a flat plane of light-absorbent material—a virtual architecture of negativity. Boullée was proud of his "invention": "This genre of architecture formed by shadows is a discovery of the art that belongs to me. It is a new career that I have opened up. Either I fool myself, or artists will not disdain to follow it."[4] Certainly his younger contemporaries were quick to seize on the sublime potentials of this abyssal vision of mortuary form. Claude-Nicolas Ledoux, in particular, made the architecture of death a point of departure for a reverie on the infinite scale of the universe and the absolute "nothingness" of the void after life.

And yet, in retrospect, what is fascinating about Boullée's account is not so much its commonplace references to darkness, nor its fashionable appeal to Egyptian motifs on the eve of Napoleon's expedition, but rather its projection of a "skeleton" of architecture from the basis of the human shadow. This shadow, or "effigy" as Boullée called it, prefiguring the disappearance of the body into darkness, was both a haunting "double" for Boullée himself and a model for imitation in architecture. On one level, Boullée was following the traditional idea of architecture "imitating" the perfection of the human body in massing and proportions, inverting the theory in order to make an architecture based on the "death form" of the body, shadowed on the ground. But beyond this Boullée created a veritable "simulacrum" of the buried body in architecture: the building, already half sunken, compressed in its proportions as if by a great weight from above, imitated not a standing figure (as classical Vitruvian theory would have demanded) but a form that was already recumbent, itself depicted on the ground as a negative space. This prone figure was then raised up, so to speak, in order to mark the facade of Boullée's temple, now become an image of a specter: a monument to death that represented an ambiguous moment, somewhere between life and death, or, rather, a shadow of the living dead. In this way, Boullée prefigured the nineteenth-century preoccupation with the double as the harbinger of death, or as the shadow of the unburied dead.

In this doubling of the double, Boullée was thus setting up a play between architecture (art of imitation, of doubling) and death (imaged in the double) in a way that gave tangible force to Enlightenment fears. As Sarah Kofman has argued in her analysis of Freud's essay on "The Uncanny," "erected to conquer death, art, as a 'double', like any double, itself turns into an image of death. The game of art is a game of death, which already implies death in life, as a force of saving and inhibition." Boullée's death image, with its shadow inscription mirroring the shape of its dark facade or "ground," plays insistently on this theme that, as Freud pointed out, has to do with "the constant recurrence of the same thing," or repetition. Kofman comments,

[Freud's] "The Uncanny" indicates this transformation of the algebraic sign of the double, its link with narcissism and death as the punishment for having sought immortality, for having wanted to "kill" the father. It is perhaps no accident that the model of the "double," erected for the first time by the Egyptians, is found in the figuration of castration in dreams, the doubling of the genital organ.[5]

Boullée, in these terms, might well have invented, if not the first architectural figuration of death, certainly the first self-conscious architecture of the uncanny, a prescient experiment in the projection of "dark space." For by flattening his shadow, so to speak, on the surface of a building that was itself nothing but (negative) surface, Boullée had created an image of an architecture not only without real depth, but one that deliberately played on the ambiguities between absolute flatness and infinite depth, between his own shadow and the void. The building, as the double of the death of the subject, translated this disappearance into experienced spatial uncertainty.

Here the limits of Foucault's interpretation of Enlightenment space become evident. Still tied to the Enlightenment's own phenomenology of light and dark, clear and obscure, his insistence on the operation of power through *transparency,* the panoptic principle, resists exploration of the extent to which the pairing of transparency and obscurity is essential for power to operate. For it is in the intimate associations of the two, their uncanny ability to slip from one to the other, that the sublime as instrument of fear retains its hold—in that ambiguity that stages the presence of death in life, dark space in bright space. In this sense, all the radiant spaces of modernism, from the first Panopticon to the Ville Radieuse, should be seen as calculated not on the final triumph of light over dark but precisely on the insistent presence of the one in the other.

Indeed, on another level, Boullée's design puts into question the generally assumed identity of the spatial and the monumental in Foucault's system. Foucault posited a virtual homology between the institutional politics of panopticism and their monumental crystallizations in the form of building types from the hospital to the prison and beyond, thus setting in motion the critique of modernist typologies that began in the late 1960s; the *spatial* dimension here seems to act as a universal flux bonding political and architectural or monumental. But our analysis of Boullée might suggest that the spatial is rather a dimension that incipiently opposes the monumental: not only does it work to contextualize the individual monument into a general map of spatial forces that stretch from the building to the city and thence to entire territories—something recognized by the situationists, and, in another context, by Henri Lefebvre—but it also operates, by way of the negative bodily projection we have described, to absorb the monument altogether.

Boullée's relentless desire to mimic the "engulfing" of the subject into the void of death, a desire itself mimicked by Ledoux when he speaks of composing "an image of nothingness" in his Cemetery project of 1785, thus ends in the engulfing of monumentality itself. For the rational grids and spatial orders that mark the laying out of the panoptical system in the late eighteenth century are, in the Temple of Death, nowhere present; there is literally no *plan* for this monument to nothingness. Its sole mark is a facade as infinitely thin and insubstantial as the idea of redoubled darkness—a facade more-over that is precariously balanced between above and below, vertical and horizontal. Here the bodily substantiality of the traditional mon-ument and the palpable spatial identity of the controlling institution dissolve into a mirror of the projection of a disappearing subject. Space, that is, has operated as an instrument of monumental dissolution.

The homology thus established between subject and space seems, on the subjective as well as on the monumental level, to emulate what Roger Caillois referred to as "legendary psychasthenia," that "temp-tation by space" that seemed to operate in the realm of insect mimicry and that offered so many analogies to human experience. Caillois was fascinated by the loss of any distinction between the insect and its surroundings during the process of camouflaging identity, its ten-dency to assimilate to its milieu; he pointed out that this did not always correspond to the best possible defense against death. The insect that looked like the leaf on which it was seated could equally be destroyed or eaten along with the leaf. Such loss of identity, he argued, would be a kind of pathological luxury, even "a dangerous luxury." As in imitation in the arts, such mimicry depended on the distortion of spatial vision, on the breaking down of the normal process by which spatial perception situates the subject clearly in space and in opposition to it:

There can be no doubt that the perception of space is a complex phenom-enon: space is indissolubly perceived and represented. From this standpoint it is a double dihedral changing at every moment in size and position: a *dihedral of action* whose horizontal plane is formed by the ground and the vertical plane by the man himself who walks and who, by this fact, carries the dihedral along with him; and a *dihedral of representation* determined by the same horizontal plane as the previous one (but represented and not perceived) intersected vertically at the distance where the object appears. It is with represented space that the drama becomes specific, since the living creature, the organism, is no longer the origin of the coordinates, but one point among others; it is dispossessed of its privilege and literally *no longer knows where to place itself*. One can already recognize the characteristic scientific attitude and, indeed, it is remarkable that represented spaces are just what is multiplied by contemporary science: Finsler's spaces, Fermat's spaces, Rie-mann-Christoffel's hyper-space, abstract, generalized, open, and closed spaces, spaces dense in themselves, thinned out, and so on. The feeling of personality, considered as the organism's feeling of distinction from its surroundings, of the connection between consciousness and a particular point in space, cannot fail under these conditions to be seriously undermined; one then enters into the psychology of psychasthenia, and more specifically of *legendary psychasthenia*, if we agree to use this name for the disturbance in the above relations between personality and space.[6]

Following the psychological studies of Pierre Janet, Caillois compared such a disturbance to that experienced by certain schizophrenics when, in response to the question "where are you?," they invariably responded "I know where I am, but I do not feel as though I'm at the spot where I find myself." Caillois seemed to be relating such spatial disorientation to the pathology of derealization discussed by Freud, and beyond this to the host of spatial phobias, from agoraphobia to acrophobia and claustrophobia, identified in the late nineteenth century. Like sufferers from agoraphobia, described by Carl Otto Westphal in 1871, Caillois saw the schizophrenic literally eaten up by space:

To these dispossessed souls, space seems to be a devouring force. Space pursues them, encircles them, digests them in a gigantic phagocytosis. It ends by replacing them. Then the body separates itself from thought, the individual breaks the boundary of his skin and occupies the other side of his senses. He tries to look at *himself from* any point whatever in space. He feels himself becoming space, *dark space where things cannot be put.* He is similar, not similar to something, but just *similar.* And he invents spaces of which he is "the convulsive possession."[7]

This spatial condition of the devoured subject Caillois assimilated to the experience, described by Eugène Minkowski, of "dark space," a space that is lived under the conditions of depersonalization and assumed absorption. Minkowski, distinguishing between "light space" and "dark space," saw dark space as a living entity, experienced, despite its lack of visual depth and visible extension, as deep: "an opaque and unlimited sphere wherein all the radii are the same, black and mysterious."[8] For Caillois, Minkowski's formulation approximated his own self-induced experience of psychasthenia, explaining among other symptoms his (much intensified) "fear of the dark," rooted once more in "the peril in which it puts the opposition between the organism and the milieu." In Minkowski and Caillois, darkness is not the simple absence of light:

There is something positive about it. While light space is eliminated by the materiality of objects, darkness is "filled," it touches the individual directly, envelops him, penetrates him, and even passes through him: hence "the ego is *permeable* for darkness while it is not so for light"; the feeling of mystery that one experiences at night would not come from anything else. Minkowski likewise comes to speak of *dark space* and almost of a lack of distinction between the milieu and the organism: "Dark space envelops me on all sides and penetrates me much deeper than light space; the distinction between inside and outside and consequently the sense organs as well, insofar as they are designed for external perception, here play only a totally modest role."[9]

The notion of an impulsion toward a loss of the subject into dark space, linked directly by Caillois both to the death drive and to certain forms of aesthetic mimicry, thus returns us to Boullée's experience of impending death in the forest outside Paris, and more directly to its monumental mimicry. We might now say that the Temple of Death, as monument, mimics the subject's own impulsion to be tempted by space, a monument that suffers, so to speak, from legendary psychasthenia.

Posturbanism

The cities I speak of . . . are towns without a past. Thus they are without tenderness or abandon. During the boredom of the siesta hours, their sadness is implacable and has no melancholy. In the morning light, or in the natural luxury of the evenings, their delights are equally ungentle. These towns give nothing to the mind and everything to the passions. They are suited neither to wisdom nor to the delicacies of taste.

Albert Camus, "A Short Guide to Towns without a Past"[1]

In the traditional city, antique, medieval, or Renaissance, urban memory was easy enough to define; it was that image of the city that enabled the citizen to identify with its past and present as a political, cultural, and social entity; it was neither the "reality" of the city nor a purely imaginary "utopia" but rather the complex mental map of significance by which the city might be recognized as "home," as something not foreign, and as constituting a (more or less) moral and protected environment for actual daily life. Thence the privileged place of monuments as markers in the city fabric; monuments that, as Alois Riegl pointed out, owed their very name to their function as agents of memory: "A monument in its oldest and most original sense is a human creation, erected for the specific purpose of keeping single human deeds or events . . . alive in the minds of future generations."[2] The recognition of a network of such monuments, assembled in an equally recognizable hierarchy, was the basis for the cultural and political constitution of a city from antiquity to the Renaissance. But it is not so much the monuments themselves, triumphal arches or columns, that construct this "meaning" so much as what they stand for; they, after all, are agents and instruments that operate, like literary figures, to say one thing by means of another. They act, in this sense, as tropes of the memory discourse they engender. Thus Alberti will speak of Brunelleschi's dome for Santa Maria del Fiore as "covering" the people of Florence, its vast size and shape standing for the population and their political and social unity. Brunelleschi's dome was, in this sense, a metaphor, whose physical presence constantly reminded the population of their metaphysical bonds. It took its place at the center of a "memory map" that was continuously reelaborated by the Florentine humanists, that contained all the major monuments of the republic.

Such a map, as Frances Yates has shown in her remarkable treatise *The Art of Memory,* was allied to similar aids to memory constructed by rhetoricians and philosophers from the time of Cicero. The orator Quintillian was quite precise in his description of how to remember: because, as he says, "when we return to a place after a considerable absence, we do not merely recognize the place itself, but remember things that we did there," it is possible to use this property of places to construct a kind of memory machine:

Places are chosen, and marked with the utmost possible variety, as a spacious house divided into a number of rooms. Everything of note therein is diligently imprinted on the mind, in order that thought may be able to run through all the parts without let or hindrance. . . . Then what has been written down, or thought of, is noted by a sign to remind of it. This sign may be drawn from a whole "thing," as navigation or warfare, or from some word, for what is slipping from memory is recovered by the admonition of a single word.[3]

Quintillian then outlines a system of reminders that was commonplace in classical thought and was to be again revived during the Renaissance, one where a sequence of places, imagined or remembered, is established in the mind, and the signs of what is to be remembered are "installed" so to speak within these places in sequence. All that is necessary to be able to recall the thing itself is to "remember" this place and its contents. The art of memory therefore requires "places, either real or imaginary, and images or simulacra which must be invented"; these places, Quintillian says, may be real or themselves invented: "What I have spoken of as being done in a house can also be done in public buildings, or on a long journey, or in going through a city, or with pictures. Or we can imagine such places for ourselves."

Yates describes the way in which more and more elaborate versions of these memory places were fabricated throughout the Middle Ages and Renaissance, leading to those strange half-real, half-imaginary loci named "memory theaters" or even, as in the case of Campanella, "utopias." The relation between the real city and the utopian city is thereby mediated by a mental map that includes the real in order to imagine the unreal, the ideal, or simply that which has to be remembered.

For our purposes, however, this relationship, which determined to a great extent the nature of the Renaissance ideal city, becomes important only at the moment when architects became aware of the possibility of transferring to the realm of reality that which they had imagined in their memory; that is, of cutting out of the fabric of the real city the sequences and places that constituted their memory maps of the city, of turning the city into a memory theater and making that theater accessible both to the inhabitants and, equally importantly, to visitors. The planning of the Rome of Sixtus V as a vast tourist city with all its monuments and memorials joined by significant paths or streets marks the true beginning of urbanism. Urbanism, in this sense, might be defined as the instrumental theory and practice of constructing the city as memorial of itself. The history of urbanism from the late Renaissance to the Second World War illustrates this definition clearly: the replanning of London by Wren and his fellow scientists and historians of the Royal Society; the replanning of Paris by Pierre Patte and the philosophic architects of the Enlightenment; the reconstruction of Paris by Baron Haussmann under the Second Empire; the various model cities and their partial implementations envisaged by the modernists from Tony Garnier to Le Corbusier; all perpetuate the myth of memory as installed for keeps, so to speak, in the heart of a metropolis that is (finally) rendered significant and speaking to its people.

Of course with modernism, a slightly different twist was given to the idea of the memory map, even as to the monuments that signified it. For the modernists made no secret of their desire to forget as well as to remember; to forget the old city, its old monuments, its traditional significance, which were all seen as being too implicated with the economic, social, political, and medical problems of the old world to justify retention. Such a forgetting would, in Le Corbusier's case, take the form of erasure, literal and figural, of the city itself, in favor of a tabula rasa that reinstalled nature as a foundation for a dispersed urbanism and made its monuments out of the functions of modern life—the bureaucratic skyscrapers. Some have called this an antiurban vision; I would suggest that its dialectical opposition in form rendered it no more than another version of urbanism, symmetrical but counter to that of the nineteenth century.

But while the models proposed for the modern *urbs* departed very little in form and spirit from those of earlier centuries, even, as in the Ville Radieuse, maintaining that central reference point, the body, as motif and organizing principle, modernism did introduce a profoundly destabilizing concept into the general idea of memory. Forgetting, after all, is a more complex activity than simply not remembering; it implies a number of procedures, from the proleptic projection explored by Proust, who, ever nostalgic for a moment that points forward to an event that never happened, founded his "search for lost time" on a systematic process of forgetting what happened, to the nihilation described by Nietzsche and elaborated by Sartre that is the foundation of an existential comprehension of the self and the world. Paul de Man has demonstrated that Proust, who, in the guise of the narrator Marcel, consistently "remembers" something only to claim that "later on he understood" it in a different light, in fact does this only at the expense of forgetting or obliterating himself as author, in favor of an allegorical narrator who, unlike Proust, might plausibly be understood to believe that this "later on" was indeed located in his own past. Such an abyss of remembering erases as much as it traces; and, indeed, the traces of erasure form a kind of negative path, a route of obliteration into a past that is, for the modernist after Bergson, always a present as well as an anticipation of a future.

Sartre thematized this in his celebrated image of the Parisian café. Questioning the relationship of negative judgment to nonbeing, he demonstrated that in fact nonbeing is not a result of a negative judgment—for example the self-conscious nihilation of something into nothing—but rather that nonbeing brings into being a negative judgment; nonbeing, that is, is the essential presupposition for a negative judgment. Thus Pierre who is not in the café: Sartre arrives at the café a quarter of an hour late for a four-fifteen appointment with Pierre. Pierre, who is always punctual, is not in fact there, and Sartre realizes this. Is this a negation founded on judgment or intuition? Certainly the café is a "fullness of being"; "its patrons, its tables, its booths, its mirrors, its light, its smoky atmosphere, and the sounds of voices, rattling saucers, and footsteps which fill it" attest to this. Likewise, Pierre, somewhere else unknown, is also a fullness of being. But in all perception there must be a figure on a ground, so if all is fullness of being there can be no ground and therefore no perception. The café, as Sartre enters it, is immediately organized *with respect to his search for Pierre on entering* as such a ground:

This organization of the café as the ground is an original nihilation. Each element of the setting, a person, a table, a chair, attempts to isolate itself, to lift itself upon the ground constituted by the totality of the other objects, only to fall back once more into the undifferentiation of the ground; it melts into the ground. For the ground is that which is seen only in addition, that which is the object of a purely marginal attention. Thus the original nihilation of all the figures which appear and are swallowed up in the total neutrality of a *ground* is the necessary condition for the appearance of the principal figure, which is here the person of Pierre.[4]

But while all this is given to the intuition, and would be so to speak fulfilled as ground with the solid appearance of Pierre, organizing the café around his presence, Pierre is, in fact, not there. His absence is everywhere in the café, a café that remains a ground in the face of his absence, presenting "this figure which slips constantly between my look and the solid, real objects of the café" and which is, precisely, a "perpetual disappearance." "Pierre raising himself as nothingness on the ground of the nihilation of the café" is offered to Sartre's intuition as the apprehension of a double negation: the expectation of seeing Pierre, the subsequent adjustment of the café as ground, its primary nihilation, causes the absence of Pierre, which happens as a real event, and thereby a second negation. "Pierre absent haunts this café and is the condition of its self-nihilating organization as ground."

This description of the double nihilation precipitated by expectation within a world that potentially exhibits the fullness of being, but which turns out to be haunted by absence instead, seems to me to operate, if not philosophically, certainly in a literary way as a parable of the dislocation of memory in the modern city. That the models of urbanism proposed by architects of the modern movement seemed to ignore such a process only indicates the extent to which they were the prisoners of the classical belief that judgment precipitates positive or negative being and not the other way round. One could say, indeed, that the modern architects entered the old city much in the same way as Sartre the Deux Magots café, in the expectation of finding modernism there; they were certainly late, they knew this, and were certain that modernity, preparing itself for more than a century, must be already there. With this expectation they regarded the old city, which immediately organized itself into the ground ready to receive modernity as figure. The city first nihilated remained in a constant state of nihilation in the face of a modernity that, as we now know, was never really there, save as an absent presence, haunting the old ground as Pierre's haunted the café. Founded thus on a double nihilation, it was no accident that modernism, where precipitated by the anxious architect, was instantly seen as the *not-modern,* or the modern *not there,* itself old and already obsolescent before its life had begun.

For no matter what the future imagined by the modernists, the figure of proleptic projection determined their efforts, a double figure including that of prolepsis, or the representation of something in the future as already done, and projection, in which objecting arguments are anticipated in order to preclude their use. The modernist, entering the café of the old city, sought the solid presence of the future, a future that was not there because already past, and in its absence the modernist attempted to state it in terms that would anticipate *its* nihilation by future objections or arguments against it. Thence the intersection of urbanism and modernism: both employed the figure, literal and metaphorical, of projection, a mechanism learned from cartography and applied by architecture since the reinvention of perspective.

The transformation of the perspective city to the figure-ground city, the Renaissance city to the modernist city, did however involve a rupture of a certain sort: where the perspective city proposed a delicate balance between two equally significant fullnesses of being— the city as such and its monuments—the one subsumed in the mental envelope of the other, the figure-ground city of modernism was founded on the erasure of two fullnesses of being, that is to say on what Peter Eisenman has termed "the presence of absence."

The angry discomfort felt at this double absence, the letdown felt by Sartre because Pierre, who was always punctual, was not in fact there, is, I believe, involved in the impossible nostalgia of postmodern attempts to retrieve fullness of being by retrospective memory, by a process much like that hazarded by Proust: the nostalgia for a moment that points forward to an event that never happened. But this attempt is profoundly altered by the very negations of modernism: the old city, doubly negated, presents itself to the postmodernist as a haunting absence, not a haunting presence. The invention of a supposed presence to stand in for this ghost can hardly result in more than a third negation, that what is being proposed as presence is neither the absence of the modern nor the presence of the past. It cannot be the absence of the modern for obvious reasons; it cannot be the presence of the past, because the past has no presence save in a retrospective memory that searches for something in the past that would have predetermined a future—somewhat in the same way that the predictions of a scientist in the time of Copernicus might now be discovered by a historian as fixing the date of return for a comet that indeed has returned, but by virtue of that "has" is now in the past. Shaky ground on which to build a secure domestic future for mankind.

Rather than such an attempt, which with Paul de Man we might characterize in Nietzschean terms as "the endlessly repeated gesture of the artist 'who does not learn from experience and always falls into the same trap,'" in the allegory of errors constituted by postmodernism, I would suggest that we are in fact in the process of entering a very different café from one faked up to look as if it had always been there. This café I would describe in very similar terms to Sartre's; indeed it looks about the same, perhaps a little more time-worn, chairs falling apart, waiters long past their prime, a café definitely in decline and with the air of having seen better years. But of course we enter it without expectation, crossing the threshold with no sense that we are going to find anything there. Certainly if Pierre was expected we have long given up hope that he would ever arrive; certainly, too, we cannot be sure that Pierre was ever there, perhaps he was no more than a fiction of our imagination. Our lack of expectation is countered by the café, which rises up toward us in implacable reinforcement that we were right not to expect anything, that nothing here is of interest. Like the narrator of Peter Handke's novel *Across,* we enter this room simply to relax and not be noticed, to become ourselves ground in the ground:

After a day of working alone, it does me good to go to some cafe, if only because of the place names that are dropped here and there in the table conversation: Mauterndorf, Abtenau, Gerlin, Iben. There, in my weariness, I manage to show that glimmer of interest in everything around me that makes me, or so I believe, inconspicuous; no one, I feel sure, will turn to me, let alone against me. When I leave, no one will talk about me. But my presence will have been noticed.

This narrator, significantly enough, tells us that, archaeologist, he has been all his life a seeker after thresholds, looking on digs "less for what was there than for what was missing, for what had vanished irretrievably—whether carried or merely rotting away—but was still present as a vacuum, as empty space or empty form." In this pursuit he acquired "an eye for transitions," became a finder of traces— "hollows, color gaps and traces of wood." For him, however, such thresholds do not simply refer to something else—the door or the gate—as a metonymy, the part standing for the whole, but rather they are zones or places in themselves, "a place of testing or of safety."

Isn't the ash heap where Job sits in his misery a threshold, a place of testing? Didn't a fugitive put himself under someone's protection by sitting down on his threshold?

In the modern world, of course, he admits there are no such certain thresholds, save perhaps between waking and dreaming:

Only in the insane does it protrude, visible to all, into daytime experience, like the fragments of the destroyed temples just mentioned. For a threshold . . . is not a boundary—boundaries are on the increase both in inner and outer life—but a precinct. The word "threshold" embraces transformation, floor, river crossing, mountain pass, enclosure. . . . But where nowadays are we to find thresholds if not in ourselves?[5]

Thresholds in these senses are both ancient (real) and modern (imaginary); they can still be found in the country and in nature: in the city "they are forgotten." But of course, Handke's city is full of thresholds, each one announcing an entrance that is in fact a passage, a place of transition, one that, defined between other places, can take on no certain character of its own, like the café between work and sleep.

Something of this sensibility, I think, marks a number of cultural observations of the contemporary city: films like *True Stories, The Last Picture Show,* or, more melodramatically, *Blade Runner* or *Clockwork Orange.* In this city, where suburb, strip, and urban center have merged indistinguishably into a series of states of mind and which is marked by no systematic map that might be carried in the memory, we wander, like Freud in Genoa, surprised but not shocked by the continuous repetition of the same, the continuous movement *across* already vanished thresholds that leave only traces of their former status as places. Amidst the ruins of monuments no longer significant because deprived of their systematic status, and often of their corporeality, walking on the dust of inscriptions no longer decipherable because lacking so many words, whether carved in stone or shaped in neon, we cross nothing to go nowhere.

This sensibility, so far removed from Sartre's optimistic nihilism in presence, we might term posturbanism. No longer "urbanism," because without proleptic projective vision; but certainly after such an urbanism, posturbanism stands clearly distinct from other sensibilities of the fragmentary, the chance, and the marginal. Previous sensibilities of the edge—whether Baudelaire's *banlieue* or Apollinaire's *zone*—have had as their referent a positive if not aggressive urbanism, one that threatened the edge and would swallow it within a system of coherences; the edge for the symbolists and the early modernists was thereby a place of release, a potential for another order, whether of nostalgic remains, destructive forces, or difference. Thus the traditional modernist call for "survival in the cracks," that Brechtian heroism of the "City Dweller" who is encouraged to "cover his tracks":

Part from your friends at the station
Enter the city in the morning with your coat buttoned up
Look for a room, and when your friend knocks:
Do not, oh do not, open the door
But
Cover your tracks.

Such tactics presupposed an underground existence with everything "gone to ground," so to speak, with no figural identity above ground; even to identify the survivor as lone antihero becomes an impossibility. In order to take Brecht's advice that

when you come to think of dying [see]
That no gravestone stands and betrays you where you lie
With a clear inscription to denounce you
And the year of your death to give you away,[6]

a clear distinction has to exist between the memorial inscription and its absence. In the posturban domain, however, we are in the realm no longer of inscriptions, lasting epigrams to the memory of people and events, but of *hypograms,* those subtexts or infratexts posited by Saussure as tropes that indicate at once signature and its erasure, prosopopeia and apostrophe, all under the sign of catachresis. Perhaps we have truly entered that city without names, described in Robert Musil's *The Man without Qualities,* where "no special significance should be attached to the name of the city. Like all big cities it consisted of irregularity, change, sliding forward, not keeping in step, collisions of things and affairs, and fathomless points of silence in between."[7] In the posturban sensibility, the margins have entirely invaded the center and disseminated its focus; "in" indeed is hard to find, under the arches and along the walls of *Down by Law,* or in the mental slippages of *Blue Velvet.* In this last film, the total breakdown of a determined sense of Bachelard's "coefficient of adversity" is marked by the continuous sliding between states of terror, amusement, and sheer banality.

This condition is, of course, given heightened significance by the loss of the original ordering device mustered for every traditional city: that of the body itself, the original paradigm of order for urbanism as for architecture. From Francesco di Giorgio's explicit analogies to Le Corbusier's direct "imitation" of Vitruvian bodily perfection in the model layout of the Ville Radieuse, the body has provided the organic tissue, so to speak, by which the city might be recognized, memorized, and thereby lived. The bond between "body politic" and the city was, for the humanist tradition at least, more than a simple comparison. The psychological consequences of the loss of such a guiding metaphor can only be approached through the notion of homesickness, the desire to return to a once-safe interior.

The political consequences of the loss of the bodily paradigm, however, are less clear. Certainly humanists and urbanists would argue that the end of urbanism also signifies the end of liberal humanism, of social conscience and a belief in the (naturally good) public realm. But it is at least arguable that in the face of the rigorous exclusions operated by urbanism at its most idealistic, and the economic supports it demanded at its most realistic, a posturbanist world would perhaps offer more inclusivity if less grand hope. Indeed, our posturban café might shelter many of those so long undesirable to urbanism: undesirable because of gender, race, or class.

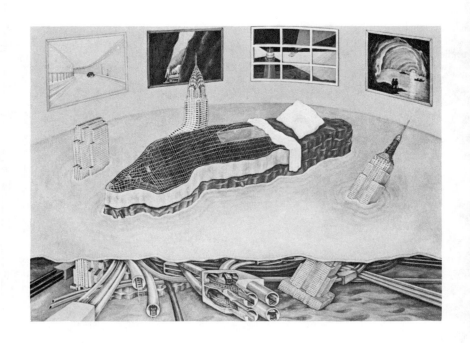

Psychometropolis

One is an artist at the cost of regarding that which all nonartists call "form" as "content," as "the matter itself." To be sure, then one belongs in a topsy-turvy world: for henceforth content becomes something merely formal—our life included.

Friedrich Nietzsche, The Will to Power

The idea of a "modern" architecture, at least insofar as it was consciously identified with the idea of the avant-garde, held two dominant themes in precarious balance. The one, stemming from the demand for cultural revolution and a sense of the exhaustion of traditional academic forms, stressed the need to remake the language of the art, to explode the conventions and out of the debris to construct a way of speaking adequate to the modern moment. The other, more tied to the tradition of utopian and materialist attempts to refashion the social world, called for a political and economic transformation that would precipitate society into a life of harmony in the new industrial epoch. Both were permeated with historicist notions of progress, inevitable development, and the *Zeitgeist*, ideas that served, for a brief period, to hold the two tendencies in tandem without apparent contradiction. Whether the "modernity" espoused was Corbusian and idealistic or Marxian and materialistic, the common cause was to reformulate language and society together: as Le Corbusier wrote to Karel Teige in 1929, "we are all at this moment at the foot of the same wall."[1]

So strong was the assumed interdependence of formal and social change that, for many decades since the collapse of the fragile treaty that linked them beneath the sign of post–World War I reconstruction, the mere promise of a new language has been seen as politically threatening, while successive attempts to postulate political utopias have all questioned the existing language of forms. As Roland Barthes noted in his inaugural address to the Collège de France, "'To change language,' that Mallarméan expression, is a concomitant of 'to change the world,' that Marxian one."[2]

In one sense, of course, this is true: no one is immune to the techniques of modernism cleverly deployed. The surrealist transposition, the formalist shock, the metaphysical "heightening of experience," the materialist deidealization, all these maneuvers and many more have their place in the repertoire of contemporary effects, whether commercially useful or culturally disjunctive. But in another sense, the simple utilization of technique, no matter how well calculated, does not in fact lead inevitably to cultural *or* political estrangement: the comforting image play of many late surrealist and recent postmodernist works bears this out. For technique in and of itself, as Clement Greenberg pointed out in the late thirties, is no more than academic and very quickly becomes kitsch. Equally, the isolation of programmatic concerns, whether reformist or revolutionary, tends toward the establishment of a kind of social positivism that, whether embodied in the zoning code or the Five-Year Plan, divorces art from social change in a way that seems to preclude any possible connection. Certainly the last decade has demonstrated the distinct separation of these two concerns, formal and programmatic, so difficultly held together by modernism. Any attempt to work on the language has, despite its own best intentions, been consumed with every other imagery; any political stance with the slightest pretension to positive effectiveness has been force to deny its "aesthetic" potentiality.

Architecture, oscillating between the endless play of formal images and the economic determinism of property and space allocation, has uneasily responded to this condition. On the one hand there have emerged voices that are committed to the internal exploration of languages; on the other there are those who recognize only the certainty of social democratic forces that predetermine the bulk, the place, and ultimately the form of building. No matter how the divide is bridged—by idealism, hermeneutics, or economics—the gap between modernist form and modernist ideology seems to be reaffirmed and a part of the inevitable conditions of the postmodern era.

The work of the Office of Metropolitan Architecture (OMA), a firm named as if to confront the modern crisis head on and fearlessly, has always resisted this great divide between program and form, social text and artistic technique. From the first narrative paintings of Madelon Vriesendorp and their accompanying texts, the conceptual project of OMA has tried to weld text and image in a reciprocal dance, a dance that in its various steps mirrors the lusts, atavisms, hopes, and horrors of the modern metropolis par excellence: New York. This project has obvious links to well-known modernist techniques, surrealist and metaphysical, but differs from these antecedents by virtue of a persistent irony that undermines both the positive and negative dialectics of the twenties in an endless play of disruptions and subversions. The techniques are, in a real sense, deployed against themselves. Thus, against the youth and fitness cults of the 1920s, and noting the desperate need for constructivist utopians to leave their homeland after 1932, the *Floating Pool* and its indefatigable swimmers (1977), backing stroke by stroke toward the center of capitalist corruption: a center of dreams realized but changed in the realization, which afforded in itself no salvation for the unsalvageable hopes of modernism. Against the pale ideals of the Great Society programs, a *Welfare Palace Hotel* (1976). It is indeed a place for the people of William Burroughs, but one they would perhaps abhor out of scorn—a Grand Hotel criticized by its guests, even. Against the mass housing projects of the twenties, and the rental speculations of the more recent past, a gigantic enigma, *The Hotel Sphinx* (1975–1976), dedicated to the delivery of cosmetic bliss. All these are projects composed under the sign of the need to escape and its impossibility.

Irony is a rhetorical figure that, in its common definition, operates by means of a mocking, pleasant or serious, of the subject: in the words of a nineteenth-century theorist of rhetoric (Fontanier), "it seems to belong most particularly to gaiety; but anger and contempt also use it sometimes, even to advantage; consequently it can enter into the noblest style and the gravest of subjects."[3] As a dominant figure of speech and mode of thought throughout the modern period, irony, naive or subtle, has permeated almost every discourse, including that of architecture. The most hopeful utopias, from Fourier to Le Corbusier, were at best saturated with ironic defense against their possible, perhaps inevitable failure. As a technique, irony would appear empty, and open to deployment by almost any ideological stance; but in itself, and because of its particular structure—the way in which it operates on text and images—it is deeply antipositivist. As the historian Hayden White has noted, "as the basis of a world view, irony tends to dissolve all belief in the possibility of positive social actions. In its apprehension of the essential folly or absurdity of the human condition it tends to engender belief in the 'madness' of civilization itself and to inspire a mandarin-like disdain for those seeking to grasp the nature of social reality in either science or art."[4] But this kind of irony, the wit of the self-conscious mind, was itself put into question by the total ironism of Nietzsche—a "world historical irony," as he called it, that even destroyed the pretensions to positivity of irony itself. Many of the avant-garde movements from dada to situationism were founded on this type of ironic awareness, the irritation of critical self-consciousness against the primordial socratic "certainty in doubt."

Irony is certainly the figurative mode of the early works of OMA and of the work that, more than any other, served to give these works a coherent "program" of their own: Rem Koolhaas's *Delirious New York*.[5] This book, with its unabashed postscript of OMA images and texts, is equally unabashed in its choice of subject matter and formal strategies, both of which are borrowed from a long tradition of modernist work on metropolis. In it is displayed a sophisticated knowledge of all the techniques by which the modern city, as unconscious artifact, was to be transformed into the self-conscious agony of the avant-garde: the sociology and psychopathology of metropolis advanced by Georg Simmel, Sigmund Freud, and Emile Durkheim; the technical ideology of metropolis from Otto Wagner to Le Corbusier; and, just as important, the mythic structure of metropolis, assayed by Baudelaire in *Le Spleen de Paris* (1855–1865) and brought to a high art of montage in the filmic texts of Walter Benjamin. This, from the hands of Rem Koolhaas, a former film maker and script writer, was predictable. What was not was the way in which these borrowings were themselves ironically subverted by the subjects treated. For how should we laugh, for example, at the spectacle of positive projects like that of the "Fighting the Flames" event on Coney Island juxtaposed to the actual fire that destroyed the fairground in 1911, a fair created for pleasure at the expense of the masses and contrasting with their degradation? Political irony, surrealist irony, supreme irony, but this, when juxtaposed to the future projects of pleasure and economic gain in Manhattan, exposed finally as nonironic. On the one hand, the facts of the case, set out with bald titles—"Foundation," "Fire," "End"; on the other, the juxtaposition—itself a time-honored montage technique—that throws everything, including the stance of the author, into doubt.

This, one might think, would make excellent, dryly humorous reading, but would not necessarily provide the foundations for any kind of building. It would seem that the very choice of such techniques arms the critically self-conscious writer against the fate of the avant-garde architect. We look for no Welfare Palace Hotel to be built on landfill—indeed, we hope for none; the irony would only operate if the mental rather than the physical image remains intact.

But build OMA will, and, side by side with the early studies in *Witz*, a number of serious projects have emerged, for hotels, resorts, condominiums, office buildings, residences, and even prisons and parliament houses. Not the stuff of irony, surely. Yet in a subtle and intriguing way, OMA has succeeded in maintaining its dominant figure, through the subjects of its new building activity. And this time it is sustained not simply by the nature of the drawing and the narrative; nor are we presented with elaborate scenarios of actions side by side with their illustration. The drawings, it is true, are exquisite, but they are in no sense the surrealistic machines of urban wit previously painted by Madelon Vriesendorp. Rather they are ruthlessly "scientific," the results of calculation and computer graphics. View after view, cutting through the received angle of vision simply by virtue of the flexibility of the machine. Analysis of sight lines, of massing, of the movement of people and objects takes its place beside the most accurate representation of reality available. These are no longer the transformations of formalist technique, dedicated to destroying our commonplaces by the unexpected, but more the realism of a natural vision, deployed ruthlessly to tell us how, indeed, it would look.

The irony no longer resides in the shock of representation, nor in the juxtaposition of text and image; it is in a real sense embodied in the formal structure of the works themselves. In these projects, almost without exception, there is a determination to absorb the didactic "form" of modern movement programmatics—the zoning code, the program itself—into the form of the building. In this process, the ultimate absurdity of the juxtapositions predicated by zoning—life/work/recreation—is exploited as a "formal" device. Modernist classificatory codes and modernist aesthetics are seen as proposing fundamentally the same "form." Thus in the scheme for the resort hotel on the island of Lesbos in Greece, the "ridiculous" separations of the different functions are pointed and emphasized as strategies in themselves. The interweaving of public and private in the Dublin Prime Minister's residence is similarly given a formal demonstration, as is the movement of the viewer around the Rotterdam apartment blocks, incorporated into the form of the towers. Functionalism here finds its expression but in an ironic manner. For these contaminations between text and image, program and form, are not developed in order to make us entirely comfortable with the architectural "resolution" of a problem. The questions of relationship between people, ideas, and buildings that arise in the normal design problem are not overcome here in any positive way. In the design for 16 villas on the island of Antiparos in Greece (1981; Elia Zenghelis, principal), the environment of Greece is not overly protected by an appeal to roots, to the vernacular, nor is it deliberately shocked by the superimposition of a "modern" object. Rather, what in experience seems to be the innocent result of contextualism becomes in plan, as painted by Zoe Zenghelis, a powerful exercise in suprematism.

In this series of projects, the references to constructivism, to the vocabulary of the late modern movement, are even clearer than in the early parodic paintings; but the measure of their difference is that they do not in themselves provide any explanatory key. Style, in the art historical sense, is rendered inoperative as an analytical device. The projects might *look* like this or that modern precedent; however, they are not, for all that, repetitions or even extensions of the modernism of the twenties and thirties. The explanation, insofar as such ironic projects allow of any, is to be found more than ever in the "nature of the project," in its idea, its fundamental aim to disrupt all previous "natures."

Perhaps a key to reading these projects might be found in the apparently obvious scheme for the renovation of a "panoptical" prison at Arnhem (1979–1980); Rem Koolhaas, principal). On one level—that is, on the level of the pictorial image—this would seem to be no more than liberal "canceling" of the old, panoptical functions of the prison. So the text of the architect tells us: the axis has cut through the all-seeing center, the heart of the disciplinary apparatus has been torn out. The postpanoptical spirit has destroyed the panoptical one. Here we find echoes of a reading of Michel Foucault, whose studies of discipline and power have strongly influenced the politics and strategies of OMA's generation. However, this would be a vulgarization of the appeal made by Foucault to the Panopticon as a physical form.

Foucault himself resisted all such reductions in favor of a generalized perception that sees in each and every act of reform a pervasive will to power. This will finds its capillary-like paths through every crack of least resistance, both institutional and environmental. The actual scheme of Bentham's Panopticon in such a prescription is only the emblem or caricature of an all-embracing system of power, institutional from the outside and psychological from the inside. According to this formulation, the act of OMA would simply read as a displacement of one form of power by another; there would be no loss of energy, no effective change, save in the outer form. A cynical mind would even perceive the superimposition of cross over circle as a restoration of another kind of power, religious over secular. But this interpretation would ignore the fact that, for the architects of OMA, all this is known and understood; in fact it is with these perceptions, in the space marked out by Foucault after Nietzsche, that the project has been conceived. That is why, for example, the organization of the new prison disappears underground and operates for all the world like the prehistory of the old; it stands, so to speak, for the archaeology of the ruined prison itself.

Should this complicated set of negations and counternegations be interpreted as anything more than dried-out cynicism, a loss of faith in modernism, while employing the husks of modernist forms? Should we conclude that irony, when wielded against itself, turns into nihilism, or, worse, into postmodernism? A partial answer would be implied in the texts on which these designs rest their case: the writings of Roland Barthes and the philosophy of Foucault. For it is under these signs that modernism, in the present, continues to operate, not as kitsch but as work.

It was Foucault who, in an early essay entitled "Language to Infinity" (1963), spoke of the transformation of myth into literature, of "Homer" into the "Marquis de Sade," of the complete heroic work into the infinite whispering of writing, of rhetoric into the library.[6] Barthes in his meditation on the "languages" invented by Saint Ignatius of Loyola to "speak" to God, by de Sade to "speak" of sexuality, and by Fourier to "speak of social harmony"—all impossible projects demanding new languages doomed to speak to no one—developed Foucault's theme.[7] Both Foucault and Barthes, sensitive to the world after Nietzsche—the former by positive reflection, the latter by writing itself—have opened the possibility of what one might call a "restricted modernism." Such a restrained art, conscious of its loss of positive ground yet intimately aware of its own procedures, is bound to speak, even though the results are not only unpredictable but also impossible to endow with any unitary purpose.

In this context OMA refuses the positive inquiry into semantics, the structural semiotics that have characterized so many attempts to develop "true" languages in recent years. Nor does it intend to anthropologize its productions with a false mask of humanism, for it affirms the complete independence of image and society. Similarly, the linguistic analogy, while affording valuable insights into the operation of signs in the classical world, no longer holds an absolute interpretative value. Even the space marked out by Nietzsche, which provided so powerful an incentive for Foucault, no longer seems for OMA an adequate space of architectural production.

Neither "words in liberty" nor the endless play of figurative mechanisms revealed as "truth" by contemporary philosophy of language operates as an effective code for inserting irony into life's present conditions. Irony, as Søren Kierkegaard observed, is inexhaustible as technique and as figure. Its effect, calculated but unexpected, is to produce results "negatively." This, of course, was one of modernism's own utopias as it attempted to reveal the reality behind appearances. But the dominance of irony was perhaps not fully realized until these utopias too had been proved barren.

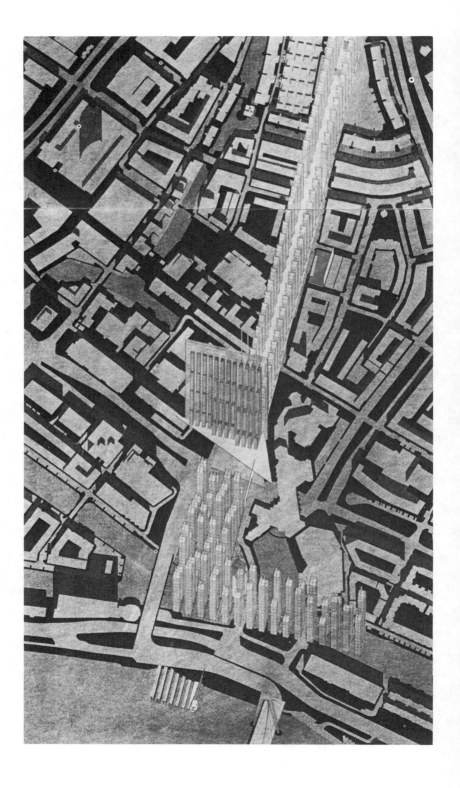

Oneirism

I am an ephemeral and not too discontent citizen of a raw modern city.
Rimbaud, Les Illuminations

The form of a city, Baudelaire noted with irony and some nostalgia in the face of Haussmann's reconstructive fury, changes more quickly than the heart of a mortal. But, as successive "modernisms" and "countermodernisms" have demonstrated, often the heart changes even more quickly than the city itself. Le Corbusier's impatience at the obstinate survival of old Paris—"Imagine all this junk, which till now has lain spread out over the soil like a dry crust, cleaned off and carted away"[1]—is only one extreme example of the radical shifts in sensibility toward the city in this century, shifts that have more often than not been resisted by the intractable nature of the existing urban fabric. More recently, debates over the fate of the "historical" city, whether couched in terms of Rossi's neorationalism or Krier's neo-classicism, have themselves foundered over the unwillingness of cities to be turned into historical museums of themselves. Maurice Halbwachs's observation that "the stones of the city . . . have a fixed place and are as attached to the ground as trees and rocks," that "Paris and Rome . . . seem to have crossed the centuries without the continuity of their life having been interrupted for a single minute," remarks written during the Second World War, seem to attest to this durability of the city, its incorrigible will to live its past in full modernity.[2]

A contemporary philosopher of urban architecture is faced then, at the end of the twentieth century, not so much with the absolute dialectic of ancient and modern posed by the avant- and rear gardes of the last eighty years, as with the more subtle and difficult task of calculating the limits of intervention according to the *resistance* of the city to change. And, as writers from Rimbaud to Julien Gracq have perceived, this resistance is not only one of stone but also, and perhaps more importantly, of mentality. In Halbwachs's words, "spatial images play such a role in the collective memory. The place occupied by a group is not like a chalkboard on which one writes, and then erases, numbers and figures."[3] The blackboard, after all, remains profoundly indifferent to the figures inscribed on its surface, while a place receives the imprint of a group, and vice versa—a salutary caution to the urban architect in front of a seemingly passive plan of streets and houses.

In the development of such a sensibility to the limits of urban change, the projects of Wiel Arets stand as evocative experiments in the intersection of the mental and the physical. From the outset, in the urban block projects designed with Wim van den Bergh (1984–1985), the traditional modern dialectic between ideal type and real context has been avoided, or rather replaced, by a more complex intercalation of intellectual narrative and material proposition. Here the city, as existing, stands as the object and generator of so many possible futures, each calculated according to the nature of its opposition to those futures. The architectural project, while crystallizing one or more of these futures, is then presented to the city, so to speak, as a whole, not as a replacement or substitute, as in the utopian urbanism of modernism, but as material to be submitted to the life and consuming power of the context. Apparently totalizing "types" will thereby inevitably be fragmented by the counterforce of the site. Thus the social "resistance" of their Moscow tower housing, imagined for a dissident population at the heart of the old city, is doubled and reciprocated by the city itself, in such a way that architecture, defining its own limits, a bulwark against the world, is in turn limited and partially invaded by its surroundings. Here Arets and van den Bergh have at once refused the image of a "modern" superimposed on a tabula rasa, or raised above it on pilotis, and also rejected any comforting simulacrum of a historical context. Their vocabulary belongs resolutely to a century of technological change, echoing while not imitating the already historicized language of the first avant-garde; but their strategy is built on a countermodern heritage, out of the

Illuminations of Rimbaud, the *vases-communicantes* of Breton, the *flâ-nerie* of Aragon and Benjamin, and, of course, the hallucinatory world of Roussel's *Locus solus*. Their contemporary "urban imaginary" is thus fabricated out of the dialectic between memory, as defined in the long post-Bergsonian tradition, and situation, as phenomenologically described by writers from Bachelard to Lefebvre.

This dialectic is perhaps most clearly evident in the later project by Arets and Joost Meuwissen for the "completion" of the Ca' Venier dei Leoni, the home of the Peggy Guggenheim collection in Venice. The historical foundations of this project, the "sea story" of an eighteenth-century palace, the very scale of which seemed already to have forbidden its completion, is here taken for the ground of a scheme intended to pay homage to two denizens of the collective memory of Venice, the musicians Franz Liszt and Richard Wagner. Physically ephemeral but mentally eternal, music becomes the preferred figure for this apparently absurd erection of (Otto) Wagnerian towers on a classical base; in one sense, both base and superstructure are mutually exclusive—if one exists, the other must be fiction—but on another level, their solid juxtaposition throws into relief the precise nature of Arets's art of memory, the forced reconciliation of present and past in an image that refuses any reduction to one or the other.

These almost archaeological superpositions, similar to those that Freud articulated in the realm of Roman memory, where two contents that *spatially* would find it impossible to locate in the same place find their reconciliation in the mind, are extended into images of territorial occupation in the OFI-sportscentre and the Columbusworld projects, again by Arets and Wim van den Bergh. In these designs, sited on apparently open ground, the land in fact plays the role we have ascribed to the city as at once ground and formidable opponent, filled equally with memory—the collective memory, as it were, of the landscape, for Greek athletics on the island of Crete, for Columbus and his discoveries in Portugal. In this latter project, which recalls Le Corbusier and Paul Otlet's vision of a Mundaneum, the attempt is to construct a form of contemporary memory theater, along the lines suggested by Giordano Bruno, that will allow the visitor to trace the multiple paths offered by the idea of Columbus, paths that both echo a history and propose a future.

Whether in city or country, these designs seem conscious of the special psychogeography of places—that complex mixture of memory, experience, and space intimated by the situationists in the late 1950s and theorized by Henri Lefebvre—in contrast to the mechanical memory lifted from history by a postmodernism that relies more on quotation than on interior strategy.

And this consciousness, it must be said, is not allowed to remain in the domain of the pictorial but, in Arets's more recent projects, is itself forced into the physical domain with technical and formal mastery. Thus the remodeling of the House and Pharmacy of Brunssum, the Medical Centre and House at Hapert, the pharmacy Keent-Moesel at Weert Zuid, and, most importantly, the Medical Centre Weert, all display a drive toward a language of simplicity, realized with a deliberately reduced technological repertoire, that allows for elegant functional solution without impeding the play of memory and experience. In this sense, Arets's often-lauded "purity" approaches the "difficult simplicity" noted by Aldo Rossi in the geometrical reductions of Boullée, and evoked by Rossi himself in early projects for schools and houses. The deceptive absence of high architecture in these built designs serves to heighten the effect of what Le Corbusier unambiguously defined as the fundamental architectural elements— light and shade articulating masses and surfaces. Here the memory theater and the architectural object find their intersection in an unobtrusive typological imagination, one that, for example in the Pharmacy of Brunssum, underlines the virtues of the Corbusian Domino model by stressing the horizontal floors and framing all interior divisions in translucent glass block, but without destroying the nature of the existing pitched roof. Typology is confronted with context as a means of measuring, once more, the necessary recalcitrance of the already built. Other projects exhibit a similar attitude toward the typical, most especially the design for the Fashionshop in Maastricht, where the space of cultural consumption is articulated by architectural elements that resist the decorative or the stylistic in favor of a simple contrast between the "loft" volume and the vertical stair. Other not yet realized designs for domestic settings, such as the Villa Romanoff, Miami, continue this precise calibration of the minimum number of architectural events necessary at once to shelter function and to liberate thought.

Perhaps the most advanced combination of architectural typology and urban discourse is demonstrated in the design for Rotterdam's North Urban Core, proposed in the context of nine schemes commissioned by Architectural International Rotterdam for the "Railway Tunnel Site." A strongly modulated but delicately inserted string of architecturally defined types, composed of diverse combinations of glass towers echoing the first urban block projects, is deployed in a city whose fabric is entirely respected yet profoundly transformed. The long thin line of glass towers leads from the center to the river's edge, marking a route and a thought at one and the same time. Yet for all the powerful visual character of this intervention, the surrounding city is left untouched, save, of course, for the mental reverberations of this "translucent" machine. The metropolis as an architectural container for individual and collective memory, "a void which is only filled with thoughts," in Arets's words, takes on, in this project, a catalytic rather than an instrumental role. In lieu of the modernist "social condenser," calculated with Benthamite fervor to transform the daily life of the citizen according to fixed ideals of bourgeois reform, Arets envisions a shimmering and broken curtain of translucent walls that reverberate with the multiple "stimuli" observed by Georg Simmel as the leitmotivs of the "mental life" of metropolis.

But this substitution, one that affirms the possibilities for urban architecture at a moment when, politically and aesthetically, the modern tradition seems in defeat and disarray, is, by the same token, more than a literal recombination and recalculation of modern architectural types. Its strategy emerges here as even more important than any (less than final) result. For the practice outlined by Arets equally privileges city *void* and city *thoughts,* a difficult dialogue to sustain but one based on a belief in the permeability of things to ideas and ideas to things. No longer are things either the result of thoughts or their simple signifiers; rather they are constituted in that ambiguous realm of memory that is at once experience and recollection of experience in such way as to remain inseparable. Thus the early design for the Farsetti garden in the Veneto, founded on a narrative recalling both a description from de Tipaldo and the more recent "garden" imagined by Roussel, transforms a literary conceit into a spatial situation so as to permit the experience and re-creation of as many narratives as there are visitors. In the Columbusworld or the Translucent City projects, despite the almost anatomical attention to the delineation and program of each separate architectural event with its corresponding metaphorical referent, the resulting composition remains open to multiple interpretations. Architecture, creating situations or events, demands a fictional starting point; the city, an "accumulation of effects whose causes are reversed," refuses any such limitation on its freedom to reconstruct the imaginary.

In other terms we might understand this procedure, so self-consciously developed by Arets, as a deliberate merging of the *locus solus* invented by the architect and the *locus suspectus,* or haunted site, of the city, a recognition that architecture and lived experience share the same sources. In this conflation, the traditional opposition between an ideal project and its real application is overcome by the essential *complicity* of the architect's project and the collective memory from which it derives. In the *unheimlich* environment that is thereby created, we might imagine that Arets's buildings take their place easily enough amidst the cacophony of walls and spaces that suffice to indicate the memory of a city; that they, following from and juxtaposed to the concrete evidence of prior imaginaries, will in turn stimulate their own; that walking in them, in the steps of Julien Gracq, we might for a moment find as much permanence in the city as in the heart:

and the town, with me, changes and remodels itself, carves out its limits, deepens its perspectives, and on this course—a form open to all the impulses of the future, the only way in which it can be within me and be truly itself—it does not cease changing.[4]

Vagabond Architecture

"To glorify vagabondage and what one can call bohemianism."
Baudelaire, Mon coeur mis à nu

In a recent publication of a journey taken to the cities of Riga and
Vladivostock, John Hejduk once more, but in a significantly different
and highly developed form, has mustered up a tribe of architectural
animals, a traveling carnival of objects gradually assembled over the
last decade; a tribe that now seems infinitely extensible. This company, without which Hejduk never travels, is composed of veterans
of former voyages—many of the sixty-seven "victims" of Berlin reap-
pear here in different guises—together with new characters invented
for specific places visited and yet to be visited. In his own words:

This troupe accompanies me from city to city, from place to place, to cities
I have been to and cities I have not visited. The cast presents itself to a city
and its inhabitants. Some of the objects are built and remain in the city; some
are built for a time, then are dismantled and disappear; some are built,
dismantled, and move on to another city where they are reconstructed.[1]

Perhaps on one level we might interpret this apparently playful,
seemingly deliberately ephemeral construction of a traveling architecture as an example of what Jeffry Kipnis and David Shapiro have
recently noted as Hejduk's difficulty in joining, in agreeing; of his
relentless drive to distance himself from contemporary fashions. We
might also see in these movable objects a generalized critique of
conventional monumentality, of fixed urban architecture, in favor of
the mobile and the nomadic. Such a countermonumentality has, as
we know, a long tradition of supporters in modernism, from Le

Corbusier to Buckminster Fuller. The modern city dweller living in houses like tents (the Maison Domino), houses like cars (the Maison Citrohan), or more radically, houses like airplanes (the Maison Voisin), was the leitmotiv of a society (as envisaged by Le Corbusier, following the futurists) literally constituted by mobility. For progressive modernists, the traditional model of a house, "heavily attached to the earth by the depth of its foundations and the weight of its thick walls," "the symbol of immutability, *la maison natale, le berceau de la famille*," was obsolete. Such a characterization of modernity, of course, was equally the burden of conservative social critics from Heidegger to Sedlmayr, who had no hesitation in placing the blame for "the lost center" on architects like Ledoux whose spherical design for a house seemed for the first time to uproot the domicile from its proper foundations.

We might be tempted to place Hejduk's mobile "homes" in this tradition, somewhere between functionalist optimism and phenomenological nostalgia. But Hejduk's strange-looking characters on wheels defy rationalist classification—the list of "victims," for example, reads like some Borgesian elaboration of a "Chinese Encyclopedia"—even as they balk at incorporation into conservative regression. Hejduk's "mobility," both in *Victims* and in *Vladivostock,* is neither the simple and functionalist invention of a mobile or quasi-mobile architecture nor an oneiric counter to modern mobilization.

Indeed, his designs stand aggressively against both past and present, acting as catalysts for critique in each of the cities they visit. Here we think of the explicit reminders, in *Victims,* of the Holocaust and the sociocultural construction of cruelty. The site itself, we are told, "had formerly contained torture chamber during WWII"; it was now to be occupied, among other objects, by "houses" for "The Identity Card Man" and "The Keeper of the Records" and their offices— "Identity Card Unit," "Record Hall"—Kafkaesque figures certainly, but given unmistakable historical context by spaces such as the "Room for Those Who Looked the Other Way."[2] Such explicit references are confirmed by the entire population of victims—"The Disappeared," "The Exiles," and "The Dead." Representations of the repressed unsaid, they act as a perpetual reminder, a kind of memory theater, of the uncomfortable past, both in the sites they occupy and the forms they assume. These structures, accompanied by laconic tales assembled in the form of a diary that merges the everyday horrors of "the news" with memories of past atrocities, are hardly invitations to Heideggerian recuperation.

Hejduk's witty, quasi-anthropomorphic transmutations, which seem to belong to something like a Grandville cartoon come to life or the modern equivalent of a medieval joust or miracle play, are thus more than simple rhetorical figures of criticism, confined to a symbolic role. With an interpretation of *homo ludens* that approaches that of Huizinga, Hejduk's play is deadly serious; it invades and repopulates the cities en route; like an original carnival, his troupe overturns daily routines and commonplace thoughts, upsetting heirarchies and crowning fools. In fact Hejduk's horde contains its own threat: emulating those vagrants, vagabonds, and *strangers* that were so distinctly disquieting to nineteenth-century social order, it invades its "host" cities like a band of ruffians. They are not here today and gone tomorrow; rather, like Georg Simmel's "stranger," they come today and stay tomorrow. This refusal to be dislodged once arrived is the source of their willed unacceptability.

Hejduk in this way associates his work with a long poetic and political tradition that has found in the characteristics of vagabondage an inherent critique of social and legal norms. For, as we know, vagabondage has had a double face in the modern period: a social and legal construction of bourgeois society that endows a "person without estate, without domicile" with all the attributes of criminality, it is also—and for this very reason—a preferred role of the bohemian, the outcast artist, the rebellious poet. Hence the interrelated meanings of *vagabond* in French: from "whatever strays" (from the Latin *vagari,* "wandering about," as in St. Justinian's characterization of "savage nations" as "those vagabond peoples, without fixed abode"), the word shifts to the pejorative and the figurative (as in "unruly, without order," applied to persons and things and, importantly, to the imagination). Thus to have a "vagabond imagination" was the desired state of the poet.

As Kristin Ross has demonstrated, the link between poetic and literal vagabondage was, in the case of Rimbaud, more than metaphorical, as the poet searched relentlessly for "infinite walks, rests, trips, adventures, wanderings, *bohémienneries,*" with a sense of being constitutionally "dépaysé." In this, Rimbaud was less the romantic poet as outsider than a normal adolescent of his generation. Pointing out that in 1889 alone, over 600,000 had been characterized as juvenile vagrants, Ross situates the Rimbaud who asserted that he was "an ephemeral and not too discontent citizen of a crude metropolitan city" as a member of that class defined by Théodore Homberg in 1880 as "outside of the society that it frightens and repels . . . a class of individuals for whom there is no family, no regular work, no fixed domicile. That class is the class of vagabonds."[3] Vagabonds, then, were guilty of no crime but that of vagabondage; *potential* criminals, outside the law not for a crime committed but for what might be committed in the future as the product of a wayward life.

In thus identifying himself with the tradition of vagabondage, Hejduk seems self-consciously to activate all its potentially critical roles, roles that derive from the confrontation of a fixed context with an unfixed and roving subject. For, like the vagabonds they emulate, Hejduk's constructions literally construct "situations" from the part-random, part-preconceived intersection of objects and subjects, insistent provocateurs of the urban unconscious. In this context, we might see them as the heirs to a long tradition of investigating the critical power of such "situations," from poets like Baudelaire and Rimbaud to the surrealists and situationists. Opposed to late modernist visions of technological progress, Hejduk follows the surrealists as they attempted to counter the modernist utopias of the nomad; like the "nightwalker" of Aragon, peasant in the strange city, or the bohemian flaneur of Benjamin, Hejduk endows his characters with the pose of a vagabond at once literal and imaginary, a sensibility that actively reads a city. What Walter Benjamin once referred to as the "colportage de l'espace" ("the peddling of space"), in describing the experience of the flaneur, is now transformed into a "vagabond architecture" that transforms the city once more into an autocritical artifact. As Benjamin noted in the *Passagen-Werk*, "Have not its incessant vagabondages accustomed the city to proffer a new interpretation of its image everywhere? Does it not transform the passage into a casino, into a gaming house?"[4]

It was Apollinaire, in his countermanifesto *L'Antitradition futuriste* of 1913, who anticipated this consummately surrealist contribution to urban psychogeography when, under the heading "Construction," he noted: "Nomadisme épique exploratorisme urbain ART DES VOYAGES et des promenades."[5] Such voyages close to home, tourisms of the city, were thence to be explored by writers from Breton to Julien Gracq, Benjamin to Franz Hessel, their half-designed, half-oneiric situations framed by snapshots and marked by found objects. Even as, in Michel Beaujour's words, "*Nadja* is the tale of an ethnological expedition toward the interior of a singularly uncanny city, a haunted Paris that unveils its spells little by little, admits its periodic and ritual human sacrifices, proffers its possessed and its mirages,"[6] so Berlin, Riga, and Vladivostock are explored and settled by the uncanny objects of their (repressed) desire.

It is as if, by some disquieting automatism, Hejduk's players roam the city not so much like tourists but more in the manner of those little groups around Guy Debord in the late 1950s and early 1960s, *lettristes* and *situationnistes,* as they stumbled into the practice of the *dérive.* As described by Debord, the theory of the *dérive* included directions on the place of chance and the random in the planned, the type and duration of movement through the streets, the precise number of *dérivistes* to be included in the party, all toward the end of developing what was defined as "a mode of experimental behavior linked to the conditions of urban society, a technique of hasty passage through varied ambiances."[7] Such a walk, mingling wandering and wayward activity, merging meanings drawn from memory and chance as well as from random associations with encountered objects and people, was an elaborate technique collaged from surrealism, the sociopsychology of Henri Bergson and Maurice Halbwachs, and more "scientific" ways of measuring the use of urban space, as proposed, for example by the urbanist Chombart de Lauwe when he traced, in his *Paris et l'agglommeration parisienne,* the routes taken by a student of the 16th arrondissement in the space of a year.[8]

Against the Corbusian schemes of modern urban renewal, the situationists posed a new mental mapping of the city, attempting to redraw the officially defined *quartiers* to conform to more enduring mentalities tied to the space of Paris. Thus the attempt of December 1958 to construct a psychogeographic description of Les Halles by Abdelhafid Khatib, who discovered a "unity of ambiance" confirmed by the internal currents and exterior communications of Les Halles at night, laboriously mapping the paths of moving vehicles and people.[9] These "maps" provided a guide to the new "science" of psychogeography: "the study of the precise effects of the geographical milieu, consciously organized or not, acting directly on the affective behavior of individuals."[10] In this way the situationists built up literal collage-maps of Paris and investigated specific areas for their spatio-mental qualities.

But this activity was hardly passive: it relied equally on the possi-bility of "constructing situations," the primary sport of the situation-ist, situations that were themselves defined as "moments of life, concretely and deliberately constructed by the collective organization of a unitary ambiance and a play of events."[11] Armed with the tech-nique of *détournement,* which specialized in literally displacing and reinscribing meaning in objects and texts (the cartoon strip with its "detourned" word balloons ubiquitously populated the publications of the *Internationale situationniste*), the situationists carried on an in-tensive campaign against all the effects of "spectacular" culture, not-ably modern architecture and urbanism.

In his "Formula for a New Urbanism," Gilles Ivain railed against the boredom of the modern city. A new architecture was necessary in order to modify present conceptions of time and space, an archi-tecture that would be at once a means of knowledge and action: an experimental architecture that would itself know how to construct situations. Citing de Chirico, who "has attacked the problems of absences and presences through time and space," Ivain called for a new vision of time and space for architects of the future, embodied in symbolic buildings figuring the desires and mental powers—a kind of Fourierism in architecture—that would finally place "psychoanal-ysis in the service of architecture." He outlined the specifications for a new, countermodern town:

This town could be envisaged in the form of an arbitrary grouping of chateaux, grottoes, lakes, etc.

The quarters of this city could correspond to diverse catalogued feelings that one meets *by chance* in current life. Bizarre Quarter—Happy Quarter—particularly reserved for habitation—Noble and Tragic Quarter (for wise children)—Historic Quarter (museums, schools)—Useful Quarter (shops, shops for equipment)—Sinister Quarter, etc. Perhaps also a Quarter of Death, not to die in but to live in peace. . . . The Sinister Quarter for example will usefully replace these holes, hell mouths that peoples once possessed in their capitals; they symbolized the evil powers of life. The Sinister Quarter will have no need to shelter real dangers, such as traps, secret dungeons, or mines. It would be approached in a complicated way, frightfully decorated (loud whistles, alarm clocks, periodic sirens with irregular cadence, mon-strous sculptures, mechanical mobiles driven by motors called *Auto-Mobiles*) and lit poorly at night, as well as violently lit during the day by an abusive use of reflection. At the center, the "Square of the Terrifying Mobile." The saturation of the market by a product provokes the devaluation of this product; the child and the adult will learn by exploring the Sinister Quarter no longer to fear the anguishing manifestations of life, but to be amused by them. The principal activity of the inhabitants will be the CONTINUOUS DERIVE. The changing of landscape hour by hour will be responsible for a complete "dépaysement."[12]

The contradictions of this theory of architectural construction became only too clear when architects themselves attempted to realize such an "architecture of the *dérive.*" The different projects of Constant, for example, for gypsy camps, however influenced by the play models of Huizinga and the researches of Giuseppe Pinot-Gallizio, fell far short of the flexible, festive space he imagined. Equally, the architectural heirs to his New Babylon were, despite his call for "a new regard for social space," the technologically utopian "moving cities" of Archigram. Inevitably the demand for "a new creativity that is to manifest itself in daily life, by means of a continually varied arrangement of the environment, in harmony with a dynamic way of life" resulted in a privileging of literally mobile architecture, one as prone to panoptical implications as that which it apparently replaced. And yet Constant's description of the experience of the citizen in New Babylon seems to echo more Nietzschean ideals of labyrinthine wanderings, free from observation: "One can wander for prolonged periods through the interconnected sectors, entering into the adventure afforded by this unlimited labyrinth."[13] As described in the fourth number of the *Internationale situationniste,* Constant's "Yellow Sector" would shelter a complete "Zone of Play" where vast communal halls, "labyrinth houses" consisting of a large number of rooms of irregular form, stairs at angles, lost corners, open spaces, culs-de-sac, would provide places of adventure. Other spaces—the deaf room, fitted out in insulating materials; the screaming room, decorated in bright colors and loud sounds; the echo room; the room of images (cinematographic games); the room of reflection; the room of rest; the room of erotic play and psychological influences—would allow for the free play of the senses. "A long stay in these houses has the beneficent effect of a washing of the brain," concluded Constant.[14]

Such might well be a description of the city of Hejduk's imaginary, a countermodern psychogeographic situation, but with the significant difference that it would no longer be constructed out of the mental response of citizens subjected to the behavioral experiments of the architect, but now out of objects that themselves are occupied in a continuous *dérive*. It is the play of these objects from city to city that forms, for Hejduk, a psychogeographic network across the new Europe, one that he is concerned should not lose the traces of its bad conscience, nor bury in forgetfulness the memory of its past victims.

Here Hejduk goes beyond the situationist obsession with the spectacle and its protopanoptical implications, to explore a new type of space, that of the nomad, as it intersects with the more static space of established urban realms. We might refer to the distinction, drawn by Deleuze and Guattari in their *Traité de nomadologie; La machine de guerre*, between "state" space and "nomad" space. A sedentary space that is consciously parceled out, closed, and divided by the institutions of power would then be contrasted to the smooth, flowing, unbounded space of nomadism; in western contexts, the former has always attempted to bring the latter under control. In this way, Deleuze and Guattari trace the struggle between a state mathematics and geometry and a nomad science based on dynamic notions of becoming, heterogeneity, the infinitesimal, the passage to the limit, and continuous variation (a science sketched, but not elaborated, by Husserl when he spoke of a "vague" or vagabond geometry). This is paralleled by the historical difference between nomad work and state work, where "nomad" associations, such as those of journeymen, compagnonnage, itinerant labor, guilds, "bands," and "bodies," have always been difficult to conquer and to bring into line with the regular order of state-controlled work. A kind of "band vagabondage" linked to a "body nomadism" has ever resisted incorporation into the divided space of capitalist development.[15]

In this context it would be possible to infer a type of nomadism that associated the body language of Hejduk's structures with the mobile space they inhabit, always unassimilable to the normal spaces of the city. This would be, so to speak, the guerrilla warfare of the tribe, operating in the interstices of the settled community, a gypsy band that strangely prefigures those newly mobile nomads released (or expelled) from the territorial regulation of the recently "liberated" states of the former eastern block. Here, in the realm of the imagination, the visions of the journeyman architect intimate possible strategies for articulating what, in an increasingly urgent argument, Michael Ignatieff has recently called "the needs of strangers."[16]

Transparency

Modernity has been haunted, as we know very well, by a myth of transparency: transparency of the self to nature, of the self to the other, of all selves to society, and all this represented, if not constructed, from Jeremy Bentham to Le Corbusier, by a universal transparency of building materials, spatial penetration, and the ubiquitous flow of air, light, and physical movement. As Sigfried Giedion observed in his *Bauen in Frankreich* of 1928,

The houses of Le Corbusier define themselves neither by space nor by forms: the air passes right through them! The air becomes a constitutive factor! For this, one should count neither on space nor forms, but uniquely on relation and compenetration! There is only a single, indivisible space. The separations between interior and exterior fall.[1]

Walter Benjamin, who copied this citation in his monumental compilation of quotes, the *Passagen-Werk,* heard in this urge for transparency a death knell for the ancient art of dwelling:

In the imprint of this turning point of the epoch, it is written that the knell has sounded for the dwelling in its old sense, dwelling in which security prevailed. Giedion, Mendelssohn, Le Corbusier have made the place of abode of men above all the transitory space of all the imaginable forces and waves of air and light. What is being prepared is found under the sign of transparency.[2]

On another level, transparency opened up machine architecture to inspection—its functions displayed like anatomical models, its walls hiding no secrets; the very epitome of social morality. In this vein,

André Breton criticized the hermeticism of Huysmans and the interiority of symbolism:

> As for me, I continue to inhabit my glass house [*ma maison de verre*], where one can see at every hour who is coming to visit me, where everything that is suspended from the ceilings and the walls holds on as if by enchantment, where I rest at night on a bed of glass with glass sheets, where *who I am* will appear to me, sooner or later, engraved on a diamond.[3]

Reading this passage, which does not entirely, as we might imagine, join Breton to his modernist contemporaries, Walter Benjamin was drawn to remark, "To live in a glass house is a revolutionary virtue par excellence. It is also an intoxication, a moral exhibitionism, that we badly need. Discretion concerning one's own existence, once an aristocratic virtue, has become more and more an affair of petit-bourgeois parvenus."[4] Such an ideology of the glass house of the soul, a psychogeographic glass house one might say, parallels the ideology of the glass house of the body—the aerobic glass house— and together the two themes inform the twenties with dialectical vigor. No wonder that Marcel Duchamp, Man Ray, and of course Georges Bataille were all in favor of a little dust. In Bataille's ironic encomium of dust:

> The storytellers have not imagined that the Sleeping Beauty would be awakened covered by a thick layer of dust; no more have they dreamed of the sinister spiders' webs that at the first movement of her brown hair would have torn. Nevertheless the sad *nappes de poussière* endlessly invade earthly dwellings and make them uniformly dirty; as if attics and old rooms were planned for the next entry of obsessions, of phantoms, of larvae living and inebriated by the worm-eaten smell of the old dust. When the big girls "good for anything" arm themselves, each morning, with a big feather duster, or even with a vacuum cleaner, they are perhaps not entirely ignorant that they contribute as much as the most positive savants to keeping off the evil phantoms that sicken cleanliness and logic. One day or another, it is true, dust, if it persists, will probably begin to gain ground over the servants, invading the immense rubbish of abandoned buildings, of deserted docks: and in this distant epoch there will be nothing more to save us from nocturnal terrors.[5]

Glass, once perfectly transparent, is now revealed in all its opacity.

Indeed, it was under the sign of opacity that the universalism of modernism, constructed on the myth of a universal subject, came under attack in the past twenty-five years. Beginning with Colin

Rowe's and Robert Slutzky's sly undermining of modernist simplici-
ties in their "Transparency, Literal and Phenomenal," transparency
was gradually discredited by the critique of the universal subject in
politics and psychoanalysis.[6] In its place, opacity, both literal and
phenomenal, became the watchword of the postmodern appeal to
roots, to tradition, to local and regional specificity, to a renewed
search for domestic security. A few years ago one might have concluded that, if the old art of dwelling had not been entirely revived,
save in kitsch imitation, certainly transparency was dead.

Yet in the last few years, as if confirming the penchant of the
century for uncanny repetition, we have been once again presented
with a revived call for transparency, this time on behalf of the apparently "good modernism," patronized by the French state in its
Parisian *grands projets*. *La transparence* is now the rage in France,
represented by the winning schemes for the new national library and
the Palais des Expositions near the Eiffel Tower, reopening questions
originally posed in the context of the first of François Mitterand's
monuments—the pyramid of the Louvre. But what seemed, in the
case of the pyramid, to be an ostensibly practical problem of making
a new monument disappear in relation to its context has been raised
to the status of principle. Transparency, in the form of the four
towers proposed for the book stacks of Dominique Perrault's library
and the three box-shaped pavilions for the expo building, is now, at
least in the minds of Mitterand, his administration, the juries and
apologists for the schemes, and, of course, the architects themselves,
firmly identified with progressive modernity. And is thus posed
against what is regarded as a regressive postmodern tendency of
historical atavism. The association is made confidently, with the apparent faith of the first avant-gardes of the twenties.

On one level, the connection transparency/modernity is easy
enough to understand. Following a decade of historical and typological exploration of "false walls" and fake stones, postmodernism,
the argument goes, has been seen for what it was—the Potemkin City
of the present—to be purified only by a renewed adhesion to the
spirit of the age. In France at least, the spirit of the age is still haunted
by the ghosts of technocratic "rational" architecture from Durand
and Viollet-le-Duc to Pierre Chareau, continued in the sixties with
the technological expressionism of the Centre Pompidou, and, more

recently, Norman Foster's Town Hall for Nîmes, next door to the Maison Carré.

Literal transparency is of course notoriously difficult (as Pei himself admitted) to attain; it quickly turns into obscurity (its apparent opposite) and reflectivity (its reversal). Despite all the researches of the Saint-Gobain glass company, the pyramid remains a glass pyramid, no more or less transparent than Bruno Taut's glass block pavilion of 1914. As for the library, the claim of transparency—books exposed to the world as symbols of themselves—was quickly suppressed in the face of professional librarians asking simple questions. The solution has been twofold: either to "fake" transparency—a falsely lit wall beyond the walls protecting the stacks from daylight—or to embrace its mirror image, so to speak, reflectively.

Why then transparency in the first place? To make huge cubic masses, monumental forms, urban constructions of vast scale—disappear? A crisis of confidence in monumentality? Certainly it seems significant that the projects were selected from models, without structure or scale—and conceptual models at that, where the expo "boxes" seem (and are) like giant perspex boxes. The conclusion would be that to work effectively, the ideology of the modern, either as *bête noire* of the postmodern or its recent replacement, would have to be a fiction in practice. Public monumentality would then be in the same position as in the 1940s when Giedion posed the question of whether a "new monumentality" was indeed possible in modern materials.

We are presented with the apparently strange notion of a public monumentality that is more than reticent—indeed wants literally to disappear, be invisible—even as it represents the full weight of the French state. And perhaps the underpinnings of the present revival should indeed be sought in the difficult area of representation, one that is no doubt joined to the problematic outlined by Gianni Vattimo, that of a "weak" or background monumentality, but also, and perhaps more fundamentally, to the self-perceived role of architecture in the construction of identity. For if it was in the task of constructing a new and modern subject that transparency in architecture was first adduced, the present passion for see-through buildings is indubitably linked to the attempt to construct a state identity of technological modernity against a city identity (Paris, Chirac) enmeshed in the tricky historicism of preservation.

Yet, coupled with this tendency, we may begin to discern the emergence of a more complex stance, one that, without rejecting the technological and ideological heritage of modernism, nevertheless seeks to problematize its premises, recognizing that the "subject" of modernity has indeed been destabilized by its worst effects. In this vein, the cube of glass envisaged by Rem Koolhaas in his competition entry for the French national library, with its internal organs displayed, so to speak, like some anatomical model, is at once a confirmation of transparency and its complex critique. For here the transparency is conceived of as solid, not as void, with the interior volumes carved out of a crystalline block, so as to float within it, in amoebic suspension. These are then represented on the surface of the cube as shadowy presences, their three-dimensionality displayed ambiguously and flattened, superimposed on one another, in a play of amorphous densities. Transparency is thus converted into translucency, and this into darkness and obscurity. The inherent quality of absolute transparency to turn into its opposite, reflectivity, is thrown into doubt; the subject can no longer lose itself in *l'espace indicible* of infinite reason or find itself in the narcissism of its own reflection. Rather, it is suspended in a difficult moment between knowledge and blockage, thrust into an experience of density and amorphism, even as it is left before an external surface that is, to all intents and purposes, nothing more than a two-dimensional simulacrum of interior space.

The qualities of estrangement that result are, on one level, similar to the uncanny effects of all mirroring, apparent to writers from Hoffmann to Maupassant. In the latter's story "Le Horla" (1887), which served as an exemplary model for Otto Rank in his book *The Double*, the narrator is tormented by the thought that he is ever accompanied by an invisible other, a spirit that he cannot see but that nevertheless resides in his house, drinks his wine, controls his actions and thoughts; he is obsessed with the idea of catching it out, often running into his room in order to seize his mysterious double and kill it. Once, on an impulse, he turned around quickly, to face a tall wardrobe with a mirror; but, as he recalled, "I did not see myself in my mirror. The glass was empty, clear, deep, brightly lit, but my reflection was missing, though I was standing where it would be cast." Then, after gazing at this large clear mirrored surface from top to bottom for some time, he was terrified, for "suddenly I saw myself in a mist in the center of the mirror, through a sort of watery veil; and it seemed to me as if the water were slipping very slowly from left to right." Convinced he had seen his double, he develops a case of what, in the context of our analysis, might be called advanced agoraphobia: barricading the windows and doors of his room with iron; leaving and setting fire to the room in order to kill the apparently trapped other. But beset with doubts as to whether he had actually killed this invisible specter, he was finally forced to kill himself.[7]

Such themes of mirror reflection and its uncanny effects were noted by Freud, who tells the amusing but disturbing story of sitting alone in his compartment in a *wagon lit*, when a jolt of the train caused the door of his washing cabinet to swing open; "an elderly gentleman in a dressing gown and traveling cap came in." Jumping up angrily to protest this unwonted intrusion, Freud at once realized to his dismay "that the intruder was nothing but my own reflection in the looking glass of the open door. I can still recollect that I thoroughly disliked his appearance" (U 244). Interpreting this scene, Sarah Kofman has concluded:

Repetition, like repression, is originary, and serves to fill an originary lack as well as to veil it: the double does not double a presence but rather supplements it, allowing one to read, as in a mirror, originary "difference," castration, death, and at the same time the necessity of erasing them.[8]

The psychoanalyst Mahmoud Sami-Ali has gone further in explaining this association of the uncanny with reflection, taking Lacan's notion of the mirror stage and arguing that the proximity, noted by Freud, of the familiar and the strange causes "a profound modification of the object, which from the familiar is transformed into the strange, and as strange something that provokes disquiet because of its absolute proximity." Sami-Ali proposes that space itself is deformed by this experience. If, as Freud had implied, "the feeling of the uncanny implies the return to that particular organization of space where everything is reduced to inside and outside and where the inside is also the outside," then the space of the mirror would precisely meet this condition: a space of normal binocular, three-dimensional vision, modified by being deprived of depth. This would lead to the conflation, on the same visual plane, of the familiar (seen) and the strange (projected). In the case of the mirror stage, this would involve a complex superimposition of the reflected image of the subject and, conflated with this, the projected image of the subject's desire—the other: "Being simultaneously itself and the other, familiar and nevertheless strange, the subject is that which has no face and whose face exists from the point of view of the other."[9]

But, while the presence of such an uncanny in Koolhaas's library project is undeniable, we have yet to account for its equally evident refusal of mirroring, its absorbency to both interior representation and external reflection. Here the unexpected manifestation of this as yet undefinable condition, erupting suddenly out of an apparently simple play of transparencies, should be distinguished from the qualities of reflectivity found in modernism as well as from any "postmodern" surface play of simultaneity and seduction. The architect allows us neither to stop at the surface nor to penetrate it, arresting us in a state of anxiety.

This condition seems to approximate not the mirror stage itself but that moment, described by Lacan, of the *accomplishment* of the stage. "This moment in which the mirror stage comes to an end inaugurates, through identification with the *imago* of the counterpart and the drama of primordial jealousy . . . the dialectic that will henceforth link the *I* to socially elaborated situations." Such socially elaborated situations were, he concluded, characterized by "paranoiac alienation, which dates from the deflection of the specular *I* into the social *I*."[10]

With this swerve from the self to the social, the subject is no longer content to interrogate its face in the mirror in the search for transparency of the soul but, following Lacan's deliberately chosen metaphor, desires to stage its self in its social relations. Here two-dimensional physiognomy, the representation of the "face," is transformed into the three-dimensional space of subjectivity, place for the staging of social activity. That is, the plane of the mirror becomes the space of a theater: "The *mirror stage* is a drama" asserts Lacan.[11]

In Lacan's wordplay, the mirror stage is staged, or, following the connotations of the French, the *stade* (or biological stage) acts in the space of a *stade* (or stadium):

The formation of the *I* is symbolized oneirically by a fortified camp, a stadium indeed—establishing, from the interior arena to its outer enclosure, its periphery of rubbish and marshes, two opposed fields of struggle where the subject is caught up in the quest for the lofty and distant chateau, whose form (sometimes juxtaposed in the same scenario) symbolizes the id in a striking fashion. And in the same way we find realized, here on the mental level, those structures of the fortified work the metaphor of which rises up spontaneously, and as a result of the very symptoms of the subject, to designate the mechanisms of inversion, of isolation, of reduplication, of annulation, of displacement, of obsessional neurosis.[12]

In this image of the self, fortified and surrounded by garbage dumps, staged in an arena, is established the parameters of what Victor Burgin in a recent article also following Lacan, has termed "paranoiac space."[13]

In the light of Rem Koolhaas's preoccupation, outlined in *Delirious New York*, with the "paranoid critical method" of Salvador Dalí, a method that anticipates Lacan's first publications on paranoia, we might be tempted to apply such a designation to the facade of the Koolhaas library project. The paranoiac space of the library would then be that which is staged through the anxiety instigated at its surface.

In his seminar on *angoisse* conducted between 1962 and 1963, Lacan himself tied anxiety directly to the experience of the uncanny, claiming, indeed, that it was through the very structure of the *unheimlich* that anxiety might be theorized. The "field of anxiety" is framed by the uncanny, so to speak, even as the uncanny itself is framed as a sudden apparition seen, as it were, through a window: "The horrible, the suspicious, the uncanny, everything by which we translate as we can into French this magisterial word 'unheimlich,' presenting itself through the skylights [lucarnes] by which it is framed, situates for us the field of anxiety." The notion of "suddenness," of the "all at once," is fundamental for Lacan in setting this scene of uncanny anxiety: "you will always find this term at the moment of entry of the phenomenon of the *unheimlich!*" In this space of the sudden, as in "that brief, quickly extinguished moment of anxiety" before the curtain goes up in the theater—the moment of the three taps of the conductor's baton—anxiety is framed; it is for a moment collapsed into waiting, preparation, "a state of alert." But, beyond the frame, anxiety is, in a real sense, in the frame; it is something already known, and therefore anticipated: "Anxiety is when, in this frame, something appears that was already there, much closer to the house, the *Heim*: the host." The host, suddenly appearing at the door of the home or on the scene of the stage, is both expected and hostile, foreign to and yet embedded in the house: "It is this rising up of the *heimlich* in the frame that is the phenomenon of anxiety."[14]

The anxiety of the subject confronted with the "soft" space of Koolhaas's surfaces is then the manifestation of an uncanny based on the newly formulated conditions of interiority and exteriority, where the "ghosting" of the functionalist "interior" on the exterior mirrors not the outward appearance of the subject but its own, now-transparent biological interior. Paranoiac space is transformed then into panic space, where all limits become blurred in a thick, almost palpable substance that has substituted itself, almost imperceptibly, for traditional architecture.

Notes

Introduction

1. Ernst Bloch, "A Philosophical View of the Detective Novel" (1965), in *The Utopian Function of Art and Literature: Selected Essays*, translated by Jack Zipes and Frank Meckelburg (Cambridge, Mass.: MIT Press, 1988), p. 245.

2. Walter Benjamin, *Charles Baudelaire: A Lyric Poet in the Era of High Capitalism*, translated from the German by Harry Zohn (London: New Left Books, 1973), pp. 128–131: "Fear, revulsion, and horror were the emotions which the big city crowd aroused in those who first observed it" (p. 131).

3. Benjamin Constant, *De l'esprit de conquête et de l'usurpation dans les rapports avec la civilisation européenne* (1814), in Benjamin Constant, *Oeuvres*, annotated with an introduction by Alfred Roulin (Paris: Bibliothèque de la Pléiade, 1957), p. 984.

4. Karl Marx, *Economic and Philosophic Manuscripts of 1844*, in Karl Marx and Friedrich Engels, *Collected Works*, vol. 3, *Marx and Engels, 1843–1844* (New York: International Publishers, 1975), p. 314. See also Marx's earlier observation in the same manuscript: "Man returns to a cave dwelling, which is now, however, contaminated with the pestilential breath of civilisation, and which he continues to occupy only *precariously*, it being for him an alien habitation which can be withdrawn from him any day—a place from which, if he does not pay, he can be thrown out any day. For this mortuary he has to *pay*" (p. 307).

5. Sigmund Freud, "The 'Uncanny'" (1919), in *The Standard Edition of the Complete Psychological Works of Sigmund Freud*, 24 vols. (London: Hogarth Press, 1955), 17:217–252. All quotations from this essay will be taken from the corrected reprint of this edition in Sigmund Freud, *Art and Literature*, The Pelican Freud Library, vol. 14, edited by Albert Dickson (Harmondsworth: Penguin Books, 1985), pp. 335–376, and will be cited in the text as "U."

6. See Otto Rank, *The Double: A Psychoanalytic Study*, translated and edited by Harry Tucker, Jr. (Chapel Hill, N.C.: University of North Carolina Press, 1971), first published in essay form as "Der Doppelgänger," *Imago* 3 (1914):97–164.

7. Sigmund Freud, "Thoughts for the Times on War and Death" (1915), *Standard Edition*, 14:271.

8. Georg Lukács, *The Theory of the Novel*, translated by Anna Bostock (Cambridge, Mass.: MIT Press, 1971) p. 41: "The old parallelism of the transcendental structure of the form-giving subject and the world of created forms has been destroyed, and the ultimate basis of artistic creation has become homeless."

9. Hubert L. Dreyfus, *Being-in-the-World: A Commentary on Heidegger's "Being and Time,"* *Division I* (Cambridge, Mass.: MIT Press, 1991), p. 37.

10. See Dreyfus, *Being-in-the-World*: "Directly contradicting his early emphasis on man's essential experience of unsettledness, later Heidegger strives to give us 'a vision of a new rootedness which someday might even be fit to recapture the old and now rapidly disappearing rootedness in a changed form'" (p. 337). Dreyfus is quoting from Heidegger's *Discourse on Thinking* (New York: Harper and Row, 1959), p. 55.

11. Theodor Adorno, *Aesthetic Theory*, translated by C. Lenhardt, edited by Gretel Adorno and Rolf Tiedemann (London and New York: Routledge and Kegan Paul, 1984), p. 262.

12. Adorno, *Aesthetic Theory*, p. 369.

13. Adorno, *Aesthetic Theory*, p. 262.

14. Freud's writing on the uncanny has recently been scrutinized for its own uncanny lapses. See, for example, Hélène Cixous, "Fiction and Its Phantoms: A Reading of Freud's *Das Unheimliche*," *New Literary History* 7 (Spring 1976):525–548 (originally published as "La Fiction et ses fantômes. Une lecture de l'*unheimliche* de Freud," *Poétique* 10 [1972]:199–216); Samuel Weber, "The Sideshow, or: Remarks on a Canny Moment," *Modern Language Notes* 88 (1973):1102–1133; Sara Kofman, *The Childhood of Art: An Interpretation of Freud's Aesthetics*, translated by Winifred Woodhull (New York: Columbia University Press, 1988), from *L'Enfance de l'art* (Paris: Payot, 1970); Sarah Kofman, "Le Double e(s)t le diable," *Quatre romans analytiques* (Paris: Galilée, 1973), pp. 135–181; Neil Hertz, "Freud and the Sandman," in Josué V. Harari, ed., *Textual Strategies: Perspectives in Post-Structuralist Criticism* (Ithaca: Cornell University Press, 1979), pp. 296–321; Jacques Derrida, "La Double séance," in *La Dissemination* (Paris: Seuil, 1972), pp. 300–301; Jacques Derrida, "Speculations—On Freud," translated by Ian McLeod, *Oxford Literary Review* 3, no. 2 (1978):84–85.

15. Jacques Lacan, "L'Angoisse," seminar, 1962–1963, unpublished transcript.

16. "We will be unceasingly drawn back [to the rereading of Freud's *Das Unheimliche*] by the paradoxes of the double and repetition, the effacement of the limit between 'imagination' and 'reality,' the 'symbol' and the 'symbolized,' the references to Hoffmann and to the literature of the fantastic, considerations of the *double meaning* of the word: 'Thus *heimlich* is a word the meaning of which develops in the direction of ambivalence, until it finally coincides with its opposite, *unheimlich*. *Unheimlich* is in some way or another a subspecies of *heimlich*.'" Jacques Derrida, "La Double séance," p. 249.

17. Jean Baudrillard, *De la séduction* (Paris: Seuil, 1979), p. 91.

18. Freud, "Fetishism," *Standard Edition*, 21:152–157. Silverman, among others, in her use of this question to open the discussion of the relation between vision, fetishism, and the castration complex in the male subject, has, by implication, provided a way to reinterpret the spatial dimensions of the Freudian uncanny in terms that finally upset the traditional categories of exteriority and interiority, public and domestic. See Kaja Silverman, *The Acoustic Mirror: The Female Voice in Psychoanalysis and Cinema* (Bloomington: Indiana University Press, 1988), pp. 17ff.

19. Julia Kristeva, *Étrangers à nous-mêmes* (Paris: Fayard, 1988), p. 277; Michael Ignatieff, *The Needs of Strangers* (Harmondsworth: Penguin Books, 1985); Tzvetan Todorov, *Nous et les autres: la reflexion française sur la diversité humaine* (Paris: Seuil, 1989).

20. Homi K. Bhabha, "DissemiNation: Time, Narrative, and the Margins of the Modern Nation," in Homi K. Bhabha, ed., *Nation and Narration* (London and New York: Routledge, 1990), pp. 319–320, 300.

21. Ernst Bloch, "Building in Empty Spaces" (1959), in *The Utopian Function of Art and Literature*, pp. 186–199.

22. Jeffrey Mehlman, *Revolution and Repetition: Marx/Hugo/Balzac* (Berkeley: University of California Press, 1977), pp. 3–7. Mehlman characterizes his book as "a meditation on the perversity of the repetition compulsion in two of its most striking formulations: 'the uncanny (*das Unheimliche*)' and the 'death instinct'" (p. 3).

Unhomely Houses

1. Edgar Allan Poe, *The Complete Tales and Poems* (New York: The Modern Library, 1938), p. 231.

2. Poe, *The Complete Tales*, p. 233.

3. Poe, *The Complete Tales*, p. 233.

4. Poe, *The Complete Tales*, p. 237.

5. Victor Hugo, *Les Travailleurs de la mer*, in *Oeuvres complètes. Roman III* (Paris: Robert Laffont, 1985), pp. 50, 51.

6. Hugo, *Les Travailleurs*, pp. 119, 120.

7. Hugo, *Les Travailleurs*, p. 51.

8. Poe, *The Complete Tales*, p. 231.

9. Edmund Burke, *A Philosophical Enquiry into the Origin of Our Ideas of the Sublime and Beautiful* (1757), edited with an introduction and notes by James T. Boulton (Notre Dame: University of Notre Dame Press, 1968), pp. 39–40.

10. Burke, *A Philosophical Enquiry*, p. 119.

11. Burke, *A Philosophical Enquiry,* p. 59.

12. G. W. F. Hegel, *Aesthetics: Lectures on Fine Art* (1835), 2 vols., translated by T. M. Knox (Oxford: Oxford University Press, 1975), 1:243.

13. "Can" comes from the Anglo-Saxon *can* or *cann,* the present indicative of *cunnan,* "to know, be able," related to the Dutch *kunnan* and the German *können,* "to know." "Canny," or "cannie," thus means cautious, prudent, knowing, watchful, and also skilled, expert. From this the meaning extends to "possessed of supernatural power"; "skilled in magic." Hence "uncanny" is mysterious, unfamiliar, frightening, preternaturally strange, eerie, and weird, joining "canny" in much the same way as *unheimlich* is affiliated to *heimlich.*

14. Ernst Jentsch, "Zur Psychologie des Unheimlichen," *Psychiatrisch-Neurologische Wochenschrift* 22 (25 August 1906):195. The second part of the article was published in the same journal, vol. 23, September 1, 1906, pp. 203–205. I am indebted to Jeannette Treiber of the University of California, Davis, for the translation of Jentsch's article.

15. Freud's lengthy display of dictionary research, as if inviting the reader to participate in his own enquiry, was of course staged—his argument was, as critics have pointed out, carefully constructed to an already determined end; but the insistent rhythm of the dictionary, its piling up of ramified "meanings," had the semblance of a legal brief. Carried by the numerous dictionary citations from biblical and German sources, it also established the uncanny in a broad cultural field, that, following Schiller and Schelling, gained force in the romantic period. The cumulative effect of these several pages of dictionary entries, reproduced by Freud more or less verbatim, was, as Hélène Cixous has pointed out, almost uncanny in itself, as Freud, by way of Sanders and Grimm, circled repetitively and obsessively around the concept, gently indulging his readers as Holmes indulges Watson, before pouncing on the slightest of clues—a single phrase from Schelling—that will emerge as the fundamental principle of the psychoanalytic uncanny. See Hélène Cixous, "Fiction and Its Phantoms: A Reading of Freud's *Das Unheimliche,*" *New Literary History* 7 (Spring 1976):525–548. Freud's text, notes Cixous, is itself "a strange theoretical novel," "a kind of puppet theater in which real dolls or fake dolls, real and simulated life, are manipulated by a sovereign but capricious stage-setter" (p. 525).

16. Daniel Sanders, *Wörterbuch der Deutschen Sprache,* 3 vols. (Leipzig: Otto Wigand, 1860), 1:729.

17. Sanders, *Wörterbuch,* 1:729.

18. Jacob and Wilhelm Grimm, *Deutsches Wörterbuch,* 16 vols. (Leipzig: S. Hirzel, 1854–1954), 4:2:874.

19. Sanders, *Wörterbuch,* 1:729 quoting from the novelist and playwright Karl Ferdinand Gutzkow (1811–1878).

20. Sanders, *Wörterbuch,* 1:729.

21. Sanders, *Wörterbuch,* 1:729.

22. Friedrich Wilhelm Joseph Schelling, *Philosophie der Mythologie*, 2 vols. (Darmstadt: Wissenschaftliche Buchgesellschaft, 1966), 2:649. Translation by Eric Randolf Miller.

23. Schelling, *Philosophie der Mythologie*, 2:649.

24. Schelling's own example of the aesthetic uncanny, outlined early in his career and now reelaborated, was that of the pediment sculptures of the Temple of Aegina, which had been the centerpiece of Leo von Klenze's Glyptotek in Munich. For Schelling these half-primitive, half-modern sculptures represented a special stage in the development of western art.

25. Hoffmann observed in a letter to Carl Reichscount von Brühl, Director General of the Royal Theater, Berlin, 26 January 1816, that no one was better suited than Schinkel, "who so deeply penetrates the true spirit of the romantic," to stage his own play *Undine;* earlier he had expressed his desire to "arouse Schinkel's interest concerning the story for *Undine.*" "I especially want him to build me a magnificent, authentic, Gothic tomb," stated Hoffmann. See *Selected Letters of E. T. A. Hoffmann,* edited and translated by J. C. Sahlin (Chicago: University of Chicago Press, 1977), pp. 254–256. The premier of this "magic opera" was staged, with Schinkel's sets, on 3 August 1816.

26. E. T. A. Hoffmann, *Der Sandmann. Das öde Haus* (Stuttgart: Philipp Reclam, 1969), pp. 46–47. The house existed at 9, Unter den Linden in Berlin.

27. E. T. A. Hoffmann, "Rat Krespel," in *Die Serapionsbrüder, Poetische Werke,* 6 vols. (Berlin: Aufbau-Verlag, 1958), 4:32–56. Quotations are from "Councillor Krespel," translated by L. J. Kent and E. C. Knight, in E. T. A. Hoffmann, *Tales,* edited by Victor Lange (New York: Continuum, 1982), pp. 80–100 and will be cited in the text as "K."

28. Schelling, *The Philosophy of Art,* edited, translated, and introduced by Douglas W. Stott (Minneapolis: University of Minnesota Press, 1989), p. 177.

29. Goethe, *Maximen und Reflexionen,* in *Werke* (Hamburger Ausgabe), vol. 12 (1953), p. 474.

30. Goethe, *Maximen und Reflexionen,* p. 474. Goethe substituted the term "silent music" (*verstummte Tonkunst*) for Schelling's "frozen music."

31. E. T. A. Hoffmann, "The Sandman," in *Tales,* pp. 277–308. All quotations of this story will be from this edition, cited in the text as "S."

32. Jacques Lacan, *The Four Fundamental Concepts of Psychoanalysis,* edited by Jacques-Alain Miller and translated from the French by Alan Sheridan (New York: W. W. Norton, 1978), pp. 102–103.

33. Maria Tatar, *Spellbound: Studies on Mesmerism and Literature* (Princeton: Princeton University Press, 1978), p. 126.

34. Hoffmann, "Der unheimliche Gast," in *Die Serapionsbrüder,* 7:103–153.

35. Thomas De Quincey, *Confessions of an English Opium Eater* (Harmondsworth: Penguin Books, 1971), p. 93.

36. The fullest treatment of the romantic chain of interpretations of the Piranesi *Carceri* etchings is Luzius Keller, *Piranèse et les romantiques français, le mythe des escaliers en spirale* (Paris: Librairie José Corti, 1966). Keller summarizes the successive Piranesi fantasies of De Quincey, Alfred de Musset, Charles Nodier, and Théophile Gautier, as well as tracing their influence on Balzac, Hugo, Baudelaire, and Mallarmé. The modernist inheritor of this myth of movement was Sergei Eisenstein, for whose treatment of the *Carceri* transformations see Manfredo Tafuri, *The Sphere and the Labyrinth* (Cambridge, Mass.: MIT Press, 1988).

37. See Mario Praz, "Introductory Essay" to *Three Gothic Novels,* edited by Peter Fairclough (Harmondsworth: Penguin Books, 1968), who notes the influence of the *Carceri* on Horace Walpole's *The Castle of Otranto* (1765), on William Beckford's *Dreams, Walking Thoughts and Incidents* (1783), and more generally on the literature of the Revolutionary period. Praz cites the two classic studies of these filiations: Jorgen Andersen, "Giant Dreams, Piranesi's Influence in England," *English Miscellany* 3 (Rome, 1952), and Luzius Keller, *Piranèse et les romantiques français* (cited above).

38. Thomas De Quincey, *Confessions of an English Opium Eater,* pp. 105–106.

39. Arden Reed, "Abysmal Influence: Baudelaire, Coleridge, De Quincey, Piranesi, Wordsworth," *Glyph* 4 (1978):189–206.

40. Jacques Derrida, "Speculations—On Freud," translated by Ian McLeod, *Oxford Literary Review* 3, no. 2 (1978):78–97.

41. Charles Nodier, "Piranèse, contes psychologiques, à propos de la monomanie réflective," in *Oeuvres complètes de Charles Nodier,* 12 vols. (Paris: Eugène Renduel, 1832–1837), 11:167–204. For a study of the topos of the library in Nodier, see Didier Barrière, *Nodier l'homme du livre* (Bassac, Charente: Plein Chant, 1989).

42. Nodier, "Piranèse," pp. 188–189 (my emphasis). The following quotations also come from this story.

43. Nodier, "Piranèse," p. 193. Nodier remarks, somewhat ingenuously after this long variation and theme on De Quincey: "The drawing of which I speak has perhaps been described somewhere, but it was Piranesi who drew it" (p. 193).

44. Nodier, "Piranèse," pp. 194–200.

45. For Nodier's struggle was, of course, that of the librarian, torn between a fetishistic bibliophilia and a bibliophobia born of his hatred for the relentless multiplication of books in the era of printing: see, for example, his short story "Le Bibliomane," *Oeuvres,* 11:25–49. On the one hand, he no doubt found a kind of comfort in this most *heimlich* of places, a site of calm study and peaceful retirement. Its central role in Nodier's topography, from the literary utopia of "Mes rêveries," written during the Terror, to the careful architecture of Maxime's library in "L'Amour et le grimoire," some thirty-two years later, marks it as an almost sacred realm (see Barrière, *Nodier,* pp. 28–31). Whether accommodated in an old castle or in rooms constructed especially for the purpose, the library is constituted by its architecture: "The whole building comprised a single long room, rectilinear, lit from the east and west by ogival windows, and opening to the south onto a garden, small, but well enough conceived in its distribu-

tion" (Nodier, "L'Amour et le grimoire," *Contes* [Paris: Garnier, 1961], p. 530). At the center of this rectangular room is a long black table that reproduces its plan, set with room to circulate around it; on the walls nothing is seen but the leather spines of books. Its proximity to the garden establishes the relation of books to the greater book of nature, itself an inexhaustible dictionary. As if anticipating the simple rectilinear form of Henri Labrouste's Bibliothèque Sainte-Geneviève, with its ground-floor entry simulating a philosophic garden, Nodier carefully constructs a precinct within which his hero might turn his back on the frivolous society of the theater, rejecting its "masks" for the "meditation" to be found in his library. On the other hand, in contrast to the controlled setting if these asylums for the bibliophile, the library takes on the more menacing form of an uncontrollable Babel.

46. Michael Riffaterre, "Hermeneutic Models," *Poetics Today* 4, no. 1 (1983):7–16.

47. Arthur Rimbaud, "Veillées [*Illuminations*]," in *Oeuvres,* edited by S. Bernard and André Guyaux (Paris: Classiques Garnier, 1987), pp. 281–282, my translation.

48. Herman Melville, "I and My Chimney," in *Pierre, Israel Potter, The Confidence-Man, Tales and Billy Budd* (New York: The Library of America, 1984), pp. 1298–1327.

49. See, for example, V. H. Litman, "The Cottage and the Temple: Melville's Symbolic Use of Architecture," *American Quarterly* 2 (1969):638ff.

50. Melville, "I and My Chimney," p. 1311.

Buried Alive

1. Wilhelm Jensen, *Gradiva: A Pompeiian Fancy* (1903), translated by Helen M. Downey, quoted in Sigmund Freud, *Delusion and Dream,* edited by Philip Rieff (Boston: The Beacon Press, 1956), pp. 175–176. Downey's translation of *Gradiva* was first published in 1917.

2. Baron Taylor, letter to Charles Nodier, "Sur les villes de Pompéi et d'Herculanum," in François-René de Chateaubriand, *Oeuvres romanesques et voyages,* vol. 2 (Paris: Bibliothèque de la Pléiade, 1969), p. 1505.

3. Chateaubriand, *Oeuvres romanesques et voyages,* 2:1475.

4. Gustave Flaubert, *Correspondance, I, 1830–1851* (Paris: Gallimard, 1973), 773, letter to Louis Bouilhet: "Ah! poor chap, how I missed you in Pompeii! I send you flowers that I picked from a brothel over the door of which is set an erect phallus. There were in this house more flowers than in any other. The sperm of ancient penises, fallen to the earth, have perhaps fertilized the earth."

5. Chateaubriand, *Oeuvres romanesques et voyages,* 2:1783, 1472; Gérard de Nerval, *Oeuvres,* 2 vols. (Paris: Bibliothèque de la Pléiade, 1952), 1:1175.

6. Théophile Gautier, "Arria Marcella, souvenir de Pompéi," in *Récits fantastiques* (Paris: Flammarion, 1981), p. 246.

7. Gautier, "Arria Marcella," pp. 240ff.

8. Schelling, *Philosophie der Mythologie*, 2:653.

9. Chateaubriand, *Oeuvres romanesques et voyages*, 2:1474.

10. Friedrich Schlegel, *Athenaeum*, fragment 206, quoted in Philippe Lacoue-Labarthe and Jean-Luc Nancy, *L'Absolu littéraire* (Paris: Seuil, 1978), pp. 126, 101.

11. Gautier, "Arria Marcella," pp. 237–238.

12. Gautier, "Arria Marcella," p. 253.

13. Gautier, "Jettatura," in *Récits fantastiques*, p. 379.

14. Gautier, "Arria Marcella," p. 243.

15. Gautier, "Arria Marcella," p. 245.

16. Freud, "Delusions and Dreams in Jensen's Gradiva," *Standard Edition* 9:1–95; corrected reprint in *Art and Literature*, pp. 33–118.

17. Freud, *The Interpretation of Dreams*, *Standard Edition* 5:452.

18. Freud, *The Interpretation of Dreams*, p. 454.

19. Freud, *The Future of an Illusion*, *Standard Edition* 21:17.

Homesickness

1. Walter Pater, "The Child in the House" (1878), in Harold Bloom, ed., *Selected Writings of Walter Pater* (New York: Columbia University Press, 1974), pp. 1–16.

2. Thus Georges Bataille, in his *Histoire de l'oeil*, would note that the insane asylum in which Marcelle was housed seemed to him to be "confusedly" a *château hanté* or haunted chateau, a sense imparted by the elision and association of the words *maison de santé* and *château;* he thereby mistook "the presence of the mad in a huge silent dwelling at night for that of ghostly phantoms." He was equally astonished to find that in approaching this sinister building, he always had the impression of going to his own home, "j'allais *chez moi*," giving him the sense of being ill at ease. Georges Bataille, *Oeuvres complètes*, 9 vols. (Paris: Gallimard, 1970), 1:41.

3. Walter Pater, "Winckelmann" (1867), in *The Renaissance: Studies in Art and Poetry* (London: Macmillan, 1873), pp. 177, 178, 220, 190, 213.

4. Pater, conclusion to *The Renaissance* (omitted in the second edition), p. 236.

5. Pater, "Winckelmann," p. 227.

6. Pater, "Winckelmann," pp. 230, 210, 210–211, 230, 209.

7. Pater, "Winckelmann," p. 226.

8. Walter Pater, *Marius the Epicurean,* edited with an introduction and notes by Michael Levey (London: Penguin Books, 1985), p. 218.

9. Pater, *Marius the Epicurean,* pp. 233, 228.

Nostalgia

1. Gaston Bachelard, *La Terre et les rêveries du repos* (Paris: Librairie José Corti, 1948), pp. 6, 95, 96. The first volume of this study was *La Terre et les rêveries de la volonté* (Paris: Librairie José Corti, 1948).

2. Theodor Adorno, *Minima Moralia: Reflections from Damaged Life,* translated from the German by E. F. N. Jephcott (London: Verso, 1974), p. 38.

3. Paul Claudel, *Oiseau noir dans le soleil levant,* quoted in Gaston Bachelard, *La Poétique de l'espace* (Paris: Presses Universitaires de France, 1957), p. 42.

4. Vladimir Jankélévitch, *L'Irréversible et la nostalgie* (Paris: Flammarion, 1983), pp. 346ff.

Architecture Dismembered

This chapter has been much informed by Elaine Scarry's *The Body in Pain: The Making and Unmaking of the World* (New York: Oxford University Press, 1985).

1. This three-stage model, here suggested for architecture, might also be recognized as a typical, atemporal model for all such embodiments of the external world. Elaine Scarry sees it as a gradually expanding field of animism. To take the case of the chair: as a body part, the chair is mimetic of the spine (as in Quatremère de Quincy's celebrated formulation of the idea of type); as a projection of physical attributes, the chair is mimetic of body weight; as a repository of the desire to will an end to discomfort, the chair, finally is mimetic of sentient awareness as a whole. Each of these three stages progressively interiorizes the body:

> To conceive of the body as parts, shapes and mechanisms is to conceive of it from the outside: though the body contains pump and lens, "pumpness" and "lensness" are not part of the felt experience of being a sentient being. To instead conceive of the body in terms of capacities and needs (not now "lens" but "seeing," not now "pump" but "having a beating heart" or, more specifically, "desiring" or "fearing") is to move further in toward the interior of felt experience. To, finally, conceive of the body as "aliveness" or "awareness of aliveness" is to reside at last within the felt-experience of sentience.

Scarry, *The Body in Pain,* pp. 285–286.

2. For a concise account of this tradition, see Françoise Choay, "La Ville et le domaine bâti comme corps," *Nouvelle Revue de Psychanalyse* 9 (Spring 1974):239–252.

3. Burke, *A Philosophical Enquiry,* p. 100.

4. Heinrich Wölfflin, *Renaissance and Baroque,* trans. K. Simon, intro. Peter Murray (Ithaca: Cornell University Press, 1966), p. 77.

5. Wölfflin, *Renaissance and Baroque,* pp. 78–87.

6. Coop Himmelblau, *Die Faszination der Stadt. The Power of the City,* with a foreword by Frank Weiner (Darmstadt and London, 1988), pp. 95, 72; the latter from "In the Beginning Was the City" (1968).

7. Coop Himmelblau, *Die Faszination der Stadt,* p. 14.

8. Coop Himmelblau, *Die Faszination der Stadt,* p. 93.

9. Coop Himmelblau, *Architecture Is Now: Projects, (Un)buildings, Statements, Sketches, Commentaries, 1968–1983* (New York: Rizzoli International, 1983), p. 106.

10. Jacques Lacan, *Ecrits: A Selection,* translated from the French by Alan Sheridan (New York: W. W. Norton, 1977), pp. 4–5.

11. Roland Barthes, *A Lover's Discourse: Fragments,* translated by Richard Howard (New York: Hill and Wang, 1978), p. 71.

12. Roland Barthes, *S/Z,* translated by Richard Miller, preface by Richard Howard (New York: Hill and Wang, 1974), p. 112.

13. Coop Himmelblau, *Architecture Is Now,* p. 11.

14. Coop Himmelblau, *Architecture Is Now,* p. 73.

15. Jean-Paul Sartre, *Being and Nothingness,* translated with an introduction by Hazel E. Barnes (New York: Philosophical Library, 1956), pp. 323–325.

Losing Face

1. Colin Rowe, "James Stirling: A Highly Personal and Very Disjointed Memoir," in *James Stirling: Buildings and Projects,* compiled and edited by Peter Arnell and Ted Bickford (New York: Rizzoli Publications, 1984), pp. 22–23.

2. Wölfflin, *Renaissance and Baroque,* p. 77; Geoffrey Scott, *The Architecture of Humanism* (1914; New York: W. W. Norton, 1974), p. 177.

3. Scott, *Architecture of Humanism,* p. 159.

4. There has been no comprehensive study of the idea of physiognomy in architecture; for a brief sketch see my *The Writing of the Walls: Architectural Theory in the Late Enlightenment* (Princeton: Princeton Architectural Press, 1987), pp. 118ff.

5. Georg Simmel, "The Aesthetic Significance of the Face" ["Die ästhetische Bedeutung des Gesichts," 1901], translated by Lore Ferguson in *Georg Simmel, 1858–1918*, edited by Kurt H. Wolff (Columbus: Ohio State University Press, 1959), pp. 276–281.

6. Simmel, "The Aesthetic Significance of the Face," pp. 278, 280.

7. Simmel, "The Aesthetic Significance of the Face," p. 281.

8. Charles-Edouard Jeanneret (Le Corbusier), "La Construction des villes," unpublished manuscript, c. 1910, quoted in H. Allen Brooks, "Jeanneret and Sitte: Le Corbusier's Earliest Ideas on Urban Design," in Helen Searing, ed., *In Search of Modern Architecture: A Tribute to Henry-Russell Hitchcock* (New York: The Architectural History Foundation and MIT Press, 1982), p. 286.

9. Colin Rowe, "La Tourette," in *The Mathematics of the Ideal Villa and Other Essays* (Cambridge, Mass.: MIT Press, 1976), pp. 186–200.

10. Colin Rowe, "The Mathematics of the Ideal Villa," in *The Mathematics of the Ideal Villa*, p. 16.

11. Sigfried Giedion, *Architecture, You and Me* (Cambridge, Harvard University Press, 1958), p. 29.

12. In a remark during a doctoral seminar sponsored by the Mellon Foundation in Princeton University School of Architecture, Spring 1988.

13. Theodor Adorno, "Valéry Proust Museum," in *Prisms*, translated by Samuel and Shierry Weber (Cambridge: MIT Press, 1981), p. 175.

14. Arnold Gehlen, "Über kulturelle Kristallisation," in *Studien zur Anthropologie* (Neuwied, 1963), p. 321, quoted in Jürgen Habermas, *The Philosophical Discourse of Modernity*, translated by Frederick Lawrence (Cambridge: MIT Press, 1987), p. 3.

15. Georges Bataille, "Musée," *Documents*, 5 (1930):300; reprinted in *Oeuvres complètes*, 1:239.

Trick/Track

1. Bernard Tschumi, "Disjunctions," in *Perspecta* 23 (1987):116.

2. Roland Barthes, "From Work to Text," in *The Rustle of Language*, translated by Richard Howard (Berkeley: University of California Press, 1989), pp. 56–64; the essay was first published in the *Revue d'esthétique* (1971).

3. Bernard Tschumi, *The Manhattan Transcripts* (London: Academy Editions, 1981).

4. David Carroll, *Paraesthetics: Foucault, Lyotard, Derrida* (New York: Methuen, 1987), p. xiv.

5. Gilles Deleuze, *L'Image-temps* (Paris: Minuit, 1985), p. 27.

Shifting Ground

1. Hegel's own problematization of origins, dedicated to the dismantling of the entire apparatus of classical theory in favor of a philosophical conceptualization of the architectural project, would require analysis of its own. See, as a preliminary approach, Jacques Derrida, "The Pit and the Pyramid: Introduction to Hegel's Semiology," in *Margins of Philosophy,* translated with additional notes by Alan Bass (Chicago: Chicago University Press, 1982), and the evocative essay by Paul de Man, "Sign and Symbol in Hegel's 'Aesthetics,'" *Critical Inquiry* 8 (1982):761–765.

2. G. W. F. Hegel, *Aesthetics: Lectures on Fine Art,* 2 vols., translated by T. M. Knox (Oxford: Oxford University Press, 1975), 2:630. This edition will be cited in the text as "HA."

3. See Peter D. Eisenman, *Fin d'Ou T Hou S,* with introductory essays by Nina Hofer and Jeffrey Kipnis (London: Architectural Association, 1985).

4. See, for example, Eisenman, "Misreading Peter Eisenman," in *Houses of Cards* (New York, Rizzoli International, 1987).

5. Neil Hertz, *The End of the Line: Essays on Psychoanalysis and the Sublime* (New York: Columbia University Press, 1985), pp. 217–239.

6. As used by Kenneth Burke in *The Philosophy of Literary Form: Studies in Symbolic Action,* 3d ed., revised (Berkeley: University of California Press, 1973), pp. 84–89. Writing of Robert Penn Warren's novel *Night Rider,* Burke notes, "At one point . . . the process of maturing is metaphorically described as the peeling away of the successive layers of an onion, which would perfectly suggest such a development by introversion, by inturning towards a non-existent core, as I would consider typical of the 'to the end of the line' kind of plot" (p. 84).

7. Burke, *Philosophy of Literary Form,* adumbrates the end-of-the-line mode suggestively: "We should also note a 'serial' quality in the 'to the end of the line' mode—a kind of 'withinness of withinness,' as the 'night' company within the 'day' company (paralleling the similar development, in the economic sphere, from operating companies to holding companies, controlled by 'insiders'). One may get the pattern in Coleridge's line 'Snow-drop on a tuft of snow.' And in *Moby Dick* there is an especially 'efficient' passage of this sort, prophetically announcing the quality of Ishmael's voyage: after walking through 'blocks of blackness,' he enters a door where he stumbles over an ash-box; going on, he finds that he is in a Negro church, and 'the preacher's text was about the blackness of blackness'" (p. 88).

8. It is certainly not coincidental that another romantic writer, Victor Hugo, came to a similar conclusion almost contemporaneously with that of Hegel.

9. Emile Zola, *Correspondance (1858–1871)* (Paris: Editions de Bernouard, 1928), p. 250.

10. Marcel Duchamp, *The Writings of Marcel Duchamp,* edited by Michel Sanouillet and Elmer Peterson (New York: Da Capo, 1989), p. 26.

11. P. D. Eisenman, *Moving Arrows, Eros and Other Errors* (London: The Architectural Association, 1986). In an exhibition of the Venice panels, the Architectural Association followed the logic of transparency by holding them up to the actual windows overlooking Bedford Square.

12. Jacques Lacan, *The Four Fundamental Concepts of Psychoanalysis,* edited by Jacques-Alain Miller, translated by Alan Sheridan (New York: Norton, 1978), p. 97.

13. These white spaces have been tellingly referred to as "nodal points" or *Knotenpünkte,* "obsessive (or 'haunting') fixed points," by Charles Mauron in *Introduction à la psychanalyse de Mallarmé* (Neuchâtel, 1950); he has further related this level of punctuation to another, lower level, noting that "beneath a romanesque church one is not astonished to find a crypt that has architectural value" (*Des métaphores obsédantes au mythe personnel* [Paris, 1964]), an observation that Jeffrey Mehlman joins to that of Kenneth Burke's image of literature as *l'ecclesia super cloacam* (*The Philosophy of Literary Form,* p. 259). See Mehlman, "Entre psychanalyse et psychocritique," *Poétique* 3 (1970). Such reflections on the subterranean are taken up in a later section of the present essay.

14. Jacques Derrida, "Freud and the Scene of Writing," in *Writing and Difference,* translated with an introduction and notes by Alan Bass (Chicago: Chicago University Press, 1978), p. 227.

15. Derrida, "Freud and the Scene of Writing," p. 230.

16. Philippe Sollers, *Nombres* (Paris: Seuil, 1968), p. 22.

17. Sollers, *Nombres,* p. 87. Perhaps one might also seek a connection between this violent moment and the title of the Romeo and Juliet project: *Moving Arrows, Eros and Other Errors,* as boxed by the Architectural Association, London, 1986.

18. Xenophon of Ephesus, *Ephesiaca,* Book III, V, 8, where Anthia, rescued by Perilaus from robbers and wishing to escape marriage to him, in order to protect her original marriage seeks a *pharmakon* from a physician, that, fortunately, turns out to be only a *thanasimon* or sleep-inducing draft. Similar narratives of the double nature of the *pharmakon* occur in Masuccio's *Il Novellino* of 1476, Luigi da Porto's *Istoria novellamente ritrovata di due Nibili Amanti* of c. 1530, Bandello's *Le Novelle* of 1554, and Arthur Brooke's *The tragicall Historye of Romeus and Juliet* of 1562. This last, which furnished the basis for Shakespeare's drama, was adapted from Pierre Boiastuau's translation of Bandello in *Histoires tragiques extraictes des oeuvres italiens de Bandel* (Paris, 1559). The particular role of the crypt in all these stories might be examined in relation to Kenneth Burke's notion of the *cloacam* beneath every church (see note 14).

19. See, for example, Benoit B. Mandelbrot, *Fractals: Form, Chance, and Dimension* (San Francisco: W. H. Freeman, 1977).

20. Duchamp, *Writings of Marcel Duchamp,* p. 79.

21. See Mandelbrot, *Fractals,* p. 87, on the "Random Walk."

22. Jacques Derrida, *Margins of Philosophy,* translated by Alan Bass (Chicago: University of Chicago Press, 1982), p. 86.

23. Lewis Mumford, "Monumentalism, Symbolism and Style," *Architectural Review* (April 1949), 179, quoted in Sigfried Giedion, *Architecture, You and Me* (Cambridge, Mass.: Harvard University Press, 1958), p. 23.

24. Kurt W. Forster, "Traces and Treason of a Tradition: A Critical Commentary on Graves' and Eisenman/Robertson's Projects for the Ohio State University Center for the Visual Arts," *A Center for the Visual Arts: The Ohio State University Competition* (New York: Rizzoli International, 1984), p. 135.

25. Sigfried Giedion, J. L. Sert, and F. Léger, "Nine Points on Monumentality" (1943), in Giedion, *Architecture, You and Me,* p. 48.

26. Georges Bataille, "Architecture," in *Oeuvres complètes* (Paris: Gallimard, 1970), 1:171, first published in *Documents* 2 (May 1929):117.

27. Rosalind E. Krauss, "Grids," in *The Originality of the Avant-Garde and Other Modernist Myths* (Cambridge: MIT Press, 1985), p. 10.

28. Krauss, "Grids," pp. 18–19.

29. Krauss, "Grids," p. 17.

30. Krauss, "Grids," p. 18.

31. Jacques Lacan, "Ecrits inspirés: Schizographie" (1931), in *De la psychose paranoïque dans ses rapports avec la personnalité* (Paris: Seuil, 1975), pp. 365–382.

32. Lacan, "Ecrits inspirés," p. 379.

33. Georges Bataille, "Informe," in *Oeuvres complètes,* 1:217.

34. Bataille, "Architecture," 172.

Homes for Cyborgs

1. Walter Benjamin, *Das Passagen-Werk,* in *Gesammelte Schriften* vol. 5 (Frankfurt: Suhrkamp, 1982), p. 513.

2. Donna Haraway, "A Manifesto for Cyborgs: Science, Technology, and Socialist Feminism in the 1980s," in *Coming to Terms: Feminism, Theory, Politics,* edited by Elizabeth Weed (New York: Routledge, 1989), pp. 174, 176. (First published in *Socialist Review,* no. 80, 1985).

3. See Alice Jardine, "Of Bodies and Technologies," in *Discussions in Contemporary Culture,* no. 1, edited by Hal Foster (Seattle: The Bay Press for The Dia Art Foundation, 1987), pp. 151–158.

4. Haraway, "Manifesto for Cyborgs," p. 176.

5. Leonora Carrington, *The House of Fear: Notes from Down Below,* introduction to the English edition by Marina Warner (New York: E. P. Dutton, 1988), p. 2.

6. Carrington, *House of Fear,* p. 72.

7. Carrington, *House of Fear,* pp. 42, 134, 135.

8. Le Corbusier, "Louis Soutter. L'inconnu de la soixantaine," *Minotaure* 9 (October 1936):62.

9. Walter Benjamin, *Passagen-Werk,* p. 573.

10. Tristan Tzara, "D'un certain automatisme du Goût," *Minotaure* 3–4 (December 1933):84.

11. Tristan Tzara, "D'un certain automatisme du Goût," p. 84.

12. Freud's interpretation of the uncanny desire for intrauterine existence was evolved from his analysis of the "Wolf Man," written down in winter 1914–1915 and published in 1918 under the title "From the History of an Infantile Neurosis" (*Collected Papers,* vol. 3, translated by Alix and James Strachey [New York, 1959]). The Wolf Man's complaint, noted Freud, "was that for him the world was hidden by a veil," a veil that could only be torn through the action of the bowels. But this veil was also a kind of mysterious generator of the uncanny: "nor did he keep to the veil. It evaporated into a sense of twilight, into *ténèbres,* and into other impalpable things." During the treatment it became clear that this veil was the response to the circumstances of his birth "with a caul" (*Glückshaube,* or "lucky hood") that, until the onset of castration fears, made him feel he "was a child of fortune":

> Thus the caul was the veil which hid him from the world and hid the world from him. The complaint that he made was in reality a fulfilled wish-fantasy: it exhibited him as back once more in the womb, and was, in fact, a wish-fantasy of flight from the world. It can be translated as follows: "Life makes me so unhappy! I must get back into the womb!" (*Collected Papers,* 3:580–581)

In this way Freud was able to explain the peculiar functions of intestinal movements that, tearing the veil, precipitated a sort of "rebirth," which was in turn connected to the primal scene of his parents' coitus, imaged in the vision of the wolves in the tree. The tearing of the veil corresponded to the opening of his eyes, and thence the opening of the window; the womb fantasy itself was linked to his attachment to his father, an indication of his desire to be inside the mother's womb in order to replace her during coitus, to take her place with regard to the father. Thus, concluded Freud triumphantly, "two incestuous wishes were united." Here, as Ned Lukacher remarks, Freud "wants to tell a story about what is prior to presence and what has always already been forgotten." (Ned Lukacher, *Primal Scenes: Literature, Philosophy, Psychoanalysis* [Ithaca: Cornell University Press, 1986], pp. 36–37.)

13. Matta Echaurren, "Mathématique sensible—Architecture du temps" (adaptation by Georges Hugnet), *Minotaure* 11 (1938):43.

14. Cited by Dalibor Veseley in "Surrealism and Architecture," *Architectural Design* 48, nos. 2–3 (1978):94.

15. Salvador Dalí, "De la beauté terrifiante et comestible, de l'architecture modern'style," *Minotaure* 3–4 (December 1933):72.

242

Notes to Pages 154–162

16. Dalí, "De la beauté terrifiante et comestible," p. 73.

17. Le Corbusier, *The Decorative Art of Today,* translated and introduced by James I. Dunnett (Cambridge, Mass.: MIT Press, 1987), p. 72.

18. Benjamin, *Passagen-Werk,* p. 680, citing Salvador Dalí, "L'Âne pourri," in *Surréalisme au service de la Révolution,* vol. 1 (Paris, 1930), p. 12. The first attempt to "take the measure of technique" was that of realism; the second, art nouveau.

19. Benjamin, *Passagen-Werk,* p. 694.

20. Benjamin, *Passagen-Werk,* pp. 693, 118.

21. See the evocative passages on Max Ernst and "mechanized adornment" in Giedion's *Mechanization Takes Command* (New York: (Oxford University Press, 1948), pp. 360–361, 387–388.

22. *Mechanization Takes Command,* p. 388. The illustration discussed (fig. 199, p. 341) is Ernst's "Night Shrieks in Her Lair . . .," from *La Femme 100 têtes* (Paris, 1929).

23. Le Corbusier, *Decorative Art of Today,* p. 77.

24. See Jean-François Lyotard, *Les TRANSformateurs DUchamp* (Paris: Galilée, 1977), pp. 46–47.

25. Jardine, "Of Bodies and Technologies," p. 157.

26. Michel de Certeau, *The Practice of Everyday Life,* translated by Steven Rendall (Berkeley and Los Angeles: University of California Press, 1984), p. 147.

27. Le Corbusier, *L'Art décoratif d'aujourd'hui* (Paris, 1925), pp. 76, 79.

28. Jardine, "Of Bodies and Technologies," p. 155.

29. Alfred Jarry, *Les Jours et les nuits* (Paris, 1897), cited in de Certeau, *The Practice of Everyday Life,* p. 151.

30. Haraway, "Manifesto for Cyborgs," p. 194.

31. See Michel de Certeau's description of the "cybernetic system," as it "moves forward on its own; it is becoming self-moving and technocratic; it transforms the subjects that controlled it into operators of the writing machine that orders and uses them. A cybernetic society." (*The Practice of Everyday Life,* p. 136.)

32. De Certeau, *The Practice of Everyday Life,* p. 146.

33. William Gibson, *Neuromancer* (New York: The Berkeley Publishing Group, 1984), p. 11.

34. William Gibson, "Johnny Mnemonic," in *Burning Chrome* (New York: The Berkeley Publishing Group, 1986), pp. 13–14.

35. See Mahmoud Sami-Ali, *Le banal* (Paris, 1980).

36. Theodor Adorno, *Stadien auf dem Lebensweq* (Jena, 1914), 1:289: "Homesickness results from distancing. The art would be to experience it at the same time as staying at home, which requires illusionistic virtuosity."

37. Jardine, "Of Bodies and Technologies," p. 171. Jardine lists four possible responses to the "cyborg orgy" depicted by Haraway. The first would be an antitechnological position, which in its back-to-nature guise would be politically to the left and in its antiabortion guise firmly on the right; the second would be a protechnological stance that would to all intents and purposes say "go ahead and be a cyborg, it's great"; the third would consider technology as a way of liberating men from real women, investing reproductive technologies with the role of finally draining the female body of the feminine; and the fourth, a kind of paranoid version of the third, would imagine machine as woman. In these last two versions, technology appears as a male phantasm of the maternal body, mythicized and accessible through psychoanalysis. None of these versions, by itself, seems to accept Haraway's attempt at a politically ironic stance, embodied in the very notion of the cyborg itself.

38. Haraway, "Manifesto for Cyborgs," p. 173.

39. In one of Haraway's more utopian moments, cyborg "sex" is depicted (in a vision that recalls Charles Fourier's dream of a third sexuality) as restoring "some of the lovely replicative baroque of ferns and invertebrates," "organic prophylactics against heterosexism" ("Manifesto for Cyborgs," p. 174).

Dark Space

1. François Delaporte, in *Disease and Civilization: The Cholera Epidemic in Paris, 1832*, translated by Arthur Goldhammer (Cambridge, Mass.: MIT Press, 1986), characterized these realms as follows (p. 80): "Living conditions affect two distinct areas, one within the body, the other outside it: organic space and social space. Social space is the space within which the organism lives and labors, and the conditions of existence within that space—living conditions—determine the probability of life and death."

2. Michel Foucault, "The Eye of Power," in *Power/Knowledge: Selected Interviews and Other Writings 1972–1977*, edited by Colin Gordon (New York: Pantheon Books, 1980), pp. 153, 154.

3. Etienne-Louis Boullée, *Architecture. Essai sur l'art*, texts selected and presented by Jean-Marie Pérouse de Montclos (Paris: Hermann, 1968), p. 113.

4. Boullée, *Architecture*, pp. 136, 78.

5. Sarah Kofman, *The Childhood of Art: An Interpretation of Freud's Aesthetics*, translated by Winifred Woodhull (New York, 1988), p. 128.

6. Roger Caillois, "Mimicry and Legendary Psychasthenia," translated by John Shep-

ley, in *October: The First Decade, 1976–1986,* edited by Annette Michelson, Rosalind Krauss, Douglas Crimp, and Joan Copjec (Cambridge, Mass.: MIT Press, 1987), p. 70. Caillois's essay was first published in *Le Mythe et l'homme* (Paris: Gallimard, 1938), and in a shortened version in *Minotaure* a year before.

7. Caillois, "Mimicry and Legendary Psychasthenia," p. 72.

8. Eugène Minkowski, *Lived Time: Phenomenological and Psychopathological Studies,* translated and with an introduction by Nancy Metzel (Evanston: Northwestern University Press, 1970), p. 427.

9. Caillois, "Mimicry and Legendary Psychasthenia," p. 72. Caillois is quoting from Eugène Minkwoski, "Le temps vécu," *Etudes phénoménologiques et psychopathologiques* (Paris, 1933), pp. 382–398.

Posturbanism

1. Albert Camus, "A Short Guide to Towns without a Past," in *Lyrical and Critical Essays,* edited by Philip Thody and translated by Ellen Conroy Kennedy (New York: Vintage Books, 1970), p. 143. First published in 1947, this essay appeared in the collection *L'été* (Paris, 1954).

2. Alois Riegl, "The Modern Cult of Monuments: Its Character and Origin," translated by Kurt W. Forster and Diane Ghirardo, *Oppositions* 25 (Fall 1982):21.

3. Quintillian, *Institutio oratoria,* XI, ii. 17–22, quoted in Frances Yates, *The Art of Memory* (London: Routledge and Kegan Paul, 1966), p. 37.

4. Sartre, *Being and Nothingness,* p. 10.

5. Peter Handke, *Across,* translated by Ralph Manheim (New York: Farrar, Straus and Giroux, 1986), pp. 27, 11, 66, 67.

6. Berthold Brecht, quoted in Walter Benjamin, *Understanding Brecht,* translated by Anna Bostock (London: New Left Books, 1973), pp. 59, 60. Benjamin is quoting from the first poem in Brecht's *Handbook for City Dwellers.*

7. Robert Musil, *The Man without Qualities,* translated and with a foreword by Eithne Wilkins and Ernst Kaiser, 3 vols. (London: Picador, 1954), 1:1.

Psychometropolis

1. Karel Teige, "Mundaneum," translated by Ladislav and Elizabeth Holovsky and Lubamir Dolezel, *Oppositions* 4 (October 1974):89. This criticism was first published in *Stavba* 7 (1929):145.

2. Roland Barthes, *Leçon inaugurale de la chaire de sémiologie littéraire du Collège de France* (Paris: Seuil, 1978), p. 23.

3. Pierre Fontanier, *Les Figures du discours* (Paris: Flammarion, 1977), p. 146.

4. Hayden White, *Metahistory: The Historical Imagination in Nineteenth-Century Europe* (Baltimore: The Johns Hopkins University Press, 1973), p. 38.

5. Rem Koolhaas, *Delirious New York: A Retrospective Manifesto for Manhattan* (New York: Oxford University Press, 1978).

6. Michel Foucault, "Language to Infinity," in *Language, Counter-Memory, Practice: Selected Essays and Interviews*, edited and translated by Donald F. Bouchard (Ithaca: Cornell University Press, 1977).

7. Roland Barthes, *Sade, Fourier, Loyola* (Paris: Seuil, 1971).

Oneirism

1. Le Corbusier, *Urbanisme* (Paris, 1925), p. 280.

2. Maurice Halbwachs, *La Mémoire collective*, preface by Jean Duvignaud (Paris: Presses Universitaires de France, 1968), p. 134.

3. Halbwachs, *La Mémoire collective*, p. 133.

4. Julien Gracq, *La Forme d'une ville* (Paris: José Corti, 1985), p. 213.

Vagabond Architecture

1. John Hejduk, *Vladivostock* (New York: Rizzoli, 1989), p. 15.

2. John Hejduk, *Victims* (London: The Architectural Association, 1986).

3. Kristin Ross, *The Emergence of Social Space: Rimbaud and the Paris Commune* (Minneapolis: University of Minnesota Press, 1988), pp. 55–59, 17. Ross quotes from Théodore Homberg, *Etudes sur le vagabondage* (Paris: Forestier, 1880), p. ix.

4. Benjamin, *Passagen-Werk*, p. 614.

5. Guillaume Apollinaire, *L'Antitradition futuriste* (Milan: Direction du Mouvement Futuriste, [1913]), pp. 1–2.

6. Michel Beaujour, "Qu'est-ce que *Nadja*?" *Nouvelle Revue Française* 15, no. 172 (April 1967):797–798, cited in Dawn Ades, "La Photographie et le texte surréaliste," *Explosante-Fixe* (Paris: Hazan), pp. 161–163.

7. "Définitions," *Internationale situationniste* 1 (June 1958):13.

8. *Internationale situationniste* 1 (June 1958):28.

9. Abdelhafid Khatib, "Essai de description psychogéographique des Halles," *Internationale situationniste* 2 (December 1958):13–17.

10. "Définitions," p. 13.

11. "Définitions," p. 13.

12. Gilles Ivain, "Formulaire pour un urbanisme nouveau," *Internationale situationniste* 1 (June 1958):19.

13. Constant, "New Babylon," in Ulrich Conrads, *Programs and Manifestos on 20th-Century Architecture,* translated by Michael Bullock (Cambridge, Mass.: MIT Press, 1970), p. 178.

14. Constant, "Description de la zone jaune," *Internationale situationniste* 4 (June 1960):23–26.

15. Gilles Deleuze and Félix Guattari, *Nomadology: The War Machine,* translated by Brian Massumi (New York: Semiotext(e), 1986), pp. 50–53.

16. Michael Ignatieff, *The Needs of Strangers* (Harmondsworth: Penguin Books, 1985).

Transparency

1. Sigfried Giedion, *Bauen in Frankreich* (Berlin, 1928), p. 85, quoted in Benjamin, *Passagen-Werk,* p. 533.

2. Walter Benjamin, "Die Wiederkehr des Flaneurs," in *Gesammelte Schriften,* 7 vols., edited by Rolf Tiedemann and Hermann Schweppenhauser (Frankfurt am Main: Suhrkamp Verlag, 1972ff.), 3:168.

3. André Breton, *Nadja* (Paris: Gallimard, 1964), pp. 18–19.

4. Benjamin, "Surrealism," in *Reflections: Essays, Aphorisms, Autobiographical Writings,* edited by Peter Demetz, translated by Edmund Jephcott (New York: Harcourt Brace Jovanovich, 1978), 180.

5. Bataille, *Oeuvres complètes,* 1:197.

6. Colin Rowe, "Transparency: Literal and Phenomenal" (with Robert Slutzky), in *The Mathematics of the Ideal Villa,* pp. 160–176.

7. Guy de Maupassant, "Le Horla," in *Le Horla et autres contes d'angoisse* (Paris: Garnier-Flammarion, 1984), pp. 77–80.

8. Sarah Kofman, *The Childhood of Art: An Interpretation of Freud's Aesthetics,* translated by Winifred Woodhull (New York: Columbia University Press, 1988), p. 128.

247

Notes to Pages 223–225

9. Mahmoud Sami-Ali, "L'espace de l'inquiétante étrangeté," *Nouvelle Revue de Psychanalyse* 9 (Spring 1974):33, 43.

10. Jacques Lacan, *Ecrits, a Selection,* translated by Alan Sheridan (New York: Norton, 1977), p. 5.

11. Lacan, *Ecrits,* p. 4.

12. Jacques Lacan, "Le Stade du miroir," in *Ecrits,* 2 vols. (Paris: Seuil, 1966), 1:94, my translation.

13. Victor Burgin, "Paranoiac Space," *New Formations* 12 (Winter 1990):61–75.

14. Jacques Lacan, unpublished seminar, "L'Angoisse," 19 December 1962.

Acknowledgments

Illustrations

Cover: John Hejduk, "House for the Homeless." From *Vladivostock* (New York: Rizzoli, 1989), p. 147.

Page 16: Victor Hugo, "La Maison visionnée" (House at Pleinmont, Guernsey), 1866.

Page 68: Coop Himmelblau, House Vektor II (Haus Meier-Hahn), Düsseldorf.

Page 84: Bottom: Karl Friedrich Schinkel, Altes Museum, Berlin, plan. *Top:* James Stirling, Staatsgalerie, Stuttgart, plan. From *Assemblage* 9 (1989): 50–51.

Page 100: Bernard Tschumi, Park of La Villette, Paris, project.

Page 116: Peter Eisenman, Romeo and Juliet Project, photograph of model.

Page 146: Elizabeth Diller and Ricardo Scofidio, "It Even Works Lying Down," installation, Cap Street, San Francisco.

Page 166: Etienne-Louis Boullée, Temple of Death, c. 1790. Bibliothèque Nationale.

Page 176: Jean-Claude Gautrand, "Les Halles," 1971, photograph.

Page 188: Office of Metropolitan Architecture (Madelon Vriesendorp), "Freud Unlimited."

Page 198: Wiel Arets and Wim van den Bergh, "Translucent City," project for North Urban Core, Rotterdam.

Page 206: John Hejduk, "Object/Subject," Riga. From *Vladivostock* (New York: Rizzoli, 198 p. 49.

Page 216: Office of Metropolitan Architecture (Rem Koolhaas), National Library, Paris, competition project, facade. Photograph by Hans Werleman, Hectic Pictures, 1989.

Publication Information

Portions of Part I, "Houses," were first published in "The Architecture of the Uncanny: The Unhomely Houses of the Romantic Sublime from Hoffmann to Freud," *Assemblage* 3, Spring 1987. "Architecture Dismembered" was published in a different form as "The Building in Pain: The Body and Architecture in Post-Modern Culture," *AA Files,* 19, 1990. "Losing Face" was published in *Assemblage* 9, 1989. "Trick/Track" was published in Bernard Tschumi, *La Case Vide,* London, The Architectural Association, 1986

250

Acknowledgments

and "The Pleasure of the Architect: On the Work of Bernard Tschumi," *A+U*, September 1988. "Shifting Ground" was published as "After the End-of-the-Line: Notes on the Architecture of Peter Eisenman," *A+U*, special issue, Spring-Summer 1988, and "Counter-Monumentality in Practice: Peter Eisenman's Wexner Center," in *The Wexner Center for the Visual Arts. The Ohio State University*, New York, Rizzoli and The Ohio State University Press, 1989. "Homes for Cyborgs" was published in a shorter version in "Homes for Cyborgs: Domestic Prostheses from Salvador Dali to Elizabeth Diller and Ricardo Scofidio," *Ottagono*, Winter 1990. "Dark Space" was published in France Morin, ed., *The Interrupted Life*, New York, The New Museum of Contemporary Art, 1991. "Psychometropolis" was first published as "The Ironies of Metropolis: Notes on the Work of OMA," *Skyline*, May 1982. "Oneirism" was published as "The Resistance of the City: Notes on the Urban Architecture of Wiel Arets," introduction to *Wiel Arets Architect*, Rotterdam, 1989. "Vagabond Architecture" was published in *Lotus International*, Spring 1991. "Transparency" was published in *Anyone*, 1992.

Index

Acrophobia, 174
Acropolis, 52
Adorno, Theodor W., 8–9, 65, 97, 163, 243n36
Agoraphobia, 6, 174, 222
Alberti, Leon Battista, 71, 80–81, 89–90, 125, 159, 178
Alienation, ix, 4–6, 7, 9, 12, 40, 223
Alphand, Adolphe, 113–114
Anthropomorphism, xi–xii, xiv, 20, 69–82, 103, 111, 137–138, 144, 209
Anxiety (*angoisse*), ix, xi, xiii, 3, 5–7, 9, 22, 34, 53, 126, 224–225
Apelles, 77
Apollinaire, Guillaume, 185, 210
Apostrophe, 186
Aragon, Louis, xiv, 201, 210
Archigram, 75, 160
Arets, Wiel, xiii, 200–204
Arp, Hans, 153
Art nouveau, 150, 153–155
Auto-mate, 157
Axonometric drawing, 106

Bachelard, Gaston, xi, 7, 64–65, 80, 186, 201
Balla, Giacomo, 74
Balzac, Honoré de, 78
Banham, Peter Reyner, 148
Barthes, Roland, 77–78, 104–108, 190, 195–196
Bataille, Georges, 85, 99, 136–138, 144–145, 218
Baudelaire, Charles, 4, 185, 192, 199, 207, 210
Baudrillard, Jean, 10

Beaujour, Michel, 211
Beckford, William, 37
Benjamin, Walter, xiii, 4, 10, 147, 151, 155–157, 192, 201, 210, 217–218, 227n2
Benn, Gottfried, 97
Bentham, Jeremy, 168, 195, 203, 217
Bergh, Wim van den, xiii, 201
Bergson, Henri, 180, 211
Berlin, xiv
    Altes Museum, 91–96
    Hejduk's "Victims," 208–211
Bhabha, Homi K., 10–11
Blanc, Charles, 87
Bloch, Ernst, 3, 4, 13
Body, x–xii, 44, 60–62, 138, 167–168, 214, 218
    animism and, 235n1
    Burke on, 72
    classical analogy in architecture, 69–71
    cyborgian, 147–149, 157–161
    fetishization of, 78–79
    Lacanian, 77
    Le Corbusier on, 90
    modernist, 74–75
    morselated or fragmented, 49–55, 74–80, 111–112
    Sartre on, 80–82
    Scott on, 86–87
    physiognomy and, 87–88, 236n4
    urban analogy to, 75–77, 186
    Wölfflin on, 72–74, 86–87
Bohemianism, 207–209
Bonaparte, Marie, 6
Borges, Jorge Luis, 208

Boullée, Etienne-Louis, 131, 169–173,
175, 202
Boyarsky, Alvin, xv, 75–76
Brecht, Bertolt, 185
Brentano, Clemens, 28
Breton, André, xiii, xiv, 119, 150–151,
201, 210, 218
Brunelleschi, Filippo, 178
Bruno, Giordano, 201
Bürger, Peter, 95
Burgin, Victor, 224
Burke, Edmund, 3, 20–21, 37, 39, 72,
169
Burke, Kenneth, 120, 238nn6,7
Burroughs, William, 191

Caillois, Roger, 173–175
Camouflage, 173
Campanella, Tommaso, 179
Camus, Albert, 177
Carcassonne, 52
Carrington, Leonora, 149–150
Carroll, David, 107
Carroll, Lewis, 101
Castration anxiety, x, 34, 54–55, 79,
152, 171, 222
Catachresis, 187
Champollion, Jean François, 44
Charcot, Jean-Martin, 154
Chareau, Pierre, 219
Chateaubriand, François-René de, 46–
47, 49, 51
Chermayeff, Serge, 150
Chombart de Lauwe, 211
Claudel, Paul, 66
Claustrophobia, 6, 43, 174
Coleridge, Samuel Taylor, 37
Constant, Benjamin, 4
Constant (Nieuwenhuys), 213
Constructivism, ix, xii, 103, 106–107,
109–112, 140, 191, 194
Coop Himmelblau, xii, 69–70, 75–76,
78, 80–82, 138
Copernicus, Nicolaus, 183
Courbet, Gustave, 120
Creuzé de Lesser, 47
Cubism, 74–75
Cybernetics, xii, 147, 159–163
Cyberspace, 10, 148, 160
Cyborgs, ix, xii–xiii, 10, 147–164,
243nn37,39

Dadaism, xii, 8, 156, 192
Dalí, Salvador, xiii, 137, 150, 153–155,
224
Debord, Guy, 211
De Certeau, Michel, 157, 160, 162,
242n31
De Chirico, Giorgio 156, 212
Deconstruction, xii, 105
Defamiliarization (ostranenie), 8
Delaporte, François, 168, 243n1
Deleuze, Gilles, 114, 214
De Man, Paul, 120, 180, 183
Dépaysement, 213
De Quincey, Thomas, xi, 37–39, 57,
232n36
Dérive, 211–214
Derrida, Jacques, x, xii, 9–10, 38, 104,
107, 108, 110, 128, 134, 228n16
Desire, 152–153
De Stijl, 141
Détournement, 212
Dickens, Charles, 4
Diderot, Denis, 126
Diller, Elizabeth, xii, xiv, 148, 158–164
Doesburg, Theo van, 103, 142
Domesticity, ix, x, 3, 10–13, 17, 23–24,
45–48, 59, 70, 80, 160–161, 164, 183,
219
Double, xiii, 3, 6, 8, 10, 12, 34–35, 170–
172, 221–222
Dreyfus, Hubert, 7
Duchamp, Marcel, 74, 119, 125–128,
130, 157, 161–162, 218
Dulwich Art Gallery, 98
Durand, Jean-Nicolas-Louis, 219
Dürer, Albrecht, 126
Durkheim, Emile, 192

Eiffel, Alexandre Gustave, 109
Eisenman, Peter, xii, 118–145, 182
Eisenstein, Sergei, 106–107
End-of-the-line mode, 120–121,
238nn6,7
Entäusserung, 5
Entfremdung, 5
Ermenonville, 113
Ernst, Max, 149, 154, 156, 158
Eros, 127–128
Estrangement, ix–x, 4–5, 8–9, 221
Exile, ix, 10–11, 19, 167, 169
Expressionism, 8, 76, 106

Face, xii, 58, 76, 85–91, 95, 221–224
Fetishism, 78, 156
Filarete (Antonio di Piero Averlino), 71, 103
Flaubert, Gustave, 46
Florence, 178
Follies, 106, 109–114
Fontanier, Pierre, 192
Forster, Kurt W., 135
Foster, Norman, 220
Foucault, Michel, 107, 160, 167–169, 172, 195–196
Fourier, Charles, 191, 196, 212
Fractals, 130
Fragments, ix, 49–51, 54–55, 77–78, 97–98, 111, 114, 141, 143–144
Francesco di Giorgio, 71, 186
French Revolution, 169
Freud, Sigmund, 10, 13, 38, 43, 45, 53–55, 64, 79, 119, 128, 135, 171, 185, 192, 201, 222
  Adorno on, 8–9
  animism, 54
  archaeological metaphor, 54
  Beyond the Pleasure Principle, 7, 38, 54
  burial alive, 45
  castration complex, 53–55, 79
  death drive, x, 7, 175
  Derrida on, 38, 128–129
  dismembering, 53–54
  dissection dream, 54
  fetishism, 229n18
  fragmentation, 54
  Future of an Illusion, 54
  Genoa, 43, 185
  gettatore, 53
  haunting, 17, 54
  homesickness, 53–55, 152
  Interpretation of Dreams, 54
  intrauterine fantasies, 54–55, 241n12
  Kofman on, 171, 222
  mirroring, 222
  "Mourning and Melancholia," 7
  "On Transience," 7
  repetition, 13, 43, 222
  "Sandman," 54
  "Thoughts for the Times on War and Death," 7
  "Das Unheimliche"("The Uncanny"), xi, 6, 7, 8–9, 14, 17, 21–27, 32–33,

53–55, 79, 129, 135, 154–156, 171, 222, 228n14, 230n15
Friedrich, Caspar David, 28
Fuller, R. Buckminster, 148, 162, 208
Futurism, 8, 63, 76, 155, 208

Garnier, Tony, 179
Gaudí, Antonio, 153
Gautier, Théophile, 47–49, 51–54
Gehlen, Arnold, 96–97
Gehry, Frank, 138
Gender, xii–xiii, 12, 147–149, 160–161, 164, 186, 243n37
Gibson, William, 10, 148, 162–164
Giedion, Sigfried, 94–95, 137–139, 156, 217, 220
Gilbreth, Frank and Lilian, 158
Goethe, Johann Wolfgang von, 28, 30–31, 53, 103
Gracq, Julien, 200, 204, 210
Greenberg, Clement, 190
Grids, 140–143
Grimm, Jacob and Wilhelm, 25
Gropius, Walter, 91
Grotesque, 13, 138, 145
Guattari, Félix, 214
Guggenheim Foundation, Venice, 201
Gutzkow, Karl Ferdinand, 25

Habermas, Jürgen, 97–98
Hackers, 161–164
Haggard, C. Rider, 54
Halbwachs, Maurice, 199–200
Hancarville, Pierre-François Hugues, baron d', 49
Handke, Peter, 183–184
Haraway, Donna, xii, 147–149, 160–161, 164
Haunting, xi, 4, 10–11, 14, 17–20, 23, 27–29, 41, 48, 53, 58–59, 63, 65–66, 80–81, 170, 181–183, 217
Haussmann, Georges, baron, 112, 179, 199
Hegel, Georg Wilhelm Friedrich, xii, 5, 21, 27–28, 42–43, 59–60, 88, 117–118, 122–124, 131–134, 136, 238n1
Heidegger, Martin, xi, 7–8, 12, 65–66, 164, 208–209, 228n10
Heimlich, x, xii, 6, 23–26, 32, 35–36, 53, 62, 80, 135, 224–225

Hejduk, John, xiii–xiv, 138, 207–211, 213–214
Hellenism, 59–60
Herculaneum, 47
Hertz, Neil, 120
Hessel, Franz, 210
Historicism, 59–60, 70–71, 102, 117–118, 137–138, 189, 220
Hoffmann, E. T. A., xi, 3, 4, 6, 27–37, 41, 53, 57, 156–157, 221, 231n25
Hölderlin, Friedrich, 28
Homberg, Théodore, 210
Home, ix, xi, xiii, 3–5, 7, 8, 11–13, 19–20, 24–26, 29–30, 36–37, 42–44, 55, 57–62, 66, 147, 150, 153, 154, 157, 160–164, 186, 225
Homelessness, ix, x, 7–10, 12–13, 160, 187
Homer, 27
Homesickness, 7, 12, 53–55, 152, 164
Horkheimer, Max, 65
Hugo, Victor, xi, 19–20, 28
Huizinga, Johan, 209, 213
Humbert de Superville, David Pierre Giottin, 87
Humboldt, Wilhelm von, 98
Husserl, Edmund, 214
Huysmans, Joris Karl, 218
Hypermaterialism, 155
Hypograms, 186

Ignatieff, Michael, 10
Ignatius of Loyola, Saint, 196
Imitation, 170
Inquiétant, 22
Insect behavior, 173
Internationale situationniste, 212–213
Intrauterine architecture, 138, 152–154
Irony, 164, 191–193, 196
Ivain, Gilles, 212

James, Henry, 63
Janet, Pierre, 174
Jardine, Alice, 148, 157, 160, 163, 243n37
Jarry, Alfred, 160
Jensen, Wilhelm, 45, 47, 54
Jentsch, Ernst, 23
Jugendstil, 155
Justinian, Saint, 209

Kafka, Franz, 8, 159
Kahn, Louis, 98
Kandinsky, Wassily, 106
Kant, Immanuel, 21, 77
Kent, William, 113
Khatib, Abdelhafid, 211
Kierkegaard, Søren, 196
Kiesler, Frederick, 153
Kimbell Art Museum, Fort Worth, 98
Kipnis, Jeffry, 207
Klee, Paul, 106
Kofman, Sarah, 1, 10, 171, 222
Koolhaas, Rem, xiii, 192–196, 221–225
Krauss, Rosalind E., 107, 142–143
Krier, Leon, 199
Kristeva, Julia, 10

Lacan, Jacques, x, 126
anxiety (angoisse), 9, 224–225
gaze, theory of the, 35
mirror stage, 77, 223–224
schizography, 143–144
space, 159
uncanny, 9
Landscape, 130–131
Laugier, Marc-Antoine, abbé, 103
Le Camus de Mézières, Nicolas, 87
Le Corbusier (Charles-Edouard Jeanneret), 46, 63, 89–91, 103, 113, 147, 150–151, 156–157, 162, 168, 186, 189, 192, 199, 202, 207–208, 211, 217
Maison Domino, 63–65, 86
Modulor, 91, 96, 147
Mundaneum (Musée Mondial), 94, 201
Palace of Assembly, Chandigarh, 93
Unité d'habitation, 64
Ville Radieuse, 75, 91, 180
Ville Verte, 64, 112
Ledoux, Claude-Nicolas, 87, 170, 172, 208
Lefebvre, Henri, 172, 201–202
Leiris, Michel, 152
Le Nôtre, André, 113
Lequeu, Jean-Jacques, 87
Lettristes, 211
Libeskind, Daniel, 138
Lissitzky, El, 106
Liszt, Franz, 201
Longinus, 21

Loos, Adolf, 103, 122
Loutherbourg, Jacques, 37
Lukács, Georg, 7, 228n8
Lynch, David, 10
Lyotard, Jean-François, 107, 157
Lytton, Edward George Earle Lytton
    Bulwer-, 47

Magritte, René, 126
Malevich, Kasimir, 106
Mallarmé, Stéphane, 101, 127, 190
Mandelbrot, Benoit B., 130
Man Ray (Emmanuel Radnitsky), 218
Mapping, 130–131
Marey, Etienne-Jules, 74
Martin, John, 38–39
Marx, Karl, 4–5, 9, 10, 227n4
Matta (Sebastian Antonio Matta
    Echaurren), 153
Maupassant, Guy de, 221
Mehlman, Jeffrey, 14
Melville, Herman, xi, 42–45, 48, 57
Memory theater, 177–180, 202, 208
Mendelsohn, Erich, 217
Mies van der Rohe, Ludwig, 141
Minkowski, Eugène, 174–175
Minotaure, 137, 151–153
Mitterand, François, 219
Modernism, xii–xiv, 8–9, 13, 63–66, 70,
    86, 89, 90–91, 94–95, 103, 106, 109–
    110, 128, 141–143, 147, 150–151,
    155–158, 168, 172, 179–182, 185,
    189–192, 194–196, 199–202, 207,
    211, 217–221, 224
Mondrian, Piet, 142
Moneo, Raphael, 98
Monstrosity, 138, 144–145
Monumentality, 86, 93–96, 105, 135–
    140, 145, 168, 172–173, 175, 207,
    217, 220–221
Mumford, Lewis, 135
Museums, xii, 7, 18, 46, 48–49, 85–99,
    135
Musil, Robert, 186

Neoclassicism, 199
Neoplasticism, 103
Neorationalism, 199
Nerval, Gérard de (Gérard Labrunie),
    47

Nietzsche, Friedrich, 26, 38, 59, 107,
    159, 180, 183, 189, 192, 195–196, 213
Nihilation, 180–182
Nîmes, 221
Nodier, Charles, xi, 38–41, 232n45
Nomadism, 207–214
Nostalgia, x, 7–8, 39, 63–66, 152, 180
Notation, 105–106, 108, 112
Novalis (Georg Friedrich Philipp von
    Hardenberg), 28

Objets-types, 147, 156–158
Objets-membres-humains, 156–157
Office of Metropolitan Architecture
    (OMA), xiii, 192–196
Ohio State University, Wexner Center
    for the Visual Arts, 135–136, 139–142
Oneirism, 199–204
Opacity, 125–129, 218–219, 221
Organicism, 147
Origins, 117–118
Orpheus, 31
Ostranenie, 8
Otlet, Paul, 201
Otto, Frei, 95

Panofsky, Erwin, 160
Panopticism, 160, 167–168, 172, 194–
    196, 217
Paraarchitecture, 107–109
Paraesthetics, 107
Paranoia, xiii, 223–225
Pâris, Pierre-Adrien, 46
Paris
    Bibliothèque Nationale, 219
    grands projets, xiv
    Hôtel de Cluny, 18
    La Villette, park of, xii, 104–114
    Louvre, 219–220
Pater, Walter, xi, 33, 57–62
    "The Child in the House," 57
    on Hegel's aesthetics, 60
    Marius the Epicurean, 59
    The Renaissance, 59
Patte, Pierre, 179
Pei, I. M., 221
Perrault, Dominique, 219
Pharmakon, 129, 239n18
Physiognomy, 87–88, 136–137, 223
Pinot-Gallizio, Giuseppe, 213

Piranesi, Giovanni Battista, 37–40, 162
Poe, Edgar Allan, 3, 4, 6, 17–20
Pompeii, 45–55
Posthistoire, 13, 97, 98, 97, 98
Postmodernism, xiv, 9, 12, 66, 91, 94,
    102, 183, 195, 202, 219–220, 224
Poststructuralism, 117
Posturbanism, xiii, 177–186
Prix, Wolf D., xii
Prolepsis, 182
Prosopopeia, 186
Prostheses, x, xii, 111, 147, 156–164
Proust, Marcel, 74–75, 78, 97, 180, 183
Pseudomonumentality, 137–139
Psychasthenia, 173–175
Psychogeography, 201, 211–214
Purism, 156

Quintilian (Marcus Fabius Quintilianus),
    178

Randon, 131
Randonnée, 131
Rank, Otto, 6, 221
Readymades, 162
Realism, 125
Reed, Arden, 38
Reflectivity, 220–224
Reik, Theodor, ix
Repetition, 12, 14, 37–40, 43, 57–58, 98,
    102, 110–111, 122, 142, 171, 185,
    219, 222
Restoration, 51–52
Richter, Jean Paul, 21
Riegl, Alois, 160, 176
Riffaterre, Michael, 41
Riga, 207, 211
Rimbaud, Arthur, 41, 199, 201, 210–
    211
Robespierre, Maximilien-François-Marie-
    Isidore de, 169
Romanticism, xi, 6, 7, 12, 18, 20–21, 27,
    29–31, 34, 35, 37–39, 47–50, 77–78,
    113, 123, 124–125, 131, 210
Rome, 45
Romeo and Juliet project (Eisenman),
    126–131, 134, 139
Ross, Kristin, 210–211
Rossi, Aldo, 199, 202
Rotterdam, 203

Rousseau, Jean-Jacques, 4, 11, 65
Roussel, Raymond, xiii, 201, 203
Rowe, Colin, 85–99, 219
Royal Society, 179
Ruskin, John, 122

Sade, Donatien-Alphonse-François,
    marquis de, 40, 49, 128, 196
Sami-Ali, Mahmoud, 222–223
Sanders, Daniel, 24–26
Sartre, Jean-Paul, 69, 80–82, 180–185
Saussure, Ferdinand de, 186
Scaling, 130
Schelling, Friedrich Wilhelm Joseph, xi,
    26–28, 31, 44, 48, 53, 231n24
Schiller, Johann Christoph Freidrich
    von, 28
Schinkel, Karl Friedrich, 28, 91–98
Schizography, 143–144
Schizophrenia, 174
Schlegel, August, 28
Schlegel, Friedrich, 28, 50
Scofidio, Ricardo, xii, xiv, 148, 158–164
Scott, Geoffrey, 86–87
Screen, 125–127, 158
Sedlmayr, Hans, 65, 208
Self, x, 3, 35–36, 77, 80–82, 173–175,
    222–225
Semper, Gottfried, 103
Shapiro, David, 207
Shelley, Mary Wollstonecraft, 77, 157
Sherman, Cindy, 76
Silverman, Kaja, 10, 229n18
Simmel, Georg, 5, 10, 88–89, 91, 192,
    203, 209
Simulacrum, 10, 169–171
Situationism, xiii, 172, 192, 202, 211–
    212, 214
Sixtus V, 179
Slutzky, Robert, 219
Soane, John, 98
Sollers, Philippe, 129
Sommerard, Alexandre du, 18
Soutter, Louis, 151
Space, ix, xii, 3, 13, 147–149, 160–161,
    163–164, 167–168
    abyssal, 37–40
    dark, 167–175
    empty, 114
    fear of, 6

gridded, 141–142
Lacanian, 159
modernist, 86
perception of, 173
repetition in, 43
schizophrenic, 174–175
transparent, 168, 217–225
uncanny, 11, 222–223
Speer, Albert, 95
Springer, Anton, 73
Stirling, James, xii, 85, 87–88, 91–97
Stokes, Adrian, 87
Stuttgart, Staatsgalerie, xii, 85, 97
Subject, x, xiv, 1, 12, 22, 60, 79, 126,
    127–129, 157–159, 169, 173–176,
    192, 193, 211, 218–221, 224, 223–225
Sublime, xi, 3, 12–13, 20–22, 26, 37–39,
    41, 48–49, 52, 58, 61, 62, 71–72, 77,
    163, 169–172
Suprematism, 106, 194
Surrealism, xiii, xiv, 8, 138, 149–157,
    190–192, 210–211
Surveillance, 148, 168
Swiczinsky, H., xii

Tatar, Maria, 36
Tatlin, Vladimir, 109–111
Taut, Bruno, 221
Taylorism, 148, 158, 161
Teige, Karel, 189
Tessenow, Heinrich, 152
Thorvaldsen, Bertel, 48
Threshold, 184–185
Todorov, Tzvetan, 10
Tokyo, 104, 107, 111
Translucency, 221
Transparency, ix, xiv, 49, 109, 125–127,
    168–170, 172, 217–224
Tschumi, Bernard, xii, 78, 101–114
Typology, 156–157, 172, 200, 202
Tzara, Tristan, 137, 151–153

Uncanny, ix, x, xi, xiii, xiv, 3–9, 10, 11–
    14, 17, 18, 20–22, 23, 26, 27–29, 32–
    41, 43–45, 48, 49, 51, 52, 54, 55, 58,
    80, 81, 135, 137–138, 152, 154–156,
    163, 171–173, 211, 219, 221–225
bio-uncanny, xii
contemporary, 3
definition of, 22

in Derrida and Lacan, 9
in film, 10
metropolitan, 6
political implications of, 14
postmodern, 9
techno-uncanny, xii
as topos, 17
urban, 4
Unhomeliness (das Unheimliche), x, 6–8,
    12–14, 17, 19, 22–27, 32, 35, 36, 37,
    41, 48, 55, 57, 135, 164, 204, 224
Urbanism, xiii, 13, 168, 177, 179–183,
    185–186, 199, 212

Vagabondage, 207–211
Vattimo, Gianni, 220
Venice, 122, 201
Verona, 127
Vertigo, 39
Villiers de L'Isle-Adam, Auguste de, 157
Viollet-le-Duc, Eugène-Emmanuel, 219
Vitruvius (Marcus Vitruvius Pollio), 71,
    72, 117, 171
Vladivostock, xiv, 207, 211
Void, 13, 37, 132, 134, 170–172, 203,
    221
Vriesendorp, Madelon, xiii, 191, 193

Wagner, Otto, 192, 201
Wagner, Richard, 74
Walpole, Horace, 37
Wells, H. G., 148
Wenders, Wim, 10
Westphal, Carl Otto, 174
White, Haydon, 192
Wiederhalle, xiii
Winckelmann, Johann Joachim, 46, 48,
    50, 59
Wölfflin, Heinrich, 72–74, 86–87, 94
Wordsworth, William, 120
Wren, Christopher, 179
Wright, Frank Lloyd, 42

Yates, Francis, 178–179

Zenghelis, Elia, xiii, 194
Zenghelis, Zoe, xiii, 194
Zola, Emile, 125, 127